analysis and cogent warning that will make you think and even think the unthinkable about America's culture, politics, government, policies, and institutions… and consequences for our future if we don't change our present course. You won't agree with all the assessments. But you will pay attention! From a respected, experienced, and astute student of world affairs."

—Chuck Hagel, 24th Secretary of Defense,
Former U.S. Senator, Vietnam Veteran

"Harlan Ullman has written what must be a massive bestseller. Collectively, we, meaning everyone on the planet, are at grave risk from this new MAD for Massive Attacks of Disruption that are potentially existential dangers to our democracy and our Constitution. And Ullman shows us how to contain, mitigate, and prevent these disruptors from creating global havoc. Read this book!"

—Anthony Scaramucci, Chairman of SkyBridge
Capital and the SALT conferences and author of
several books including *Trump, the Blue-Collar President*

"I once suggested Harlan Ullman combines Clausewitz and Tom Clancy. His new book goes even further. We inhabit a new world that we do not yet understand—and we must. After reading this extraordinary book, the reader will face the future better armed and much better informed."

—Lord Michael Dobbs of Wylye,
author of *House of Cards*

"When Harlan Ullman writes in *The Fifth Horseman and the New MAD* that Massive Attacks of Disruption threaten America, Americans, the Constitution, and our way of life, I believe him, and we should all listen closely…especially the Biden Administration. COVID, cyberattacks, climate change, environmental disasters, and the January 6th assault on the Constitution are the precursors and cannot be ignored. Our only hope is to respond immediately and coherently to these looming existential dangers if the nation is to be kept safe, secure, and prosperous."

—General John Allen, USMC (Ret), commanded NATO forces in Afghanistan; President of the Brookings Institution, his latest book coauthored with Lt. Gen. Ben Hodges and Dr. Julian Lindley-French is *Future War and the Defence of Europe*

the FIFTH HORSEMAN *and the* NEW MAD

HOW MASSIVE ATTACKS *of* DISRUPTION
BECAME *the* LOOMING EXISTENTIAL DANGER
to a DIVIDED NATION *and the* WORLD *at* LARGE

HARLAN ULLMAN

Post Hill
PRESS

A POST HILL PRESS BOOK
ISBN: 978-1-63758-139-1
ISBN (eBook): 978-1-63758-140-7

The Fifth Horseman and the New MAD:
How Massive Attacks of Disruption Became the Looming Existential Danger to a
Divided Nation and the World at Large
© 2021 by Harlan Ullman
All Rights Reserved

Post Hill Press
New York • Nashville
posthillpress.com

Published in the United States of America
1 2 3 4 5 6 7 8 9 10

*This book is dedicated to the Great Americans of the unique
and irrepressible bicentennial National War College Class of
1976 and the extraordinary year we spent together.*

When government becomes destructive, it is the right of the
people to alter or abolish it and establish a new one.

The Declaration of Independence
July 4, 1776

A house divided among itself cannot stand.

Abraham Lincoln
June 16, 1858

Then we fucked up the end game....

Charlie Wilson
From *Charlie Wilson's War*

[Technological advances]...*bring not only new possibilities*
to improve life, but also new problems and dangers.

Vladimir Putin
December 1999

Charlie Wilson and Vladimir Putin were correct: coronavirus and COVID-19
were the last warning. And indeed we fucked up the end game. It was massive
disruption and not China or Russia or terror that did us in. It was us!

Anne Jackson Bennett
President of the United States (2029–2037)

Contents

Contents

Author's Note

WHO WILL TAKE NOTICE; WHO WILL ACT?

Warnings, however prescient, too often go unheard and unheeded. As a young Swift Boat skipper serving in Vietnam in mid-1967, I and two other Army and Marine officers were summoned back to the White House to brief President Lyndon Johnson on how we thought the war was going.

In the pre-briefings, it was clear the president wanted to hear good news. He did not get it from me. I bluntly told him we were getting the "shit kicked out of us" and had two choices: get out or get in. We did neither at the time.

A quarter of a century later, I found myself in profound disagreement along with more distinguished colleagues over the Clinton administration's decision to expand NATO without that leading to an eventual rift with Russia. It did.

In 2002, I argued that Iraq did not have weapons of mass destruction. The evidence came from many sources, including the International Atomic Energy Agency, the studies done for prior

Central Command commander Marine General Anthony Zinni, and access to foreign officials who discredited the alleged proof offered by the Iraqi general code-named "Curve Ball" of the existence of those weapons. We still invaded.

During the Obama administration, I tried to change the thrust of its first major security review called the "Afghanistan-Pakistan Study" to focus on the real center of gravity: Pakistan. That, too, failed. When President Obama chose to use the right to protect to lead from behind in attacking Libya to save Benghazi from a threat that did not exist, I protested. But no one listened.

My critique of the Trump administration extended to at least fifty columns and articles. Those, too, had little impact.

Today, a deeply disunited United States faces perhaps the greatest set of crises in its history, extending far beyond the coronavirus/COVID-19 and the death, disruption, and dislocation wrought by the pandemic. In an intractably politically divided nation, the Constitution and the American way of life are at grave risk to supercharged forces that have emerged in what I term the era of the new MAD—Massive Attacks of Disruption.

Disruptions have always had great and often massive impact. The reason why today is profoundly different from the past is because in an age of globalization and the diffusion of power, states, governments, and people have become uniquely vulnerable to disruption whether from man or nature. Unlike the Cold War's MAD—Mutual Assured Destruction and the threat of thermonuclear annihilation—many of the new MAD's disruptors are not deterrable, and if deferred, may not be preventable.

But who is taking notice? And who is taking action? So far, the answer is no one.

The purpose of this book is to persuade the American public to do both. If not, the conditions Anne Jackson Bennett faced as president in 2029 could come to pass. Despite my dismal track record, I hope that this time these warnings will take hold.

Harlan Ullman
Washington, DC
June 1, 2021

Author's Guide for the Reader

The central argument of this book is that a new, more virulent version of the Cold War's MAD—Mutual Assured Destruction and thermonuclear Armageddon—is a specter haunting the world at large. It is the specter of a new MAD, for Massive Attacks of Disruption, that is a looming existential danger confronting mankind.

The first draft was completed in late 2020, a year before the book was published. During this interregnum, the proof and evidence of the presence and power of this new MAD could not be overstated.

The arrival in early 2020 of the coronavirus/COVID-19 followed by the SolarWinds cyberattacks, presumably from Russian sources, against the US government later that year and then the shutdown of the Colonial Pipeline that supplied the bulk of gasoline to the US east coast in Spring 2021; the unprecedented January 6, 2021 insurrection and the storming of the Capitol building, America's cathedral of democracy; and the subsequent unrest accompanying the inauguration of Joe Biden as president and Kamala Harris as vice president two weeks later based on the "big lie" of a stolen election were stunning and shocking harbingers of the presence and power of this new MAD.

And I expect that in the time between the completion of the final editing of the book and its publication, even more evidence and proof of the power of MAD will be further shocks to the system, for good or ill, such as those arising from the chaotic evacuation of non-combatants taking place in late August 2021 as many tens of thousands fled to Kabul Airport in hopes of obtaining safe passage out of Afghanistan.

Chapter 1 describes how a confluence of unprecedented forces has created a Fifth Horseman of the Apocalypse armed with the new and unique Massive Attacks of Disruption. Chapter 2 poses scenarios of how the new MAD and its seven main disruptors threaten both the United States and world at large by targeting political, economic, cultural, and societal vulnerabilities including, for the first time since 1861, the Constitution, many inadvertently and ironically created by the benefits of globalization and the diffusion of power.

Chapters 3 through 5 critically examine from a contrarian perspective how Russia and China perceive the domestic and international environments and conditions of what will be later described as a post-Westphalian world.

Chapter 6 compares the 1918–1920 Spanish flu and the 2020 coronavirus/COVID-19 pandemics. Chapter 7 provides case studies of profound transformative inflection points, perhaps similar to the arrival of MAD, before and after two world wars, the end of the Cold War, and September 11. These are reminders of past failures and successes that can serve as future guides if leaders choose to listen.

Based on analyses of the strengths, vulnerabilities, and weaknesses of the US Constitution, Congress, and the executive branch under the threat of MAD, Chapters 8, 9, and 10 offer organizational and policy recommendations for government and for new national security, defense, and foreign policy strategies to corral and contain the Fifth Horseman and MAD.

If undertaken, perhaps one fundamental paradox of the past sixty years can be reversed. The US military has won virtually every battle it fought. But the US still lost all the wars it started.

To empower a national economic recovery, a National Investment Fund was proposed. The Biden administration's COVID Relief Bill was passed by Congress and signed into law. But the bills for Jobs, Families, and Infrastructure faced heavy Congressional opposition. This proposed fund, named the 1923 Fund for the greatest economic boom in American history following the 1918–1920 pandemic, remains a viable alternative for several compelling reasons described in later pages.

The book's endnote issues a final warning. If the dangers and threats posed by MAD and its seven major disruptors to the nation, the Constitution, the American Dream, and our way of life are ignored, dismissed, or underestimated, then the dire conditions described in the Preface will prove altogether too prescient. But who will listen? And who will lead?

Preface

STATE OF THE WORLD, 2029

Noon, January 20, 2029, An Undisclosed Location

President Anne Jackson Bennett took the oath of office to support and defend the Constitution of the United States, becoming America's forty-eighth chief executive. She faced a country ravaged by multiple crises, many arising from routine shortages of the most basic human needs for food, water, medicine, and electricity.

The nation's condition was worse than at any time in its history, from the depths of the Civil War, the Great Depression, the early days of World War II, the Vietnam War, and September 11 to the arrival of coronavirus/COVID-19 nine years before. Because of its massive federal debt, the country was unable to pay its bills.

Superstorms, tornadoes, floods, and droughts crippled the already obsolete national power grid, denying millions of Americans access to electricity for extended periods of time measured in weeks, not days. Extreme weather brought havoc to the agricultural and farming sectors. Access to the internet and cell phone service was regularly disrupted because of the antiquated state of the nation's infrastructure.

Riots and protests over shortages of basic goods that governments at the federal, state, and local levels were unable to provide kept police forces and National Guard units occupied on a near permanent basis.

Only one hundred million Americans voted in November 2028 because of restrictions on movement, difficulties in obtaining absentee ballots due to domestic unrest, and coronavirus/COVID-28 forcing massive stay-at-home orders.

The election of President Joe Biden in 2020 had the potential to reverse many of the catastrophic mistakes and misjudgments of the prior administration. But vitriolic partisanship intervened with the occupation of the Capitol on January 6, 2021 and riots two weeks later during the inauguration—in part over the second impeachment of Donald Trump—cut the political honeymoon short on January 21, 2021.

Biden called for a national revival based on several pieces of legislation—the Relief, Jobs, and Family bills totaling $6 trillion to promote each and new technologies for healthcare; climate change and the environment; and for major rejuvenation of the nation's infrastructure. These were the most transformational proposals since FDR's New Deal.

But Republicans and Democrats in Congress could not agree. The massive proposed debt increases were worthy of a full debate. However, political expediency and political scorched earth policies to manipulate the forthcoming 2022 elections to advantage and litigating or forgetting (or forgiving) the role of former President Donald Trump in inciting the January 6, 2021 insurgents overrode principle and acting in the nation's and not the party's best interest. Full funding was never approved. Biden was not reelected. Nor was his successor. And the nation continued to suffer over the failure of its government to govern.

Despite the widespread euphoria over the approval of COVID vaccines in late 2020 and early 2021, the vaccination process took longer than anticipated because of failure of the earlier administration to plan for distribution and later large numbers of "anti-vaxxers" who refused inoculation. With the spread of COVID 2028 eight years later, hackers attacked the vaccine refrigerator distribution systems required to store the drugs at -94° Fahrenheit, ruining millions of doses and derailing the inoculation process for months. The hackers were never identified nor brought to justice, even though these actions probably led to hundreds of thousands of unnecessary COVID deaths. Millions of Americans still refused to be vaccinated, preventing a quick end to the new pandemic.

Delays may have caused COVID to mutate, becoming even deadlier and spreading beyond humans. What happened with the COVID transmission to Denmark's mink population in late 2020 erupted elsewhere. Livestock, crops, plants, and trees were infected in this second viral pandemic, inducing even greater food shortages.

Climate change generated more intense and destructive storms, accelerating the melting of polar ice caps. With the unexpected rise in sea levels, hundreds of thousands of Americans fled the coasts to safer regions. Mexico and Canada closed their borders with the United States to prevent this exodus from spilling over into both nations.

Cybercrimes exceeded all murders, robberies, muggings, rapes, and sales of illicit substances combined. Social media was the vehicle for organizing often daily protests and riots by the legions of unemployed, hungry, scared, and desperate citizens.

In increasing numbers, radical and extremist groups employed terror to disrupt and destroy with cyber, social media, modern weapons, and drones. An anarchist group calling itself DAN, for Destroy America Now and modeled after the radical organizations that seized the Capitol building back in January 2021, had simultaneously struck the White House, Capitol, and other government buildings with hundreds of drones carrying explosives.

The new White House, moved to a secure location, was literally a concrete iceberg with virtually the entire interior buried deeply below ground. Congress had transferred to the safety of Fort Lesley J. McNair at the southern tip of Washington, DC, at the junction of the Potomac and Anacostia Rivers.

But the greatest challenge facing the president and the nation was the inability to govern under the Constitution of the United States. Could the constitutional checks and balances still work with intractable divisions between two intractably polarized and partisan political parties without any means of reconciliation?

Abroad, China was dominant. The great-power competition put the United States and China on a collision course that was far more damaging to America than to China. The Regional Comprehensive Economic Partnership (RCEP), signed in 2020 among fifteen Asian states including many of America's allies, began this road to Chinese supremacy, followed by the new trade agreement renegotiated with the European Union in 2022. Although 250 million Chinese died in the years after a more virulent form of the coronavirus hit, China's economy eventually surpassed America's. The coronavirus attack dispelled the theory that China had developed the virus as a weapon to use against the West or had engineered it to infect non-Chinese.

The majority of deaths were among the poorest Chinese. The impact, ironically, reduced pressure on China's economy for double-digit annual growth to raise standards of living, strengthening the control and power of the ruling Communist Party. With RCEP in place, Asian states turned away from the US and joined China's Belt and Road Initiative. America became even more dependent on the Chinese supply chain.

Taiwan was absorbed into the mainland, and "One China" was finally achieved as the US Navy was incapable of breaking the embargo placed around the island by the Chinese maritime militia and fishing fleets. China's technology continued to outstrip America's.

And, perhaps most humiliating for America, the renminbi replaced the dollar as the global reserve currency.

North Korea's Kim Jong-un was assassinated in 2025. Over the next three years, North Korea moved closer to China. Just as Hong Kong was assimilated into China in 2020, North Korea became a de facto Chinese province.

Vladimir Putin celebrated his seventy-seventh birthday in Kyiv in 2029 following what Moscow termed as "Ukraine's reaccession" to Russia that was a de facto annexation. The Trump decision in 2020 to withdraw substantial troop presence from Germany sent NATO into decline. By 2029, it was in disarray.

Hungary had formally seceded from the alliance. France withdrew from NATO's Military Committee, repeating Charles de Gaulle's action sixty years before, as did Turkey in 2024. NATO was hardly a debating society and no longer a serious military alliance.

In the Persian Gulf, the US policy of maximum pressure and the failure to revive the Joint Comprehensive Plan of Action (JCPOA) that would have prevented Iran from obtaining a nuclear capability gave Tehran the reason and excuse to develop nuclear weapons. In 2029, American intelligence estimated Iran possessed at least one hundred nuclear warheads, a substantial number carried by hypersonic missiles bought from China.

With Iraq and Syria as surrogates and Shia-dominated Bahrain an Iranian ally, Saudi Arabia was forced to defer to Tehran. Iran became the regional superpower. Its reach extended to Israel. Facing annihilation, Israel had no choice except to return the West Bank to Jordan and the Golan Heights to Syria. That transfer coincided with the release from prison of a third former Israeli prime minister convicted of bribery, extortion, and perjury.

In her abbreviated inaugural address, the new president rephrased the Kennedy theme of do not ask what your country can do for you. Instead, she asked, "The question is not how we got here or even how we will extricate ourselves. The question is, can we unify a disunited United States?"

Of course, these scenarios sound wildly implausible. But on New Year's Day 2020, was a global pandemic, subsequent widespread protests over the murder of a black American that would lead to a racial reckoning, or the only sacking of the Capitol since the British attack in 1814 on anyone's mind?

Yes, it can happen here.

Chapter One

THE FIFTH HORSEMAN, MAD, AND A DISUNITED 51% NATION CALLED THE UNITED STATES

A house divided cannot stand, especially when
political termites are at work.

Make no mistake: the arrival of the coronavirus/COVID-19 pandemic was not only a once-in-a-century event. Yes, the pandemic metastasized into a massive international crisis and personal tragedies for many hundreds of millions, if not billions, of global residents who were infected, died, or whose lives were fundamentally disrupted by the virus. But the pandemic was the precursor of profound and even greater tectonic changes that so far have not been fully recognized or understood by governments and the public.

Powerful and invisible forces had arisen to challenge and threaten the safety, security, health, and prosperity of American society at large beyond what has become the great-power competition with China and Russia.

These forces combined the most potentially disruptive, destructive, and insidious challenges, threats, and dangers to the nation since the Civil War, taking the form of a Fifth Horseman of the Apocalypse armed with a new MAD. This was not the Cold War's Mutual Assured Destruction that threatened thermonuclear war.

This new MAD is Massive Attacks of Disruption. And, as with viruses, the new MAD does not respect borders or boundaries nor does it distinguish between domestic and international politics.

The Fifth Horseman and MAD were inadvertent and dangerous by-products of the diffusion of power and globalization. Two consequences are of greatest significance. By the first decade of this century, the combination of the diffusion of power and globalization unraveled the old state-centric Westphalian system—the notion that countries exercised exclusive sovereignty over their own territories and were the ultimate legitimate users of force—that had dominated international politics for 350 years. The centrality of states has been displaced and in part replaced in importance by this horseman and the new MAD.

The second and more dire consequence arose from the central paradox of the new MAD era. During the final decades of Westphalia, standards of living greatly improved for most citizens around the world. Ironically, however, in this process, greater vulnerability and fragility to all forms of disruption were created by both man and nature.

Worse, for the United States, as MAD was taking hold, political divisions had not been as intractable possibly since 1860. How America became so disunited is part of this story. And this extreme divisiveness has created its own unique vulnerability that exposed potential flaws and weaknesses in the Constitution and the system of checks and balances to disruption, further crippling the ability of the government to govern. It is this unprecedented vulnerability and viability of the

Constitution that may prove the most daunting challenge to American democracy in a century and a half.

Beyond sounding this dire warning about the gravity of these conditions, the purposes of this book are threefold. The first is to tell the story and the history of how a Fifth Horseman of the Apocalypse, armed with the new MAD, displaced the Cold War's MAD as the organizing strategic paradigm for national security.

Second is to demonstrate how and why the new MAD and its seven major disruptors differ in magnitude from past disruptions and pose potentially existential challenges, dangers, and threats at least as great or greater than those of traditional state and nonstate actors because of the MAD paradox. As societies advanced and standards of living increased due to globalization, vulnerabilities and fragilities multiplied geometrically.

Third and most importantly are the recommendations for necessary changes to the organization, policies, and strategies of the US government to fulfill the aspirations of the preamble to the Constitution "to form a more perfect Union, establish Justice, insure domestic Tranquility, provide for the common defense, promote the general Welfare, and secure the Blessings of Liberty to ourselves and our Posterity" in a MAD-driven age.

One engine empowering these reforms and recommendations is this book's argument for a national private-public investment fund of up to $3 trillion. The fund, if approved, would support investments in healthcare, the environment and climate change, high-technology areas from artificial intelligence to genome research, and the nation's failing infrastructure.

The Biden administration has proposed a different approach in the form of three bills totaling $6 trillion that do not include public-private partnerships. Full approval by Congress of the Jobs and Families bills will not occur. Hence, at some time in the future after this book is published, the necessity for a National Investment Fund should resurface.

The United States has, over the past decades, become a 51 percent nation, divided almost equally over virtually every issue and thus fractured and disunited. That has made America and Americans extraordinarily more susceptible to all forms of disruption because its government and political system are increasingly unable to respond to extraordinary stress and make difficult, unifying decisions.

To compound and complicate the dangers of MAD, historically, American presidents too often failed to exercise appropriate strategic thought, judgment, and empathy in domestic and foreign policy decision-making. Adequate knowledge and understanding of conditions and situations were not always sought or were ignored and dismissed before decisions were made. Examples of these failures follow.

Whether embarking on military interventions and adventures for the wrong reasons such as in Vietnam and the second Iraq War or diminishing or dismissing crises such as the virulence of pandemics in 1918–1920 and 2020 as two presidents have, bad outcomes were assured. These failures are likely to be made worse in a MAD-driven information age. A principal reason, as will be argued, is that not only are knowledge and understanding often lacking in decision-making, but truth and fact are now missing in action as well in a 51 percent divided nation.

These continuing failures are manifested in the current great-power competition with China and Russia, a competition that will prove unsustainable, unaffordable, and unexecutable. The military aims of the US National Defense Strategy of 2018 (NDS) and continued by the Biden administration are "to compete, deter, and, if war comes, defeat China or Russia or North Korea or Iran and violent extremism." Nowhere, however, are "compete," "deter," and "defeat" defined. No operational concepts and plans yet exist to achieve these ends. No "off-ramp" exists to prevent a future confrontation or conflict.

Nor is any time scale offered as to whether or not this competition has an end date and how that might be determined.

As the Cold War's Mutual Assured Destruction was an outgrowth of the specter of thermonuclear war and societal annihilation, the new MAD is a product of seven current major disruptive forces. The first two are potentially the most dangerous: failed and failing government and climate change. The remaining disruptors—cyber, social media, drones, terrorism, and debt—should not be underestimated in the damage and dislocation each can cause.

MAD and these disruptors target societal vulnerabilities and fragilities. Chapter 2 presents how each of the disruptors can impose great damage, disarray, and destruction in detailed scenarios drawn from actual events carrying on from the world of 2029 described in the preface.

Surprisingly, MAD has a beneficial side. The industrial and information technological revolutions have been profoundly yet creatively disruptive. So too were the American and French Revolutions. Human ingenuity, innovation, imagination, and inspiration are as unlimited as Einstein's view of the universe: finite but unbounded.

Revolutionary technologies—from artificial intelligence and machine learning to quantum physics, 3D printing, and DNA research—are creating more knowledge on a routine basis than has existed throughout history. Each offers potential and dramatic breakthroughs that can better society and mankind or disrupt and divide it further.

The Gordian knot–like problem is corralling the dangerous side of the new MAD to exploit the power of positive disruption while not neglecting traditional security threats and challenges that are also likely to exploit MAD, knowingly or not. Solutions will need new and perhaps revolutionary intellectual, conceptual, strategic, political, and practical approaches and ideas.

Yet today, why have governments been oblivious to the potential and obvious vulnerabilities and fragilities of society to MAD?

One answer is that human nature is inherently optimistic. Cynicism and skepticism are not politically acceptable characteristics to most voters and publics. Absent crisis, governments do not embark on radical or major changes, especially expensive ones. And last, making predictions, especially about the future, is inherently elusive.

Disruption has never been viewed as a or even *the* major factor in protecting and assuring national security. Other, more direct threats were, including war, nuclear proliferation, terrorism, crime, poverty, drugs, mass migration, and adversaries out to do harm to the nation. In essence, the danger of disruption was hidden in plain sight.

THE SEVEN DISRUPTORS

The fear and reach of MAD are propelled by seven powerful disruptors noted earlier: failed and failing government, climate change, cyber, social media, terrorism, exploding debt, and drones. The impact of any or all of these disruptors can be massive for three reasons.

First, the basis for the US Constitution is checks and balances. In 2021, as will be shown, both were becoming increasingly unchecked and unbalanced due to extreme partisanship and political polarization reflected in a 51 percent nation, divided on virtually every issue, large or small. Governance under those circumstances was in gridlock.

MAD exacerbates this gridlock to an even greater level of paralysis because of the limitations of government to recognize or cope with these disruptors and their debilitating effects. The takeover by a mob of the Capitol building on January 6, 2021 and the unprecedented second impeachment of Donald Trump were the unmistakable symptoms of a broken government and a Constitution under attack.

Second is the synergy and interconnectivity among these disruptors. Any one can and has exacerbated and magnified the impact of the others—and vice versa.

Third, technology makes the seven disruptors ubiquitous with the ability to affect, in real time, significant swaths of society for good or ill with unprecedented impact.

Further, a collective failure to understand and learn from the past persists in the human psyche. Y2K, the potential crisis that postulated computers would be unable to accommodate the transition of centuries from 1999 to 2000, never erupted. Hence, the possibly disastrous consequences were dismissed with relief. COVID is not Y2K, and after the 1918–1920 Spanish flu, the United States basically exercised collective amnesia. Will that failure be repeated?

A brief overview of how these disruptors are attacking a house divided offers an initial appreciation of their seriousness and reveals the flagrant absence of corrective actions. The next chapter describes in detail some of the likely MAD-induced scenarios arising from these seven disruptors.

Climate change has already wrought massive destruction through droughts, floods, fires, and superstorms. In some cases, these disruptions created extraordinary humanitarian disasters, forcing millions of refugees and evacuees to seek safety, food, and shelter. Yet many Americans deny the impact or the existence of climate change.

The massive SolarWinds cyberattacks in 2020, presumably from Russian sources and undetected for months, could have crippled electrical grids, financial networks, and businesses as the subsequent cyber shutdown and shakedown of Colonial Pipeline did. If nonstate actors or individuals decide to disrupt the power grid—and Chapter 2 raises this scenario—cyber is not their only tool. Physical destruction of major transformers or downing power and other distribution lines can be crippling. Overloading or disrupting electronic financial transactions is already occurring with flash trading in stock markets.

Yet the nation lacks an effective national cyber strategy. Merely calling for greater resilience to disruption is not a strategy.

Filled with disruptive and malign activity, social media has a powerful role to play in spreading disinformation, misinformation, outright lies, and chaos. False videos called "deep fakes" can fraudulently depict individuals in comprising positions and the worst possible light. Conspiracy theories already flood these virtual spaces. Much of the January 6 insurrection was organized through social media.

Promoting panic across any media is not a new phenomenon; social media and the internet just make it much easier. Even attacks by little green men from Mars can instantaneously circle the global commons via social media and the internet. Something similar occurred in 1938, when Orson Welles and his Mercury Theatre actors presented a radio program on another Wells, H. G., and his book published three decades before, *The War of the Worlds.* Despite repeated announcements that the program was fictitious and there was no attack from Mars, many listeners believed Earth was being invaded. In 2020, posts on social media asserting COVID-19 mutated to an even more contagious and deadly form were made. This capacity for deception and disruption is a growing fact of life and to be ignored only at our own peril.

Yet no modus operandi for regulating social media exists.

Drones are ubiquitous, easily and cheaply manufactured in basements and garages. Drones can fill nearly unlimited tasks from the most mundane housekeeping and home delivery chores to conducting intrusive surveillance and dropping bombs and missiles on targets. Regulations for owning and operating drones are in place. But these still are immature at best, even though the government updated some of these rules in late 2020 for the two million unmanned vehicles in the hands of private citizens.

Preventing large-scale interference with aircraft and other drones, for example, is still unfinished business. (One drone came close enough for Air Force One to take evasive action.) Yet no comprehensive rules of the road for drones have been established.

Massive acts of terrorism far more destructive than September 11—possibly with nuclear, biological, chemical, drone, or cyber weapons—can utterly disrupt our way of life. Terrorist attacks provoked US military interventions into Afghanistan, Iraq, Somalia, and other hot spots of violent extremism. A greater worry is homegrown terrorists, either native-born or naturalized. With the exception of a Saudi officer undergoing flight training who carried out a shooting in Pensacola, Florida in 2019, every act of terror in the United States since September 11 has been committed by a US citizen.

Right-wing militias and cults such as QAnon threaten people of color, immigrants, "the deep state," and "the swamp." The 1995 bombing of the Murrah Federal Building in Oklahoma City by Timothy McVeigh, a Gulf War veteran awarded the Bronze Star, is suggestive that violence is contagious and deadly. McVeigh's complaint was directed at a corrupt government. Yet has sufficient attention been paid to this homegrown terrorist threat?

The effect of exploding debt reaching in excess of $30 trillion (or one and a half times the US 2020 gross domestic product) as coronavirus/COVID-19 is contained or dissipates could be financially catastrophic. Interest rates will not remain close to zero indefinitely. As rates rise, interest payments will become financial weapons of mass destruction, forcing massive budgetary cuts to basic services.

Entitlement payments for Social Security, healthcare, and other safety nets will be vulnerable to reductions. Current annual defense spending of $715 billion for the 2022 fiscal year will be unsustainable especially as the Biden administration has tentatively proposed a $6 trillion budget for 2022. In these circumstances, will new budget priorities reflect the constraints of the debt and deficits or maintain the status quo as politically more expedient despite the costs? And no matter the priority, what decisions will be politically acceptable or viable? Will the debt be allowed to swell unchecked?

WHAT VULNERABILITY MEANS
FOR YOU AND FOR US

Before the internet and smartphones transformed society, electricity had the equivalent effect of modernizing America in the early twentieth century. Like most Americans, I am entirely dependent on these and other information technologies. At the height of the pandemic in 2020, our internet at home failed. Repair was not immediate and throughout much of the fall, we were intermittently without the internet and email. The impact was immediate and daunting.

While self-quarantining to protect against coronavirus infection, life became almost entirely dependent on the internet. All sorts of business that had previously been done in person was conducted virtually. Zoom and other connections provided means for electronic meetings and virtual doctor's appointments. Online ordering services became essential for delivery of items from food to toilet paper to Christmas gifts. Bills were paid electronically. Where would we have been without Amazon, Netflix, and Hulu to pass the many hours at home in self-isolation?

The temporary disruption of our internet in late 2020 was a crisis threatening our quality of life. Fortunately, internet service was restored after several weeks. However, the vulnerabilities and consequences were evident, frightening, and chastening. Some people are desperate after misplacing or losing a cell phone even for a short period. Suppose internet and smartphone services and electrical power were massively disrupted for considerable periods of time across societies and around the globe. What would happen then?

How have societies managed to become so vulnerable and fragile concurrent with the extraordinary advances in living standards made across the globe? What do these broader vulnerabilities and fragilities mean for protecting national security and for those in government responsible for assuring public safety, health, and well-being?

While lip service has been plentiful and pandemics have long been regarded as potential threats, this nation and most others were totally unprepared and unready for its spread, as COVID-19 has underscored. Likewise, vulnerabilities and fragilities of the electrical power grid, food and water supplies, and critical infrastructure have been understood and identified as such for decades. Yet despite the creation of a Department of Homeland Security, how seriously was preventive and protective action taken?

Even with intelligence and other unmistakable warnings about pending disruptive attacks, the history of effective responses has been bleak. None was sufficient to force taking advance or preemptive action before disaster struck. Pandemics, for example, had long been predicted and war-gamed to death. Yet COVID-19 spread around the world unchecked.

Bill Clinton downplayed the 1993 al-Qaeda attacks in New York that did virtually no damage and chose to treat terrorism only as a law enforcement matter.

George W. Bush ignored warnings about Osama bin Laden, the impact of Hurricane Katrina, and the "what next" question after invading Afghanistan and Iraq.

Donald Trump, despite admitting he was well aware of the danger, initially dismissed the coronavirus so as not to panic the nation, and lost precious months in preventing its spread.

So far, the Biden administration has not been in office long enough to permit an objective assessment, although his proposed spending bills and budgets are potentially transformational. Whether that will be for better or worse remains a looming and daunting question.

Vulnerability and fragility are easily exploited. Normally, weaknesses are assumed as surrogates for vulnerability and thus subject to disruption, denial, damage, or destruction. People of advancing age and with preexisting conditions are most vulnerable to coronavirus. In politics, candidates are vulnerable to allegations of wrongdoings (true or not), misstatements, adverse votes, opposition research, negative campaigning, and past and present foolish errors and mistakes.

Elections are vulnerable to fraud, interference, and manipulation even though the 2020 American presidential elections were declared the most secure ever. Homes and buildings in areas prone to forest fires, floods, storms, and earthquakes are vulnerable. Businesses are vulnerable to reverses in economic cycles, labor strikes, and, perhaps most of all, competition. Societies are vulnerable to the Four and now Fifth Horseman. And people are vulnerable to a wide spectrum of untoward and unwanted acts from accidents, gossip, and the vagaries of life.

Strengths also can become potential vulnerabilities. Jujitsu turns an opponent's strength into weakness. Nature does so in life. The steamship *Titanic* was deemed unsinkable and thus invulnerable. It was not.

Fragility is the capacity to break or be easily damaged. Fine porcelain is fragile. But care is taken to protect fragile objects. The distinctions are important.

Simply because something is fragile does not produce vulnerability unless outside factors make it so. In a geostrategic or political sense, the most fragile objects are not always the most vulnerable. And while the Twin Towers were not fragile, it turned out those skyscrapers were highly vulnerable to terrorists.

Interdependence and interconnectivity obviously create dependencies, some of which can become highly disruptive vulnerabilities. Ordinary dependence on energy, water, and food, as well as electricity and the internet, can become vulnerabilities if access is denied.

Supply chains are prime examples. Assembly of most products—from cars, TV sets, and airplanes to computers, cell phones, and pharmaceuticals—relies on individual parts and components made in countries where labor is much cheaper than in advanced states. That has produced disruptions that have become powerful factors in the political debate. The shortage of computer chips in the wake of COVID-19 is another example of supply chain vulnerability.

Comparative advantage, defined by the great economist David Ricardo three centuries ago, explains this phenomenon. Why pay more for goods or products that can be grown or manufactured less expensively elsewhere provided national security is not endangered and access to these sources is maintained? Yet one consequence is the transfer of jobs to lower-cost sources for these products.

Unless compensated with new jobs or some form of workers' insurance, growing unemployment translates into anger and resentment, with clear political implications. Donald Trump understood this disruptive power, which he translated into "America first" policies and commitments to bring jobs home. China became the poster child for theft of American jobs along with vast amounts of intellectual property.

Further, virtually all markets are linked, so disrupting supply chains and markets can have catastrophic effects. After the 1973 Arab–Israeli War, the oil embargo imposed by OPEC member states had a particularly disruptive impact on America and its economy. Long lines for gasoline were synonymous with this disruption. And the grounding of a massive merchant ship blocked the Suez Canal for nearly two weeks in early 2021, disrupting commerce as ships took at least an extra week having to transit around South Africa's Cape of Good Hope.

COVID-19 underscored the calamitous effects of MAD on the normal way of life, including impact on the food chain, businesses, schools, government, and virtually all aspects of society. Although Russian interference in US presidential elections did not affect the 2016 and 2020 outcomes, it still attempted to exploit the vulnerability of an open society—complete ease of access and openness.

Russian interference may have had a decisive effect in the Brexit vote in the UK in 2016. Some evidence suggests Moscow used social media to influence upwards of two million British citizens, unaffiliated with any political party, to vote Leave—a huge vulnerability to the Remainers. That tactic paralleled the Conservative Party's information campaign targeting the same cohort of undecided Britons.

Cyber, internet, and social media link all parts of the globe. Vulnerabilities and fragilities of individuals, societies, organizations, and governments to hacking and assaults by bots and trolls are well known. Governments, corporations, and ordinary citizens spend huge sums protecting against hacking and other malicious electronic interventions.

THE END OF WESTPHALIA AND THE RISE OF MAD

This history begins with the erosion of the 350-year-old state-centric system of international politics and the subsequent emergence of a Fifth Horseman of the Apocalypse armed with the new MAD. The critical difference between the two MADs is that during the Cold War, thermonuclear war was deterrable and thus deterred. The new MAD may be contained and mitigated. But much of MAD is not deterrable.

Few understood that the end of the Cold War sounded the death knell for the Westphalian system. Globalization and the diffusion of all forms of power accelerated that demise. Smaller states, nonstate actors, nongovernmental organizations (NGOs), and individuals were empowered by these forces at the expense of traditional states.

Globalization connected virtually all states, markets, and peoples, in many cases greatly raising standards of living. But globalization had a downside and a dark side. The downside hurt the industrial labor sector in advanced nations, where lower-cost foreign workers and goods eliminated millions of domestic jobs. One highly negative consequence was a backlash to globalization and the rise of populism.

The dark side created many societal vulnerabilities and fragilities often extremely susceptible to acts of massive disruption. The diffusion of power proliferated unprecedented capabilities and opportunities for nonstate groups and individuals to exploit, whether in pursuit of destructive or noble aims. In large part, unimpeded access was available either through global networks and the internet or the nature of free and open societies whose restrictions on entry could be circumvented. Some of the nineteen al-Qaeda hijackers did so by undergoing pilot training at civilian American flight schools.

This diffusion of power, combined with information technologies, also had an even darker side, weaponizing social media and cyber as noted earlier. Hugely disruptive attacks without attribution can be launched from anywhere on the planet with a computer or a smartphone, a distinctive aspect of MAD. Disruption wrought by cyber and social media does physical as well as reputational harm, facilitating virtual crimes that steal data or money outright or deny service until money is paid.

At no time in history has such ease of disruptive access been available to so many, nor has attribution been so easy to hide. Facebook, Instagram, and Twitter, among other technologies, extended the reach of billions of people anywhere on the globe to many more billions online everywhere, every day.

The colored revolutions in Europe and the Arab Spring in North Africa in the first decade of the twenty-first century were driven by social media. The 2011 Egyptian revolution culminating in hundreds of thousands of protestors gathering in Tahrir Square was spontaneously organized through cell phones and social media. Those protests forced long-standing president Hosni Mubarak to step down from office. Mubarak's long-term replacement was another general and democracy was not established. However, the power of this medium has been underestimated in the West in terms of impact and in taking countermeasures, unlike the potential or actual adversaries of the United States who are readily exploiting this weaponization.

If the spring 2020 protests and riots that spread across America over the killing of a black man by Minneapolis police officers had been as fueled by social media as Tahrir Square was, would the consequences have been as dramatic and sweeping in forcing change as occurred in Cairo or North Africa? One wonders.

Even before he was president, Donald Trump had many millions of followers on Twitter, something no prior president enjoyed. Until his account was cancelled following the Capitol takeover on January 6, 2021, Trump had an extraordinary and unprecedented communications platform. On Twitter, Trump transmitted, in real time, messages to his base; issued orders for running the government such as to remove American troops summarily from Syria; and fired senior appointees without consultations with advisors.

Likewise, social media has transformed how traditional politics are conducted. Campaigns for or against any issue and running for office now depend more on social media than using traditional television, radio, and newspaper outlets. Junior and newly elected members of Congress with tens of thousands of social media followers in many ways can exercise more influence than far more senior representatives who lack that same access. Dealing with this social media phenomenon may exceed the ability of government to provide sensible policies and guidance without impinging on free speech, the freedom to assemble, and other constitutional rights.

MAD AND AMERICAN POLITICS

The United States endured a civil war, fought world and lesser wars, dealt with economic and financial crises and depressions, grappled with problems of race and gender inequality, overcame political divisions, and survived at least one pandemic. The difference today is confronting current and future challenges, dangers, and threats with a divided 51 percent nation and a political structure that, by many accounts, seems ill-prepared if not ill-suited for the coming decades of the MAD-driven twenty-first century.

When the coronavirus struck without warning in early 2020, the United States was at far greater jeopardy and risk than its citizens realized. As the pandemic dissipated and vaccines and treatments became universally available by summer 2021, the nation seemed to return to some degree of normality. However, after the Spanish flu epidemic ran its course by 1920, its memory was quickly erased.

Will this amnesia be repeated? Or will the Biden and future administrations learn from it that MAD will not disappear and in many ways is far more dangerous than its Cold War predecessor? It cannot be fully deterred, merely contained, mitigated, and in some cases, prevented.

In a 51 percent nation, unlike the past, external crises such as the attack on Pearl Harbor that rallied a deeply divided nation over entering World War II, are unlikely to have the same unifying effect. MAD is crisis-rich, affecting virtually all sectors of society. Yet, COVID-19 in many ways disunited a divided nation as much or more than it generated consensus on containing and preventing the pandemic.

One accelerant for this divisiveness was the personality and politics of Donald Trump. Past presidents would certainly have been more empathetic to the ongoing tragedies caused by the pandemic (or the murder of George Floyd and other African Americans by police and would-be vigilantes). All would have listened more closely to expert medical and science advice and not rely on instinct (or Fox television) to set health and other policies.

The forty-fifth president initially refused to follow guidelines from the Centers for Disease Control and Prevention (CDC) about wearing a protective face mask in public. Many Americans followed that example. He took hydroxychloroquine as a prophylactic measure against the advice of his own Food and Drug Administration, which has since been banned for experimental use. And he threatened to deploy the US military to quell the protests and riots sparked by George Floyd's murder because, as Trump pronounced, "When the looting starts, the shooting starts," presumably meaning American soldiers could be firing on American citizens.

After the presidential election, President Trump's refusal to allow the transition process to proceed for more than three weeks was spiteful and unhelpful for the new administration in preparing to assume office. Further, he lied to his base and to the public claiming he had won a "landslide" electoral victory and then had the results stolen.

But no matter what Donald Trump said or tweeted, some two-fifths of Americans supported him in virtually all circumstances. Seventy-four million votes received in 2020 is an impressive number. An overwhelming majority of Republicans believe Trump and his team responded well to the pandemic. Democrats (and some three-fifths of Americans) did not.

In the last week of his presidency, Donald Trump was impeached for inciting insurrection, enraging a mob, and encouraging its takeover of the Capitol building. His Senate trial raised grave questions as to constitutionality and whether the nation would be further and possibly irreconcilably divided given the size of public support for Trump and the extraordinary acceptance of the lies and falsehoods made over an election that was declared to be free and fair by the Trump administration itself, if not its leader. He was acquitted on almost a strict party line vote.

Personal animosities make politics even more pernicious. That the last president and the Speaker of the House refused to speak for months was not symptomatic of good political health. These cleavages magnified the tensions between public safety and civil liberties over the pandemic.

After the first several months of self-quarantine in 2020, public unrest grew. A substantial number of Americans believed that the right to work or assemble was more important than protecting public health. The president and his party seemed to support these protesters. Democrats did not, further accentuating the political divide.

The new MAD has attacked more than just people; it has also constituted a frontal assault on the basic political structures of nations, especially democracies, and the ability to govern. In America, MAD has intensified the threat to the Constitution by widening political divides, forcing checks and balances to become increasingly unbalanced and unchecked.

Succession of leadership was another critical issue raised by the pandemic. The Twelfth, Twenty-Second, and Twenty-Fifth Amendments to the Constitution modified by the Electoral Count Act of 1887 and the Presidential Succession Act of 1947 were approved decades and centuries before MAD or COVID-19 was ever envisaged. In line after the president are the vice president, the Speaker of the House, and the Senate president pro tempore.

Suppose that President Trump (or a future president) had been incapacitated by COVID-19 or another ailment, as Woodrow Wilson was felled by a stroke in 1919. Trump, of course, had a case of COVID-19 that was far more serious than first reported. Under the Twenty-Fifth Amendment, a majority of the cabinet or two-thirds of Congress must vote to make the vice president acting president until such time as the president recovers. But suppose the vice president was stricken too? It is not an unimaginable scenario since the virus had already infected the White House.

Would a Republican cabinet bestow the acting presidency on a Democratic speaker? Or would a Democratic cabinet do the same for a Republican speaker? No rule book applies here either. To complicate matters, the next in line during the Trump years, the president pro tempore of the Senate, was eighty-seven-year-old Chuck Grassley of Iowa, who also tested positive for COVID.

These potential flaws were underscored in the aftermath of the 2020 election. The temporary occupation of the Capitol building on January 6, 2021, led to unprecedented security precautions for the January 20 inauguration. Yet the top three elected officials—the president-elect, the vice president-elect, and the Speaker of the House—were on the stage at the same time. The president pro tempore was in a secure location and at noon on January 20, when the new team took office, was eighty-year-old Senator Pat Leahy.

Next in line for succession is the secretary of state, followed by the remaining members of the cabinet. But the Biden administration had no confirmed secretaries prior to assuming office. Had the top four principals been incapacitated for whatever reason, theoretically the United States would have had no president. While this scenario is exceedingly unlikely, it is not impossible. That condition must be addressed.

WHAT NEXT AND WHAT HAVE WE LEARNED?

Let me be blunt: America's forty-sixth president, Joe Biden, was dealt the worst hand of any incoming chief executive since Franklin Delano Roosevelt took office during the Great Depression in 1933. In early 2021, the nation faced a series of crises: a once-in-a-century pandemic that had not run its course, a nation as politically torn and divided among itself as at any time since 1860, a hostile Republican Senate minority, and the unnoticed emergence of a new and so far unrecognized constellation of threats that extends well beyond traditional state-centric challenges of the past.

If this prospect was not sufficiently daunting for the president and the nation, America's economy had not recovered from COVID-19 even though stock markets hit new highs as 2020 ended and continued into 2021. Relations with Russia and China remained frigid. According to most opinion polls, America's international standing and influence were in tatters.

The nation suffered the most contested election arguably since 1876. President Biden's political honeymoon was cut short. And his list of appointees navigating the confirmation process in Congress took more time than that of his predecessors. By mid-2021, only a relative handful of some 1,400 Senate-confirmed positions had been filled.

Repairing and closing the seemingly intractable political divides of a disunited United States bitterly split on virtually every issue would test the combined skills of the Founding Fathers and Abraham Lincoln. Before the arrival of MAD, America was already metastasizing into a starkly polarized 51 percent nation.

Political consensus was virtually nonexistent. Intractably divided along party lines, clear means of reconciling these differences likewise were missing in action. How the nation reached this critical stage of such disunity is a separate story and largely a function of failed and failing government.

Since the beginning of US involvement in the Vietnam War with the Gulf of Tonkin incident in August 1964, over the next decades, Americans became increasingly distrustful of government as well as other institutions, from the media and Boy Scouts to the Catholic Church. Americans grew frustrated, angered, disillusioned, and often desperate as the government's failure to meet basic needs and expectations grew larger and larger. After George H.W. Bush, four relatively inexperienced presidents succeeded him. One consequence was a further deterioration of the government's ability to govern adequately. Twenty years of endless wars did not help and drained the treasury and American patience.

During these decades, both political parties gravitated to more radical left and right positions, abandoning the traditional center-right, center-left politics favored by most Americans. Donald Trump became the symptom and a cause of the disruption that aimed to drain "the swamp" in Washington and destroy the "deep state," preventing and impeding progress in responding to public needs. Millions of Americans were attracted to or mesmerized by Trump and perhaps an equal number was drawn to his opposition.

This polarization achieved the impossible: politicizing the coronavirus/COVID-19 pandemic. In a rational world, it would seem inconceivable that in the midst of a global pandemic, both political parties could take diametrically opposed sides on the dangers and seriousness of the disease, on vaccinations, and even on the wearing of protective masks. It was, however, what happened.

These partisan divisions grew deeper with the 2020 presidential election and the former president's assault on the legitimacy of the voting process, threatening the checks and balances that are foundational to the Constitution and America's democracy.

COVID-19 rightly dominated the attention of governments and publics. As it stands today, the disease in America was not dissipating as only half the adult population was vaccinated. Excessive focus on this most imminent disruptor now, however, will not provide solutions for the potential of MAD to impose further dislocation and destruction across societal and structural vulnerabilities.

These vulnerabilities apply to the private and public sectors and to the government and individuals. Chapter 8 focuses on the domestic implications. The effects of vulnerability and disruption of national security are at least as frightening.

In 1980, a study released by the Center for Strategic and International Studies concluded that the most vulnerable sector of American infrastructure was the national electrical power grid. Forty years after the CSIS study, the electrical power grid is even more vulnerable to cyberattack. Replacing a single transformer on which much of the grid depends to distribute electricity takes at least a year, the time needed to construct a new one (most likely in Germany) and transport a machine of that physical size thousands of miles.

Failure to understand the extent of the threat was evident in the little read but very important report from the congressionally mandated Cyberspace Solarium Commission. The commission's findings came out in March 2020 in a blistering critique of the absence of appreciation and awareness of the very clear and present danger in terms of hacking, theft, and physical damage from cybercrime. As with many warnings, this one, too, may collect dust and lie fallow on bookshelves or distant reaches of cyberspace.

A study on US Navy and Marine Corps cyber vulnerability commissioned by the secretary of the navy in 2017 was reinforced by the Solarium Commission's findings. Released in March 2019, the navy study concluded that the Chinese cyber threat was "existential" to naval forces.

The secretary of the navy's study did not get wide press or attention. One assumes the rest of the Department of Defense is not much better off in its vulnerability to Chinese cyber. The CSIS, US Navy, and Solarium studies are indicative of the range of potential vulnerabilities that will also affect the private sector and individuals. Chapter 2 presents a number of very troubling scenarios showing vulnerabilities to the various disruptors.

Vulnerability very much applies to even the most powerful of our nation's security instruments: the US military. How might a potential foe or malign nonstate actor attack the most powerful military in the world? The simple answer is through its vulnerabilities.

Two Chinese Air Force colonels answered that question in a 1999 book titled *Unrestricted Warfare*. The colonels argued for an asymmetric strategy to disrupt both an enemy's networks and its command and control. Since the US plans to fight "away" wars, it is both dependent on and vulnerable over deploying forces and logistics to distant areas.

Suppose an adversary penetrated the Pentagon's classified and unclassified networks as the navy study implies and many war games have shown is possible. Disruption produces chaos. The so-called Time Phased Force and Deployment List (TPFDL) that is the logistical operational order for mobilizing and deploying forces in a crisis, along with the entire Transportation Command, would be hacked.

Tanks or aircraft destined for an embarkation port on the East Coast could be rerouted to the West Coast. Ammunition needed for naval forces in the Mediterranean could end up in Alaska or Asia. And the integrity of command and control could be compromised or disrupted once networks were penetrated.

The growth of vulnerabilities and the susceptibility to MAD is a clear and present national security danger, not reflected in current plans and actions. At a granular level, military forces that have been the bedrock of national security and the defense of nations face daunting challenges posed by MAD. A virus can immobilize a giant nuclear aircraft carrier. What about ground and air forces that train, operate, and fight in proximity where "social distancing" is impossible?

Allied and Central Powers faced this conundrum in 1918 when the Spanish flu would claim more lives globally than all of World War I. A similar fate awaited American marines on Guadalcanal from August 1942 to February 1943 when malaria inflicted more casualties than the Japanese Army did. When that campaign ended, of the nearly twenty thousand Japanese dead, the bulk had succumbed to disease and starvation.

America's allies confront the same pressures of MAD. Future resources for defense will be constrained at best, given deficit spending to keep economies and people financially afloat. But will the same limits apply to China, Russia, North Korea, Iran, and terrorist groups? How will China and Russia evolve when COVID dissipates?

What about crises elsewhere between nuclear adversaries, specifically India and Pakistan, or in the Persian Gulf, where Saudi oil facilities were struck by Iranian drones in 2019 and where Israel and Iran are waging an undeclared cyberwar? The eleven-day war between Israel and Hamas in May 2021 could have exploded regionally and fortunately did not. Venezuela was in Washington's sights while much of South America and the Southern Hemisphere were feeling the wrath of COVID-19. NATO allies France, Greece, and Turkey are on opposite sides in the ongoing Libyan civil war.

After the attacks of December 7, 1941 and September 11, 2001, citizens had immediate means to respond. After the battleship fleet was sunk at Pearl Harbor, Americans enlisted en masse in the military, bought war bonds, took jobs in defense industries where women played a dominant role, and planted victory gardens. Similarly, Americans rallied in 2001 with direct action to join the military or other national security organizations.

Responses from these and other past crises no longer fit today. Enlisting in the military, buying war bonds, or growing victory gardens will not defeat a virus. Washing one's hands, keeping space from others, wearing masks, self-quarantining, and remaining calm are not direct means of confronting and ending this invisible threat. As America and much of the world literally shut down, the cumulative social and psychological impact may not be apparent for a long time. And what happens if other crises strike?

History offers a broader perspective, too often ignored or forgotten, about future choices, challenges, and consequences and for economic rejuvenation.

Three important insights from the 1918–1920 Spanish flu, used as a ubiquitous reference to today's pandemic, have been forgotten or ignored and are highly relevant, especially to generating a potential renaissance.

First, that period was far more violent, turbulent, and disruptive than today. In 1918, World War I was raging. In America, labor was rioting and women were powerful voices demanding the vote. The nation panicked first over the so-called Red Scare and then, more so, over two dozen terrorist letter bomb attacks that killed only two people, both leading to massive arrests and partial suspension of *habeas corpus*.

Second, after the pandemic passed in 1920, the nation experienced the greatest economic recovery and boom in its history.

Third, failure to prepare for the longer term after 1918 would lead to a second world war, the 1929 stock market crash, and the Great Depression.

Will any of this history be repeated once COVID-19 abates?

What must be done to resolve these imminent crises as well as deal with the traditional threats and challenges that continue to disunite a divided United States?

First, the impact of a MAD-driven world must be understood and acknowledged.

Second, a new model for strategic thinking incorporating MAD must be put in place that reflects the realities of the twenty-first century and rectifies misjudgments and mistakes of the past that produced failure. In that regard, the absence of strategic empathy, that is the ability to understand the other, produces fatal consequences. Vietnam, Afghanistan, and Iraq are case studies of American failures due in large part to a lack of knowledge and understanding.

Third, sweeping changes in American domestic and foreign policies accompanied by major reorganization of many of our political and governmental institutions and structures are crucial if the destructive power of the Fifth Horseman armed with MAD is to be prevented, mitigated, and contained.

To paraphrase Shakespeare, these are *the* questions. Will the president, Congress, and the public recognize the overarching dangers that not only challenge the Constitution and our republic but our way of life posed by MAD that go beyond the traditional Westphalian threats of state actors?

Should the president's proposed sweeping, and some say radical, social, political, economic, and cultural transformations inherent in his spending plans, the greatest since FDR's New Deal, be defeated or greatly reduced, what is the alternative to ensure the vital need for modernization of the nation's largely obsolete infrastructure can still be accomplished?

In July 1945, Winston Churchill was vacationing in France after Germany's unconditional surrender that May. Japan was close to capitulation. Elections in Britain were taking place, and Churchill expected to win. He did not.

Churchill's coalition government was defeated. Labor, under socialist Clement Attlee, won an outright majority in the Commons. Clementine Churchill comforted her husband, suggesting that this defeat could be a "blessing in disguise." Winston pouted that "if this were a blessing, it is indeed well disguised."

COVID-19 has profoundly and incontrovertibly shown how dangerous the new MAD is. Unless we seize the "well-disguised" blessing to learn from and react to this new danger and the reality of a Westphalia II world, Charlie Wilson's lament, noted on the title page, will be proven correct.

Chapter Two

CORONAVIRUS, CLIMATE CHANGE, CYBER, SOCIAL MEDIA, TERRORISM, DEBT, DRONES, AND FAILED GOVERNMENT DRIVEN BY TECHNOLOGY

In the long run, we are all dead.
—John Maynard Keynes
1923, in the Great Debate

The proliferation of mass destruction weapons, mass migration, trade wars, crime, social injustice, and bad luck are highly disruptive and destructive. One significant difference with the Cold War is that the new MAD creates a synergy in which one or more of these major disruptors can exacerbate, magnify, or provoke the others.

Cyber, along with social media, terrorism, and drones, form a toxic mix in that regard as each empowers the others. In the case of cyber and terrorism, the former enables the latter to telecommunicate, plan, and execute operations while recruiting new cohorts. Drones extend the destructive reach of cyber and of terrorism to another physical dimension.

This chapter examines the seven major MAD disruptors that threaten and challenge our safety, security, prosperity, and the government's ability to govern.

THE NATURE OF DISRUPTIONS

At one level, disruptions are part of life—bad weather that forces cancellation of a golf match or baseball game; forgetting to bring a wallet, credit card, misplacing a cell phone, or checkbook when making a major purchase; robocalls that interrupt dinners and family life; and many such seemingly trivial incidents are inconveniences that are tolerated or accepted. However, certain disruptions are far more consequential and even existential.

A heart attack or serious illness, crippling accidents, loss of a job, expulsion from school or university, failure to pass a bar examination, lawsuits, unlawful arrest or detainment, and being victimized by serious crime are higher forms of disruption. The Fifth Horseman evokes even more frightening images of disruption that are potentially existential to societies and governments' ability to govern.

The coronavirus is the latest in a long history of pandemics. Diseases and plagues are as old as mankind. The Black Death in medieval times, the importation of Western diseases to the Incas and Aztecs of Central and South America by Spanish conquistadores in the early sixteenth century, and even the use of smallpox-infected blankets during the French and Indian Wars in England's North American colonies (1754–1763) are part of this history.

What is profoundly different today is the extraordinary increase in vulnerabilities and fragilities that are inherent in a globalized world and the dependencies and interdependencies linking virtually every state economically, financially, socially, electronically, and culturally that make any contagion explosive and disruptive. In comparing the Spanish flu pandemic of 1918–1920 to coronavirus/COVID-19 in Chapter 7, the vulnerabilities and fragilities of society are examined as each evolved over the last century.

COVID-19 has attacked not only public health but the sinews of society, from hospitals and healthcare workers to restaurants, travel, entertainment, transportation, schools, sports, social gatherings, retirement homes, and governments. Underplayed so far is the devastating effect pandemics and diseases could have on livestock, poultry, fish and sea life such as coral reefs, agriculture, farming, and even plants and trees. As the preface noted, the coronavirus migrated to Danish minks.

In 2006, Britain faced foot and mouth disease outbreaks in which two hundred thousand cattle had to be destroyed. In the 1950s, the Dutch elm disease depleted Washington, DC's trees. Wheat, cotton, fruit, rice, and other sectors have never been disease-free. And the use of antibodies in the meat and poultry industries has raised questions about the potential dangers for human consumption.

This conclusion is important: The reach of pandemic infections extends far beyond humans. Indeed, wiping out wheat, corn, or rice crops would be existential to societies dependent on these foods for survival. This potential vulnerability cannot be obscured by the current focus only on COVID-19 and human health.

Further, pandemics can be greatly exacerbated by changing climate and natural conditions from storms, floods, fires, earthquakes, and droughts to warming and cooling trends. The Dust Bowl of the 1930s eviscerated American farming and agriculture throughout the

Midwest with sustained massive droughts. Suppose a pandemic struck the remaining crop and animal populations.

CLIMATE CHANGE

Irrefutable evidence of the power of MAD is found in climate change. While contentious arguments persist over climate change and global warming (which also causes global cooling in other regions), the scientific evidence is overwhelming in the affirmative that both are occurring. Despite heated denials too often reflecting political divides between Republicans and Democrats, the facts are unarguable even though some critics claim that climate change and global warming are functions of weather patterns. Certainly, the Earth's climate has changed throughout history.

Over the past 650 millennia, seven cycles of glacial advance and retreat have been recorded. The last was the end of the Ice Age occurring about twelve thousand years ago. The cause of many of these cycles was small changes in the Earth's orbit that altered solar radiation, hence warming and freezing, and huge meteor strikes. Upon impact, immense dust cloud and debris storms rising into the atmosphere to block sunlight quickly formed. The prolonged absence of warming sunlight sent surface temperatures falling well below freezing. A crucial difference today from past cycles is man-made greenhouse gases.

For nearly the past million years through 1950, CO_2 levels never rose above 300 parts per million (ppm). Today, CO_2 levels are over 430 ppm. As the Intergovernmental Panel on Climate Change concluded, scientific evidence for warming of the climate system is unequivocal. The conclusion drawn by virtually all scientific bodies as well as US government agencies led by NASA is that, with more than a 95 percent probability, this warming is caused by human activity and is proceeding "at a rate that is unprecedented in history."

The evidence is physical and readily observable. Satellites have photographed changes in ocean levels, the decreasing size of polar ice caps, and the increasing frequency of extreme weather events. All the symptoms of climate change are present. That greenhouse gases cause heat to be retained within the Earth's atmosphere and warm the Earth's surface has been known since the mid-1800s.

Additionally, scientific evidence drawn from glaciers as well as data found in ocean sediment, coral reefs, tree rings, and rock formations documents that current warming is increasing at an order of magnitude (ten times) faster that post–Ice Age recovery. Since the late 1800s, the average surface temperature of the planet has risen by about 1.62 degrees Fahrenheit or 0.9 degrees Celsius. The majority of this warming has occurred since the mid-1980s. Each successive year since 2010, records for warmest year in history have been broken.

Similar trends affect the oceans. Over the past fifty years, temperatures have increased about 0.4 degrees Fahrenheit in the upper two thousand feet of ocean levels. Shrinking ice masses and sheets have also been recorded. The rate of Antarctica ice mass loss has tripled since 2010 and is about 130 billion tons per year. Greenland loses nearly 300 billion tons of ice mass a year. The same phenomena apply to glaciers, snow cover, and Arctic Sea ice.

As a result, over the past century, global sea levels have risen about eight inches. More worrying is that since 2000, the rate of sea level rise is doubling and accelerating slightly each year because of the loss of ice mass. The oceans are also affected by acidification. Since the late 1700s and the Industrial Revolution, ocean acidity grew by about a third. It is estimated that the amount of carbon dioxide absorbed by the oceans is growing by about two billion tons per year.

Extreme weather has substantially increased. Hurricanes and typhoons are more frequent, persistent, and powerful, imposing greater levels of storm damage and flooding. Tornadoes and cyclones likewise are increasing in intensity and frequency. Droughts, floods, and fires are more commonplace. While part of California and the Pacific Northwest battled extreme fires in 2019 and more disastrously in 2020, conditions in Siberia, Brazil, and Italy were comparable.

All this scientific and recorded evidence underscores how climate is both causing and accelerating massive attacks of disruption. Interestingly, further proof of the damaging effects of man-made greenhouse gases is in how smog and haze that reduced visibility to close to zero in cities such as Los Angeles and New Delhi evaporated during the long pandemic shutdown. The reason was evident: When fewer vehicles were on the road, fewer greenhouse gases were emitted.

Whether this lesson will be appreciated and have impact remains problematic in a society so politically divided over most issues and especially climate change. Perhaps the worst fires and heat in the history of California and the Pacific Northwest will make a difference. And the superstorm that incapacitated power in Texas in early 2021 was a result of climate change.

Climate change and global warming could obviously have catastrophic and even existential effects on society. Sri Lanka is literally sinking into the sea. While it is too soon to predict that Tallahassee in central Florida or Arizona will become seafront properties, a rise in sea levels is indeed threatening too many coastlines.

Superstorm Sandy imposed catastrophic damage on the Northeast in 2015. Indeed, the storm surge was so powerful that it flooded underground transformers in New York City, cutting off electrical power for many of its citizens for days. Similarly, what happens when superstorms such as Sandy or Katrina strike during a pandemic?

At the end of 2020, when colder weather arrived, COVID-19 infections accelerated asymptotically. Bad weather also adds to restricting outdoors activities. Society will face potentially massive disruption as disease and extreme weather collide, each exacerbating the other.

Perhaps more troublesome, coronavirus and climate change merge in the crosshairs of partisan politics. Despite the history of the Republican Party that has been highly mindful of the environment and supportive of conservation from Theodore Roosevelt through Richard Nixon, who created the Environmental Protection Agency (EPA), and John McCain, leaders in the current GOP largely regard climate change as a hoax and COVID-19's danger as exaggerated. Former President Donald Trump predicted in late February 2020 that the coronavirus would simply disappear, inferring sooner or later.

As the Democratic Party moved left, climate change likewise became politicized with the Green New Deal, a multitrillion-dollar plan ultimately to produce zero carbon emissions. No matter the spirit and intent of the Green New Deal as proposed, it was dead on arrival because of expense and the impossibility of achieving political approval and passage into law. Still, climate change remains an ultimate potential disruptor and black swan event.

CYBER AND SOCIAL MEDIA

Cyber has huge disruptive capacity. In most countries, publics are dependent upon and linked through the internet and social media. With social distancing to mitigate the spread of the coronavirus, the internet and social media became even more important for ordering food and essentials as well as sustaining interpersonal and virtual connections and communications.

In China, for example, cash has become virtually obsolete as financial transactions are conducted by smartphone. Recently, two penniless farmers from the provinces desperate for money attempted to rob a convenience store in Shanghai. The pair was foiled because the store had no cash on hand, as it was unnecessary for transactions.

In states such as Estonia, banking is virtual. About five years ago when Russia disrupted Estonia's internet, the country was temporarily disabled, unable to conduct business transactions. During the Ukrainian conflict, the Russian military was determined to eliminate a senior Ukrainian officer whose battlefield prowess was taking a toll on the Moscow-supported rebel forces. The diabolically clever ploy was to use cyber. Russian forces texted the Ukrainian officer's mother with an urgent message to call her son. She complied. Russian electronic intelligence tracked the call, pinpointed the officer's location, and targeted and killed him with a barrage of artillery and rocket fire.

What does this mean for Americans beyond the unlikely event of being targeted by cell phone despite the ease of tracking? Imagine you check your bank account and find it emptied. Imagine your identity and Social Security number are stolen and you have been billed many tens of thousands of dollars for purchases you did not make.

Suppose your computer is hacked, your files encrypted, and you are faced with a ransom note for payment to unlock your data. Suppose "deep fakes" are posted on the internet of you or your family in compromising positions or engaged in unsavory acts that are entirely contrived. Worse, suppose postings allegedly made by you slandered others, bringing lawsuits by offended parties that are both costly and difficult to rebut.

Suppose you receive an e-mail from the Internal Revenue Service demanding tax payments for $50,000 or from your state or city government that likewise order you to pay a bill or risk losing your home or having water, electricity, and other utilities terminated. Or suppose similar demands are made over allegations of money owed by a spouse or child.

Finally, suppose you receive an email from your doctor or hospital advising you that you have contracted a life-threatening disease and that it is essential to order certain and costly medication via an attached website link. How will you respond?

These cyber vulnerabilities and scenarios apply at every level of society. Cities and states have been ransomed by hackers who have encrypted key files or taken down computer and information systems until payment is received.

A more imaginative cyber scheme was to steal $500 from a million accounts administered by fund managers and banks with balances of at least $250,000. The expectation was that these relatively small thefts would go unnoticed. That amounts to a half billion-dollar crime!

Obviously, more than individuals and nonstate actors inhabit cyberspace. In the next chapter, Russian "active measures" and Chinese cyber meddling will be examined as part of coherent strategies to disrupt adversaries and to advance the interests of both states. But an overview of cyber is important to demonstrate its relationships with MAD and other disruptors.

Cyber sits at the crossroads of privacy and security in which the internet has become indispensable to literally billions of people and to the flow of goods, services, trade, and finance. Social media is used by billions and obviously is a target for hacking and exploiting the vulnerabilities and fragilities of society, even underdeveloped states.

The past record of governments, companies, and individuals being hacked on a daily basis is voluminous. One obvious and still not fully realized conclusion is the essential need for cyber hygiene.

While hackers are often clever, unless or until governments, businesses, and individuals employ scrupulous levels of cyber hygiene to protect valuable data and records—akin to washing hands and practicing social distancing to prevent the spread of coronavirus—hackers retain the advantage. That said, "cyber" has been difficult and elusive to define. Nor has a thorough analysis been done to identify the greatest cyber vulnerabilities and fragilities as well as how to exploit its more beneficial qualities.

A starting point is an effective national cyber strategy setting out specific actions across government, the private sector, and for individuals to deal with this disruptor. After decades, this task remains unfinished business. My last book, *Anatomy of Failure: Why America Loses Every War It Starts*, proposed a strategy and three conceptual models for organizing a cyber framework.

The first was the maritime rules of the road to ensure good and safe seamanship. Cyber rules of the road make sense. Second was the analogy of nuclear deterrence. Within several years of the first uses of nuclear weapons on Japan, nuclear deterrence theory had been well defined along with a strategy for implementing it in practice.

The most applicable analogy is the domestic and international monetary and financial systems and how each operates and is regulated and overseen. The parallels are clear. Cyber and money are ubiquitous. Both are vital to the economy. Both have to contend with thieves, villains, hucksters, and con men. Both need to be kept secure and safe. By and large, the regulatory, legal, and international agreements have done this for the monetary system. To minimize the impact of the new MAD, a national strategy that sets out a cyber regime is vital.

Ticking cyber time bombs are everywhere. The Department of Defense regularly experiences millions of attempted hacks on a routine basis. The White House Offices of Management and Budget and Personnel have had millions of records compromised. And the well-known hacks of Estonia in 2007, Georgia in 2008, and Iran's nuclear facilities with the Stuxnet virus in 2010 have been publicized, as has North Korea's hack of Sony Pictures in retaliation for a satirical depiction of Kim Jong-un.

As noted, a review for the secretary of the navy concluded China's cyber threat was "existential" to naval forces. The secretary himself had grave concerns about China's ability to attack and shut down communications networks and even hack directly into units of the fleet. A vignette makes this point.

In 2018, at a war game at the Naval War College in Newport, Rhode Island, one of the participants made an extraordinary claim. A lieutenant serving aboard a nuclear attack submarine that had been pier side for nearly four years awaiting funds for an overhaul decided to study cyber hacking. He challenged and indeed dared his group to pick any US Navy warship. Armed only with his cell phone, this officer then declared he could fire that ship's Tomahawk cruise missiles remotely.

His challenge was referred to higher authority. But articles in the unclassified press, including China's, suggest that this assertion of cyber intrusion directly into a warship from a seemingly ordinary external source was far from impossible, even if it seemed more suitable to a James Bond action movie.

Scenarios that demonstrate the synergy and interactions between all these disruptors follow in the discussion on terrorism and drones. However, the threat of cyber imposing MAD is growing. A proposal for a new cyber framework to deal with the new MAD follows in a later chapter.

Social media has become a magnet for influence operations, criminal activities, and countless disruptive as well as benign activities, as will be noted below. Of the major "adversaries," it is clear how each is using a combination of cyber and social media. From the Chinese perspective, the intent is to gain information and intelligence and, where necessary, steal both. Further, China is out to penetrate as many major civilian and official or governmental networks as possible, up to the most sensitive and classified.

Russia's aim is to use the combination to disrupt and sow chaos, confusion, and disinformation. Regarding theft and espionage, Russia uses cyber to gain information. However, it is Russian crime syndicates that are more actively engaged in these illegal activities.

Iran is perhaps the most interesting case. The Iranian government has funded a robust private cyber sector, ironically with a decidedly capitalist orientation. This capacity exceeds the Iranian government's own cyber assets. At some stage, however, this commercial sector will be more efficiently harnessed by its government.

North Korean cyber is almost entirely criminal in nature, although as with the hacking of Sony Pictures, it can be used to retaliate against regime critics. And, of course, extremist groups employ cyber and social media as the nerve and circulatory systems of their networking to influence operations, command and control, and recruiting.

A final warning: In late 2020, the US government announced that it had detected massive cyberattacks and hacks throughout many of its agencies and networks, presumably from Russian sources, which Putin denied. The attacks had started around March 2020. A linking software provider, SolarWinds, had been the entry point. It was unclear how much damage was done and the extent of data and intellectual property (IP) stolen. Then came the hack of Colonial Pipeline in early 2021 and later the JBS meat packing giant.

As noted above in terms of disruptions, if these attacks had interrupted or stopped service to electrical power, water, transportation, internet, cell phones, and other essentials of daily life for extended periods, America would have been in chaos. The Colonial Pipeline hack reaffirmed the proximity of this threat. Combined with social media that was used to organize the January 6 Capitol Hill riot, the power of these disruptors to conduct MAD is self-evident and made even more potent by the growing vulnerabilities and fragilities of nations in an information age.

TERRORISM

About terrorism, and many decades before the emergence of MAD, Lenin put it bluntly: The purpose of terror is to terrorize. The American effort in the misnamed Global War on Terror after the September 11 attacks was directed against violent extremism emerging from radical Islamist ideology that was Wahhabi in character. The Wahhabis practiced highly conservative forms of Islam for centuries. Wahhabism became imbedded in the culture when that family merged with the House of Saud in the mid-eighteenth century that would formally create the Kingdom of Saudi Arabia in 1932.

Linking any variant of Islam with a terrorist connotation can wrongly imply condemnation of a religion when only a tiny fraction of Muslims embraces violence and radical extremism. Assume that this violent cohort is one-tenth of 1 percent of all Muslims. Given about 1.4 billion Muslims worldwide, that exceedingly small group amounts to 1.4 million people, male, female, young and old. And 1.4 million potential extremists represent a very significant potential problem.

Terrorism and terrorists are not limited to extremist religious groups such as al-Qaeda that emanate outside the United States. Very disturbing is the emergence of both far-left Antifa (anti-fascist) and more dangerous far-right neo-fascist clans under the guise of populism, neo-nationalism, and racial hatred and distrust of immigrants and nonwhites. During the protests and riots following the death of George Floyd in Minneapolis, then President Trump declared Antifa a terrorist organization, violating a law that prohibits domestic organizations for being so labeled. Nothing was done against right-wing groups.

For the far or alt-right and, more recently, the cult QAnon, violence is not new. Timothy McVeigh destroyed the Murrah Federal Building in Oklahoma City in 1995, killing more than a hundred people. McVeigh was a Gulf War I veteran awarded the Bronze Star in that brief campaign. His terrorist act was derived from the psychological need to attack the US government to protest some bizarre fantasy he had concocted. Since then, right-wing groups have used violence from Charlottesville to Charleston to Charlotte principally to attack black and brown minorities.

Just prior to the 2021 inauguration, the major US law enforcement and intelligence agencies led by the FBI warned that right-wing, white supremacist, and related groups posed the greatest domestic terrorist threat to America and Americans. Hundreds of arrests were made of group members following the assault on the Capitol and the inauguration. Combined with social media and encrypted communications, domestic terrorism could be formidable, highly and dangerously disruptive, and subject to manipulation by foreign governments and actors, another reminder of the chaos of the 1918–1920 period.

The outbreak of COVID-19 exacerbated these passions and reasons to worry about domestic terrorism. In the US, protests favoring individual freedom over the shutdown of schools, businesses, and activities such as wearing masks to limit contagion increased, many peaceful. In some cases, ultra-right- and left-wing groups led these protests. Violence loomed, reflecting the tension and dilemma of protecting individual freedom and civil liberties in a nation with more guns than citizens.

Cities with Democratic mayors—Los Angeles, Portland, Minneapolis, and New York—were singled out by former President Trump as examples of how violence would spread if Joe Biden were elected president and his party took control of Congress. Of course, those allegations were incendiary, baseless, and representative of Trump's refusal to regard fact and truth as relevant.

Since September 11, with one exception noted earlier of a junior Saudi officer undergoing pilot training who was recruited by al-Qaeda, all domestic acts of terror have been carried out by American citizens, some who were native born and one who was a major in the US Army. As cited, in January 2021, the FBI and the National Counterterrorism Center declared extreme right-wing groups as the most dangerous violent domestic terror organizations.

Reference has been made to the 1919–1920 terror bombings. At the time, two dozen letter bombs were posted throughout the country.

A night watchman was killed by one, as was one of the bombers in Washington, DC, who set his charge off prematurely. Later in 1920, a bomb exploded on Wall Street in front of J.P. Morgan's headquarters, killing thirty-eight. But more panic, domestic unrest, and violence ensued over these relatively small acts of domestic terrorism than after September 11.

The response by Attorney General A. Mitchell Palmer was in clear violation of the Constitution and basic rights of all Americans. Citing the Espionage Act of 1917 and the Sedition Act a year later, tens of thousands of Americans were arrested without probable cause or due process. Thousands were deported, also without due process. Mail and speech critical of the government or reporting on the Spanish flu were censored. But the perpetrators of the letter bombs were never caught, and violence over labor unions, women's voting rights, Prohibition, and the Red Scare wracked the nation at the same time.

One conclusion is that terrorists of any ilk will rely on the new MAD to achieve their ends. Terror no longer is to terrorize. Its power is to disrupt massively.

Osama bin Laden never comprehended how the disruption of his attack would become so widespread. He didn't expect the Twin Towers to collapse, but merely stand as smoking ruins and vivid reminders of the attack. He did not anticipate how MAD would have eradicated trillions of dollars of stock value, fortunately recovered since. Nor did he expect that the US would hunt him for ten years to exact its revenge.

DEBT

With good reason, debt and more debt are ticking fiscal and monetary time bombs that to the degree history is relevant can explode interest rates and inflation, creating Massive Attacks of Disruption on governments, economies, and publics. Currently, the United States public debt—what government has borrowed and at some stage must repay—is well over $30 trillion and growing, half again as large as the annual $20 trillion GDP. That borrowing will continue given the Biden fiscal year 2022 $6 trillion federal budget and the three Relief, Jobs, and Family bills that add another $6 trillion to the debt.

Fortunately, interest rates are below 1 percent. That will not last. If and when interest rates return to more "normal" levels, the federal budget will not be able to fund legally mandated nondiscretionary obligations such as transfer payments and entitlements such as Social Security, Medicare, and Medicaid and discretionary payments for national security at current levels. And accompanying interest rate increases will be inflationary as more cash floods into the economy. Confounding this future condition is the pressing matter of debt reduction to disarm these MAD time bombs.

The only way government can pay down debt is for receipts to exceed expenditures. The surplus then can be used to retire debt. Raising taxes and/or cutting spending are the only available means if substantial economic growth cannot be achieved to provide sufficient revenues for a surplus. And here is another conundrum.

Raising taxes can too easily retard economic growth. This is a principal argument against the Biden plan to pay for his huge spending by increasing taxes on corporations and individuals making over $400,000 a year. On the other hand, the argument that the best (or only) means of stimulating sufficient economic growth to pay down debt is through tax cuts, defies reality and history. Despite all the tax cuts since the end of World War II, the national debt has only increased.

As Apollo 13's astronauts warned NASA, "Houston, we have a problem." America has an equally terrifying debt problem.

DRONES

A further technology that empowers MAD cannot be ignored: drones. The highly effective 2019 attacks against Saudi oil facilities were conducted by drones and cruise missiles. For those who missed the 2018 Winter Olympics held in South Korea, at one stage several thousand drones flew in close formation performing a complicated and impressive light show. The current record, held by the Chinese, was operating 3,200 drones simultaneously. Autonomous drones are ubiquitous. Interestingly, at one point, the largest shop at Frankfurt Airport in Germany was a drone store.

The use of drones for all purposes is evident. Their ability to disrupt is limitless. Drones are cheap and easy to obtain, operate, and build. Simply by their presence, drones can interrupt flight and traffic patterns. Armed drones can attack virtually any aboveground target, from antennas to zoos.

A series of coordinated and simultaneous drone attacks throughout any country against government buildings, schools, power grids, highways, airports, and virtually any infrastructure would be devastating. In 1919–1920, a dozen letter bombs panicked the country. Suppose drones dropped white powder that social media reported as anthrax, even if it were a benign substance such as talcum or flour.

Or suppose the forty-eight continental statehouses were attacked simultaneously by drones. Disruption would be instantaneous. As noted, the electrical grid is vulnerable. Drone strikes against stock exchanges surely would be MAD on steroids. As societies grow more vulnerable and, in some cases, fragile, drone technology reflects the Janus sides of MAD. Where, then, is the contingency thinking and planning about drones?

While war games and other scenarios have examined the disruptive and destructive potential of drone strikes by themselves or in conjunction with cyber and terrorism, are governments as ill-prepared for these possibilities as they were for COVID-19? With over two million FAA-registered drones and about 170,000 "pilots," more attention must be given to the regulation, operation, and control of drones in private hands.

Will "drone shows," as with gun shows, be unrestricted? Will rules that apply to aircraft and automobiles be required of drones as well, to include insurance? The FAA updated rules for drones in late 2020. More must be done.

When drones interact with cyber, social media, and terrorism, the results can be catastrophic. Most Americans have seen the chilling and precision accuracy of military drones in Afghanistan and Iraq. One scenario, of many, follows to show how deadly a combination of MAD can be.

THE DEADLY MIX

The dark side of MAD becomes even darker and more daunting where, how, and when one or more of these and other disruptors interact and the combination reaches a critical mass that can cripple swaths of society. Three of many plausible scenarios represent the possible levels of disruption and destruction that can be imposed.

Twenty years ago, I led a study that wrote nightmare scenarios for five geopolitical crises: political implosions in Russia and China, global financial collapse, war between Pakistan and India, massive terrorist attacks, and a humanitarian crisis in Mexico combining horrific storms and cyberattacks.

The Mexico scenario hypothesized that a drug cartel was marked by the Mexican government for elimination. The cartel understood (because the government seemed immune to bribery) that its survival depended on regime change. The question was how to collapse the government and replace it with a more cartel-compliant and controllable one short of an armed revolt that would almost certainly fail.

Unusually powerful and frequent storms, intensified by El Niño, regularly hitting Mexico provided the solution. It was hurricane season in Mexico. Storms from the Atlantic and Pacific were battering both coasts. The cartel only needed to wait for a monster storm to build. That wait did not take long.

A Katrina-level superstorm soon struck. The cartel applied cyber and social media in two ways to weaponize the storm. As the storm began imposing enormous damage, forcing hundreds of thousands of citizens to flee, the cartel used social media to declare an impending and invented emergency: a massive earthquake about to unleash a tsunami of further destruction.

Then, as literally millions of Mexicans flooded highways and roads to escape the storm and earthquake, the cartel launched a cyberattack disabling Mexico's electrical power grid. The combination of the social media–invented natural disaster and the loss of electrical power created national panic.

With no safe refuge in Mexico, this hoard headed north to the US border, believing the cartel's additional social media messages that refugees would be welcomed by a more humanitarian friendly American government after the disastrous border policies to close off access across the Rio Grande. This sea of desperate Mexican refugees quickly overwhelmed the ability of authorities to provide food, shelter, and medical support and to stem this unprecedented flow of humanity. A political and humanitarian nightmare rapidly unfolded on the border far worse than in 2021.

The cartel's employment of social media hyped the magnitude of the crisis and the failure, impotence, and incompetence of the Mexican government to react. Political pressure on both sides of the Rio Grande to quell this disaster became excruciating. Unable to mount an effective response and faced with massive rioting and looting, the Mexican government fell and one amenable to the cartel assumed office, ironically promising law and order and restoring electrical power—which the cartel promptly did.

If this scenario played out today, not only would the Mexican government be at great risk. Given the intense debate over legal and illegal immigration and border security in America, such a scenario would be politically disastrous for the party in power. In today's MAD world, it is not only a desperate, powerful drug cartel that might find this toxic mix of fear and panic in the face of a crisis useful in unseating a president and driving the party in power out of office.

While any scenario can be challenged, crippling the Mexican (or other) power grid is very feasible, as is hacking into most networks. Mass migration likewise is a major disruptor. A decade and a half after this scenario was envisioned, the civil war in Syria forced twelve million refugees and displaced persons to flee to safety.

This human flood overloaded the capacity of bordering states to assimilate the flow. Domestic crises arose in several European countries as housing and feeding these refugees far exceeded the available resources. Populism and political divisions were exacerbated. Unknowingly perhaps, Russia's intervention in Syria in 2014 that created this migration probably did as much damage to European cohesion as any of Moscow's active measures.

CYBER, SOCIAL MEDIA, AND MAD

The recurring MAD nightmare scenario reflects the vulnerability of critical infrastructure and internet users to cyberattacks. And businesses are fair and lucrative game. Consider how to make a fortune illicitly and virtually as the second scenario.

For public companies, such things as data and quarterly reports, balance sheets, and profit-and-loss tables are particularly vulnerable.

Once hacked, all can be altered electronically. In this scenario, hackers penetrate several public companies, gaining access to vital business documents. Decimal points in balance sheets and profit-and-loss tables can be moved several places to the left or right, with powerful consequences. Hackers then can exploit this manipulation two ways.

First, hackers can exaggerate profits and revenues. That would mean going "long" in buying stocks on the basis that the value will greatly appreciate. Conversely, stocks can be "shorted" on the basis that the company will fare badly. Shares can be bought or sold on the basis of doctored data and the effects on future valuations. Dummy trading companies would be established in jurisdictions with favorable disclosure, extradition, and immunity laws for these counterfeit transactions. By the time the hacks were discovered, the stocks would have been traded.

Such activities can be massively profitable and massively disruptive of financial markets. This is not an isolated scenario. Hackers can access the most closely held corporate records unless strict cyber hygiene is practiced. As the navy cyber study demonstrated, China has already hacked into classified American networks.

While "shorts" have long tried to manipulate markets by planting false press releases and rumors to discredit targeted stocks or buying or selling large quantities to drive prices, cyber offers a new dimension for illegal and malign purposes. Manufacturing similar scenarios in which financial cybercrimes are committed is part of Hollywood's playbook.

Data alteration, cyber fraud, and pandemics are ripe for further disruption and exploitation. The infamous Theranos Corporation provided a pre-pandemic case study in this type of fraud. Theranos was a biotech company started by Elizabeth Holmes about twenty years ago on the proposition that a droplet of blood could be sufficient to identify virtually any known disease.

By 2014, Ms. Holmes, the daughter of a former Enron executive (that might have been suggestive for greater due diligence given that company's demise), was highly praised and regarded as a pioneering entrepreneur. Theranos market value soared to $9 billion, and Ms. Holmes was America's youngest billionaire. The board included such notables as Hillary Clinton, Betsy DeVos, Henry Kissinger, James Mattis, William Perry, and George Shultz.

But by 2015, it was becoming clear that Theranos did not have any magical solution to detect all or any diseases from blood droplets. The bulk of the blood tests were outsourced to other companies, and supporting data appeared to have been fraudulently manipulated. The company would fold amidst numerous acrimonious lawsuits and allegations of criminality. Whether Ms. Holmes was a biotech Bernie Madoff out to loot or a visionary who became deluded by her product remains an open question.

In the age of COVID-19, Theranos could be a useful model for cybercriminals to emulate for profit and/or to create panic. First, substantial amounts of money could be raised, probably from largely unsophisticated and unsuspecting investors, for a revolutionary drug that treats or cures COVID-19 or a mutation. Second, given the urgent need for a universal cure, the revolutionary effectiveness of the particular medication would be hyped much as President Trump praised hydroxychloroquine. The company's value would soar to atmospheric levels.

And if terrorism is the objective, that too is possible. Just as a handful of letter bombs terrorized America in 1919–1920, these drugs in fact could become terrorist weapons if infected with dangerous or fatal side effects. Once that story broke, panic and chaos would follow. The integrity of the drug industry and regulatory process would be under intense fire and criticism.

Advanced states have far stricter regulations regarding drugs that would have to be circumvented or bypassed (as Theranos did) or subjected to fast-track approval as what occurred with the Pfizer and

Moderna vaccines. Hence the targeted markets would most likely be developing or third and fourth world states.

Still, given the high price of drugs in the US, lower-cost generic medications would find borders as permeable as did the coronavirus. The perpetrators could also offer free samples of these "life-saving" drugs to already financially stressed countries to prime sales. As hydroxychloroquine has been praised as a preventative against coronavirus, no doubt many in Europe and North America might be tempted to buy or use this dangerous drug. After all, as Donald Trump famously boasted, "What harm can it do?"

Just as the poisoning of Tylenol bottles in the 1980s provoked panic, this scenario would be far worse. The perpetrators could retreat behind the safety of the internet, hiding in literally hundreds of servers and routing protocols. And while this scenario would be a "one-off," it is still plausible. Recall that Theranos had no problem raising hundreds of millions of dollars for its fraudulent product.

The combination of coronavirus, cyber, and terrorism with the internet and social media offers great opportunity for criminals, fraudsters, extremists, and others simply with malevolent intent. Misinformation, disinformation, deep fakes, and outright falsehoods—to include spreading conspiracy theories that border on the ridiculous, outrageous, and otherwise unbelievable—are already in use.

How nonstate actors such as al-Qaeda and the Islamic State as well as China, Iran, North Korea, and Russia can exploit these disruptive intersections is an urgent national security matter, covered in the next chapter. As noted, the SolarWinds hack is another final warning that will go unheeded.

Add to this mix drones and some of the scenarios already noted and the toxicity intensifies. The nightmare scenario is a campaign that would bring the US to even a greater standstill than COVID-19 caused. Cyber and social media would be the means to warn of a pending massive terrorist attack without specifying the source or targets. In a hierarchy of rationales for malign or criminal behavior, blackmail and ransom fit one category.

The most diabolical and disruptive third scenario would be simultaneous drone attacks against specific infrastructure sectors such as power or transportation. If the latter, then airports, railroads, bridges, and choke points would be ground zeroes. Drones could also drop chemical or biological weapons. During the anthrax scare in Washington in 2001, suppose drones and not letters transmitted the chemicals? For moviegoers, the extent of possible scenarios would keep the Bond series in business for years.

In the preface, the reason why President Bennett was at a secure location was that drone strikes had destroyed the White House, Capitol, and other government buildings. For doubters, consider the use of drones in the Libyan, Syrian, Yemeni, and Nagorno-Karabakh wars to understand their effectiveness.

With the peaceful protests, riots, and looting in parts of America following George Floyd's murder, social media did not rise to the level of impact it had in the colored revolutions and in Egypt. That does not mean it will not. At a time when the nation is under great stress over COVID-19 and law enforcement is stretched thin, social media could have concocted the perfect storm. Fortunately, that did not happen…so far.

Just as bin Laden unknowingly attacked the Constitution on September 11 by exploiting the tensions between civil liberties and physical security, COVID-19 is striking at the political as well as physical health of the United States and its huge partisan divides. While climate change is inanimate, it too is infecting political differences between the parties. And while dependence on cyber and the internet is virtually existential for many, both are being used to leverage the new MAD.

Each of these disruptors will be affected for good or ill by advancing technology that can actually exploit MAD to the benefit of all.

Sequestration of coal and the entry of electric vehicles could negate or mitigate many of the effects of climate change provided the electrical power needed to recharge these vehicles did not produce more greenhouse gases than fossil fuel-driven cars emitted. Quantum computing could lead to networks that are impenetrable to hacking, thereby securing cyber and social media from attacks. Genome research combined with AI could lead to the rapid invention and production of vaccines and cures, making disease far less widespread and deadly.

Advances in healthcare, environmental sciences, and infrastructure revolutions to build smart cities can create millions of jobs and reduce the disparities between rich and poor while raising living standards and possibly reducing the grounds for terrorism. On the other hand, each of these technologies can have negative consequences as well. And the one disruptor where technology may not offer any grand solutions is the most dangerous of all: failed and failing government.

FIXING A FAILED GOVERNMENT

There are many reasons why governments fail. Complexity of governing is not necessarily one of them. At most points in history, governing was complex and complicated. America in 1789 or 1860 was surely as difficult a period for governing or more so than 1929, 1941, and other crisis years.

First, every political system has inherent flaws, vulnerabilities, and weaknesses. The notion of the divine right of kings was not compatible with industrialization or social equality. Authoritarian states required repressive means to remain in power. Parliamentary systems necessitated a working majority, either numerically or congealed by crisis. Britain in World War II fits the latter. Constitutional checks and balances do not work without political control of all branches of government, a rallying crisis or civility and compromise to close the divides.

A compelling consideration is whether the American Constitution has outlived its usefulness and relevance as the basis for governing. A further reinforcing criticism applies to the current organization of our government that has contributed to failure. While making profound change to the Constitution is impractical if not impossible, arguments make the case that the Senate in its current form may have outlived its purpose.

Originally, the Senate was intended to ensure a representative republic and not a true democracy determined by majority vote. The House was to represent the "people," narrow as that constituency was. The Senate was to represent the states as part of federalism and as a counterweight to the executive branch exceeding its authority as King George III had.

Further, political parties were eschewed as "dangerous factions" by the Founding Fathers. But as political parties became foundational to politics and more states were added to the original thirteen, over time and probably by the late 1990s, senators were becoming more beholden to parties for reelection and control of that chamber than to the original purpose of representing states as a balance to the federal government.

In practical terms, finding remedies is difficult but not impossible, provided what Thomas Paine described as Common Sense can be applied. This, indeed, may be among one of the greatest tests for the American political system.

Second, governments survive on legitimacy, credibility, and trustworthiness. In 1964, prior to the Gulf of Tonkin incident that set the US on a disastrous course in Vietnam, a Gallup poll found about three-quarters of Americans trusted the federal government to act in the nation's best interests. By 2021, that figure was reversed with almost four-fifths of those polled distrusting of government.

Third, governments cannot function if political extremism dominates both parties. In American politics today, the two parties have veered sharply left and right. But most Americans (60 to 65 percent) are of the broad center. Who represents them when the 10 percent on either extreme have assumed control of the debate? And where is the incentive to close these huge political differences when what passes for debate is caustic, abrasive, and determined by whether one is for or against and not with?

Fourth, if democracy is to remain healthy and even functioning, the public must be educated on and engaged with the issues. Unfortunately, social media and cable television have become educational surrogates. Combined with ideology and political associations, these factors now determine where one stands on issues more than informed decisions.

That the US government is failing results from each of these vulnerabilities. The 2020 elections did not correct and indeed worsened these failures by widening these divides with one party narrowly in charge and the leader of the other still disputing the electoral outcome. MAD exacerbates these tensions and political divides because both parties refuse to agree on solutions.

In economics, the Tinbergen Rule, named for 1969 Nobel Prize winner Jan Tinbergen, argued that a single policy solution best applies to resolving only one problem. On one hand, like Theranos, beware universal cures. On the other, strategies and policies for dealing with each of the major disruptors—coronavirus, climate change, cyber, terrorism, and drones—that are approached in isolation, individually and not collectively and without regard for their interconnectivity are almost certainly headed for failure.

Ask who in government has the responsibility for these scenarios and contingencies or dealing with MAD. Is it the Department of Homeland Security, Justice, Transportation, Commerce, Treasury,

Interior, Defense, or the White House? Extending this line of inquiry, is the National Security Act, first passed in 1947 as amended, still effective or relevant in the twenty-first century? The answers are not comforting.

What should be clear from answering these basic questions is the need for an overarching, searching, and comprehensive re-examination both of the threats, dangers, and uncertainties of the twenty-first century facing the nation and the world at large and of current US policies and strategies. If that is not undertaken or conducted along partisan lines, the nation will remain in great danger at least as much within these shores as beyond them. MAD will only add to these dire forecasts.

Chapter Three

DRAGONS AND BEARS I: RUSSIA

Suppose a nuclear-armed Canada, Mexico, and the other countries of Latin America formed a military alliance directed against the United States with the aim of deterring and, if war comes, defeating us. How would the US react? Then place yourself in Russia's position. Or ask Lenin, were he alive today, what the US should do vis-à-vis Russia.

SOME COMMON LINKS BETWEEN PRESIDENTS PUTIN AND XI

Before beginning the analysis and evaluation of Russia, China, and the current antagonisms with the US and others, the ascent to and seizure of power by both Russian president Vladimir Putin and China's Xi Jinping provides more comprehensive and useful insights and understanding of the thought processes and aspirations of both leaders in a MAD-driven world. In essence, Putin and Xi are twenty-first century versions of earlier Russian/Soviet and Chinese leaders in one very important aspect: both know, have learned from, and respect history.

To deal successfully with the many disruptive centrifugal forces that threatened the existence, integrity, and stability of both states, Lenin and Stalin in the USSR and China's Mao Zedong understood the life-and-death necessity of imposing disciplined and highly autocratic regimes to maintain tight political control and, indeed, for personal and regime survival.

That need for near absolute political control, from Putin's perspective, was reinforced by the more complicated and disruptive world of MAD. It was no accident that Putin regarded the dissolution of the Soviet Union as the worst geostrategic disaster of the last century. His reasoning was that a second dissolution would threaten the existence of a coherent future Russia that emerged after the USSR imploded.

In the mid-1960s, when Mao was losing the fight for party control, he countered with the Great Proletarian Cultural Revolution. This titanic disruption was designed to restore Mao's political control by the upheaval it would cause, ultimately purging and eliminating his opposition. Stalin brutally employed the secret police, purges, and the Gulag to eliminate rivals and perceived opposition that numbered in the many millions. Putin likewise ruthlessly eliminated first the oligarchs and then political opponents and critics, but selectively and with less bloodshed than Lenin and Stalin.

Xi likewise consolidated power beginning with his election to the Politburo in 2007. He now heads the three principal levers of power: the government, the Communist Party, and the military. In achieving these posts, Xi completely departed from collective leadership practiced since Deng Xiaoping, who held no formal government post, and his successor, President Jiang Zemin. Three successive American administrations failed to appreciate the consequences of Putin and Xi's need to gain near or total control of power.

Certain characteristics are remarkably common to Putin and Xi. Both are of a similar age (Putin was born in 1952 and Xi in 1953). Both grew up at a time of great domestic hardship—the USSR and People's Republic of China (PRC) were still recovering from World War II, when twenty million Russians died and at least as many Chinese. Both were facing powerful enemies in the United States and NATO in Europe and similar alliances in the Pacific with significant American forces stationed in both regions. Putin did not come from the Russian elite, mirroring prior Soviet leaders and the two other Russian presidents: Boris Yeltsin and Dmitry Medvedev. Even in high school, Putin was considered an "outsider," aloof from contemporaries.

Xi was a "princeling." His father was a founding member of the Communist Party and Chinese Civil War hero until purged in the Cultural Revolution. After his father was denounced and arrested, Xi was exiled to Shanxi Province at age fifteen. He disdained life in the hustings and soon fled. Xi was arrested and sent to a work farm for reeducation. Premier Zhou Enlai intervened to rehabilitate Xi's father in 1974 for his prior revolutionary service so that, after ten attempts to join the party, Xi was finally admitted that same year.

Putin found his upward mobility not through the Communist Party but the KGB, the study of the law, and his mentors. In Leningrad/St. Petersburg, the combination sponsored his progress ultimately to appointment as deputy mayor. Boris Yeltsin saw promise in the young Putin and promoted him first to head the KGB and then as acting president beginning January 1, 2000, a remarkable rise to power.

Although not a university graduate as Putin was, Xi used the party and a series of key local and provincial assignments for his upward mobility, ultimately becoming "People's Leader," a title only granted to Mao. Xi is now China's president for life. Understanding the thinking and experiences of both leaders should be seen through the lens of the chaotic history of both Russia (and the USSR) and China and the impact of centuries of disruption.

That history has led both leaders to recognize that holding great individual power was necessary to contain the destructive external and domestic forces that, over centuries, threatened the survival of both countries and, in the minds of many Russians and Chinese, continue to do so today. In the West, centralization of power in an individual or even a small group is viewed as directly antithetical to genuinely representative and democratic government. Less liberal Western democracies such as Austria, Hungary, and Turkey seem headed in the opposite direction.

A flaw in American strategic thinking both inside and out of government has been the hubris to assume that rational people think or should think and reason as we do. If not, then these individuals were in need of education to reach this level. Hence, to avoid repeating this error, understanding how the thought processes of other leaders have been shaped must also incorporate the powerful influences of culture, history, language, and values.

Where hindsight is more accurate than foresight, what leaders said actually turned out to be what was meant and done in practice. Had Washington and the West understood and taken more seriously public pronouncements, statements, documents, and warnings issued by Russia and China, perhaps fewer surprises would have resulted. That did not happen.

Putin's 1999 and 2007 speeches and a variety of Chinese statements to include China's 2015; Made in China 2025; its national innovation-driven plan; and defense white papers should have left little question about future intentions of both countries. The 1999 book, *Unrestricted Warfare*, written by two PLA Air Force colonels, Qiao Liang and Wang Xiangsui, is mandatory reading because it laid out in graphic detail China's plan for military modernization based on Sun Tzu's principle of defeating the enemy's strategy.

Russia and China share common backgrounds far different from that of the United States as well as unique cultures shaped by history.

In part, because of a four-thousand-mile border and past unpleasantries, Russia and China have been wary, if not occasionally paranoid, about the other. Russia and China were autocracies first ruled by tsars anointed by God and emperors with heavenly mandates; then by general secretaries; and today, by powerful dominant presidents.

Because of geography, both Russia and China often fell victim to invasions and interventions dating back millennia. Only until after World War II and the collapse of the Nationalist Chinese government in 1949 were the Soviet Union and the People's Republic of China able to mitigate the threat of direct foreign intervention. However, as technology and globalization bypassed borders and boundaries, electronic intervention from the ether and then the internet would be viewed as a new threat.

Both states suffered from periods of national shame and foreign infringement and occupation. For Russia, it stretched from the 1917 revolution until the formation of the USSR in 1922 and the end of Allied occupation in 1925 to its collapse in 1991 that led to a weakened and fragile Russia. China's century of humiliation dates from the Opium Wars of the mid-1800s. Too often, Americans fail to appreciate how much impact this disruptive and traumatic history persists in the memory, culture, and psychology of Russia and China, their leadership, and many of their citizens.

Whether Russia and China have adopted disruption as merely expedient or from a Hegelian dialectical process that drives thesis versus antithesis to derive synthesis from this tension as a tool is a less important consideration. No matter the answer, MAD plays well into the policies of Beijing and Moscow and Presidents Putin and Xi.

A BIT OF HISTORY

The argument has been made that too often, American policy has been decided without complete knowledge and understanding of the circumstance, especially regarding the use or threat of use of force. The Vietnam War and second Iraq War are two of the most bitter examples of this failure. However, given the emergence of this great-power competition, an earlier and surprising case study of this failure is relevant and illuminating.

The analysis flies in the face of accepted history and lessons regarding the 1962 Cuban Missile Crisis. Unfortunately, in a MAD-driven world where acts of nature as well as man are the cause célèbre of crisis, future failures of knowledge and understanding are likely to be at least and even more consequential.

The Kennedy administration arrived in office later advertised as a modern-day Camelot filled with bright, energetic, highly accomplished people, all male, prepared to "pay any price and bear any burden" in the pursuit of liberty. Listening to his generals, President John Kennedy allowed what would be the catastrophic April 1961 Bay of Pigs invasion of Cuba to remove President Fidel Castro to proceed. It was a fiasco, tarnishing the credibility of the young president and the new administration.

That lesson did not prevent another, far worse miscalculation ultimately provoking the Cuban Missile Crisis in October 1962. While the United States claimed to have won a major victory and success, in fact, it was Pyrrhic. But that crisis was a decade in the making and was not inevitable.

On assuming office in January 1953, President Dwight Eisenhower believed that the military competition with the USSR could be conducted more sensibly and less expensively so as not to bleed the economy. Ike's strategic "new look" stressed nuclear deterrence over more costly conventional forces. Despite Moscow's brutal repression of uprisings in Poland and Hungary in 1956, Ike kept to his plan and cut defense spending. By 1959 and firmly in power, Soviet leader Nikita Khrushchev became convinced that the Soviet Union could follow suit and reduce defense spending.

In January 1960, the Soviets announced a reduction in reserve forces by a million troops. Through disgruntled GRU Colonel Oleg Penkovsky, the West was well informed on a near real-time basis of Soviet decisions to shift resources from defense to the civil sector. Penkovsky microfilmed the General Staff's top secret *Voenny Mys'l* ("Military Thought") journal and passed it on to British MI6's Moscow agent, Greville Wynne. Code-named "Ironbark," the material covered the fiery debate in which the military steadfastly opposed the Khrushchev-directed change in strategy and allocation of rubles.

The 1960 US presidential campaign would mark the inadvertent beginning of the Cuban Missile Crisis. The Kennedy election team invented a missile gap with the Soviet Union that was nonexistent. The aim was to run to the right of opponent Richard Nixon, accusing the Eisenhower administration of being "soft" on the Soviets.

After taking office in January 1961, based on his promise to close this fictional missile gap, Kennedy ordered a series of immediate and dramatic arms buildups through three supplemental defense spending bills sent to Congress. The missile gap was real, but decidedly in America's favor. Had the Kennedy administration accepted accurate intelligence rather than inflexibly honoring a campaign promise, who knows how long the Cold War would have persisted, and would that have made a difference?

JFK's defense secretary, Robert McNamara, admitted to me years later that the intelligence would not have mattered. Kennedy would have fulfilled the promise regardless of evidence. That rigidity was not unique to JFK.

Khrushchev's response to this unexpected and unprecedented American peacetime rearmament was clever, but not clever enough. The crucial question for Khrushchev was how the USSR could outflank the lopsided American strategic nuclear advantage at minimal cost. The simple solution was a covert plan to station shorter-range nuclear-tipped missiles in Cuba, offsetting America's superiority.

Soviet intermediate-range ballistic missiles in Cuba were capable of targeting and striking America's East Coast. By nullifying America's strategic lead, the Soviet Union could be spared the burden of an expensive arms race to even the highly uneven nuclear balance. Khrushchev would be able to continue diverting money from defense to the civilian sector.

As American short-range Jupiter missiles were based in Turkey and aimed at Moscow, this seemed a fair quid pro quo to the Kremlin. After badly intimidating Kennedy at the June 1961 Vienna summit, Khrushchev believed Kennedy would not have any choice except to accept this fait accompli. This was a classic failure of understanding by the other side.

Khrushchev's ploy failed. In early October, the plot was discovered by U-2 reconnaissance flights over Cuba that photographed Soviet missile installations. These revelations forced Kennedy into a cul-de-sac. For thirteen days, the crisis dominated both the White House and the Kremlin. With few good options and none regarding a military strike that could guarantee 100 percent elimination of the nuclear-armed missiles, Kennedy refused to be cowed. His administration imaginatively created the famous "quarantine" enforced by the US Navy, cutting off all seaborne routes to Cuba.

Caught red-handed as it were, Moscow had no choice. As Secretary of State Dean Rusk said, "I think the other fellow just blinked." Faced with military inferiority and geographic disadvantage, Khrushchev ordered Soviet missiles, nuclear weapons, and troops removed. While the US agreed it would not invade Cuba and removed its own Jupiter missiles from Turkey, to most observers this was a significant victory for Washington.

But it was not. The Soviet Union embarked on a major military rearmament program that eventually would close the so-called missile gap, giving Moscow nuclear parity and perhaps conventional force superiority. The Cold War hardened and would grow hotter. And two years later in October 1964, the Politburo would fire Khrushchev.

As a student of history, Putin is well aware of the dangers of failing to appreciate an adversary, especially when embarking on a risky or potentially foolish enterprise.

FROM IVAN TO PUTIN

Summarizing a thousand years of Russian history and eight decades of the Soviet Union illustrates how both affected President Putin's thinking and actions in contemporary Russia. Yet for Americans, despite a civil and two world wars, a depression, and in 2020 the danger of three crises—COVID-19, a 51 percent nation, and MAD—life was less disruptive than in Russia or, for that matter, China and most of Europe.

Russia dates from the ninth century AD, China to at least 1600 BC, and America from 1776 or 1789. Two oceans protected the fledgling America from European encroachment and involvement in overseas wars. Russia was the frequent victim of geography. A crossroad for invasions in Eurasia plagued Russia since before the original Rus or Slavic rowers first settled around the tenth century AD.

By his own admission, Putin is intimately familiar with this history and that of Russian tsars and Soviet secretaries-general. Russia has been an autocracy, sometimes bordering on a dictatorship, since Ivan IV, known as Ivan the Terrible (1530–1584), became Russia's first tsar (along with the first secret police, or *oprichnina*, in 1565).

Rule under tsars, Soviet general, and first secretaries, and now Putin was often brutal, highly dependent on loyal elites—courtiers, boyars, party members, oligarchs under Yeltsin, or today's *siloviki* (former KGB and security colleagues of Putin)—and not the public nor its consent. Privileges were accordingly awarded even though tsars were more profligate in luxurious living than commissars. With the dissolution of the Soviet Union and the emergence of the *siloviki* and oligarchs made rich by plundering the former Soviet state, that relative frugality of Soviet leaders disappeared.

Of former Russian tsars, two were "great": Peter and Catherine. Putin likewise assimilated their reigns into his thinking. Peter the Great (1672–1725) and Catherine the Great, a German born princess (1729–1796) both modernized and established Russia as a major power.

Peter was the father of the Russian Navy. So too Putin has presided over the rebuilding of the Russian military and in particular, like Peter, its navy. Peter had his own version of the secret police, or Preobrazhensky Prikaz, headed by Prince Fyodor Romodanovsky, that coped with the Streltsy uprising of four disenchanted army regiments in a bungled attempted coup in 1690. Putin is ex-KGB and has dealt with dissidents and opposition with his secret police and expanded security forces as well.

Like Catherine, Putin has been considered an outsider coming from Leningrad and KGB postings in the relatively obscure East German city of Dresden rather than more elite assignments. Putin also knew that after Catherine, succession was a problem that would eventually end the dynasty. Her incapable son, Paul I, reigned from 1796 to 1801, when he was assassinated. The reigns of Alexander I (1801–1825), Nicholas I (1825–1855), and the last tsar, Nicholas II (1868–1917), were ruinous.

Through a lengthy period of geographic expansion, Russia once covered nearly eight million square miles at the beginning of the disastrous Crimean War (1853–1856). It covers 6.6 million square miles today. Alexander II (1818–1881) replaced his father in 1855. Facing possible mutiny and revolution fomented by the serfs, for centuries indentured to the land owned by feudal lords, Alexander freed some twenty-five to thirty million people in 1861, or about a third of Russia's population of seventy million. Five decades later, freed serfs would become a political power base that metastasized into a revolution, toppling the Romanovs. Alexander was assassinated in 1881 by the nihilist organization People's Will.

Alexander III's reign was short (1881–1894), terminated by liver cancer, bringing his son Nicholas II to the throne. Nicholas presided over the Russo-Japanese War (1904–1905) that bloodied and exhausted both countries, culminating in the 1905 naval battle at the Tsushima Strait separating Korea and Japan, a catastrophic defeat for Russia. Admiral Zinovy Rozhestvensky's Baltic Fleet was annihilated by the Japanese Imperial Navy under the command of Admiral Togo.

Nine years later, Austria-Hungary archduke Franz Ferdinand and his wife, Princess Sophie, were assassinated in Sarajevo in June 1914. Nicholas came to Austria's support, gratuitously declaring war on Serbia and unloosing the guns of August. Russia would lose the war and strike a peace with Germany.

Riots in Petrograd in early 1917 would end the Romanov Dynasty when Nicholas was forced to abdicate that March. Germany, aiming to end the war in the east, dispatched Vladimir Lenin from Switzerland on the so-called secret train to Finland and then to Russia. The German expectation was that if Lenin's revolution succeeded, Russia would leave the war.

Following the tsar's abdication, Russia briefly experienced an attempt at democratic government under Alexander Kerensky. But the October Revolution intervened and would bring the Bolsheviks to power after a bitter civil war first against the Mensheviks and then the White Russians. Seeking to end the war to save the revolution, Russia was forced to sign the infamous Treaty of Brest-Litovsk on March 3, 1918, forfeiting about 1.3 million square miles (about one-quarter of Russia, to include Ukraine), about one-third of Russia's population of sixty-two million, a third of Russia's most arable land, and over half of its industrial capacity and resources to the Central Powers.

The Treaty of Versailles invalidated the Brest-Litovsk Treaty, and the Soviet Union reacquired what it had lost plus a bit more. However, the memory of that treaty was not easily forgotten.

The civil war ended in 1922 with the establishment of the Soviet Union. However, nearly two hundred thousand allied troops from a dozen powers occupied parts of Russia supporting the Whites and would not leave until 1925. And many in the West were violently opposed to the establishment of a communist and potentially revolutionary state in Russia, especially the USSR's most vocal foe, Winston Churchill.

FROM LENIN WITH LOVE

After the October Revolution and civil war, unifying and controlling what had been Tsarist Russia was existential for Lenin and his colleagues. The Soviet Union was in economic, political, and social disarray and disrepair. The Soviet leadership was far from unified over solidifying the country or pursuing a revolutionary agenda to export socialism.

Leon Trotsky, one of the revolution's intellectual fathers, demanded "permanent revolution" as a top priority. Trotsky argued that extending socialism to other states was crucial to preserving the Soviet Union. By creating revolutionary allies and dissent in the West and states opposed to the existence of the Soviet Union, domestic pressures would prevent or restrict anti-Soviet policies. But the Soviet Union was far too weak to dilute its precious resources in activities beyond its borders.

Pragmatism won. Trotsky lost the debate, sent into exile in-country in January 1928, and exiled to Turkey a year later. Trotsky would be assassinated in Mexico in 1940 with an ice pick, a reminder that Russia's enemies and traitors were never beyond reach. With Lenin's death in January 1924, the struggle over leadership would be won by Joseph Stalin before decade's end.

Lenin invented and practiced "active measures" to seize and consolidate power. Active measures incorporate the means to disrupt, influence, confuse, misinform, and disinform as tools of the state. The unsuccessful attempt by the Soviet Union to occupy Tallinn in Estonia in 1924 (first by seizing the command-and-control center of the day—the telephone exchange) and the infamous Zinoviev letter meant to influence the British general election the same year in favor of Labor were the first of many active measures to come. Establishment of the Comintern (Communist International) and later its replacement, the Cominform (Communist Information), were also part of active measures.

The United States recognized the Soviet Union in 1933. The Soviet Union fought against its ideological enemy, the Nazis, and Francisco Franco's Nationalists in the Spanish Civil War (1936–1939). That war did not prevent the USSR, however, from signing the Molotov-Ribbentrop Pact in 1939 with Nazi Germany. That nonaggression pact gave Hitler the assurance of a one-front war to the west that, after winning, he could turn east. In the process, with the invasion and occupation of Poland by the Nazis, Stalin also was awarded a piece of Poland.

After Hitler had occupied most of France by June 1940, on June 22, 1941, Operation Barbarossa, the invasion of the Soviet Union, was launched. Ideologies aside, the USSR became an ally of the West, but only a temporary one. The Soviet Union proved vital in grinding down the Wehrmacht, losing twenty million soldiers and citizens in the war. Yet after the war, cynical self-interest and paranoia over its security would lead to the Cold War and the clash between "the free world" and the communists.

In the Cold War, the Soviet Union mastered Lenin's active measures in its ideological struggle with the West. But these tactics were embedded in the Russian DNA well before Lenin, dating back to Ivan IV and the first days of the Romanov Dynasty. As a former KGB officer, Putin has a deep understanding of active measures, or what the West calls hybrid warfare or gray area activities.

Like prior Soviet chiefs, Putin set about gaining and maintaining a dominant leadership position. Like Stalin and Leonid Brezhnev, Putin aspired to ruling for an indefinite basis. Stalin died in March 1953, the year of Putin's birth. Nikita Khrushchev became primus inter pares in 1955 until he was deposed in an October 1964 Politburo coup because of the Cuban Missile Crisis folly.

Leonid Brezhnev, Khrushchev's replacement, lasted eighteen years, certainly the last three or four years in ill health. Preceded by three geriatrics who lasted a total of four years, a youthful Mikhail Gorbachev took control in 1986 as general secretary and later president from 1990 to 1991. During Gorbachev's years in power, *perestroika* (restructuring) and *glasnost* (openness) would implode the Soviet Union in 1991. Putin was keenly aware of and learned from this history.

Hence, Putin's millennium address of December 1999 and his February 2007 Munich Security Conference lecture are important and incisive statements that laid out his path forward. Both revealed his thinking and how it was influenced. History, culture, his upbringing in postwar Leningrad, KGB background, education, the Cold War, and the implosion of the Soviet Union shaped the future Russian president's thought processes and intellect.

Beyond a certain naivety assuming Russia would become more democratic and open, that the West and the US did not take Putin's speeches, subsequent pronouncements, and press conferences seriously and respond accordingly, explains in part why relations have so deteriorated. Hubris and the lack of knowledge and understanding were major contributors. That did not excuse, however, Putin's aggressive acts.

The 2008 intervention into Georgia was the first proof of concept for Putin's disruptive strategy that would become central to Putinism. In reestablishing Russian influence, Putin used Georgia as an operational laboratory for what would take place in Ukraine six years later and then in Syria and elsewhere. Part of the strategy reflected Lenin's dictum to drive the bayonet as deeply as possible until it struck bone. The more sophisticated aspect was to combine physical and nonphysical means of imposing influence, of which active measures were central.

What should have been learned from the nearly 3,200 words in Putin's 1999 speech? This was an explicit recitation of how Putin meant to govern, how he viewed the organization of Russia's government and its relationship with the Russian people, how Russia and Russians required a unified and coherent state, and how to avoid the perils of both communism and the modern world.

In this speech, Putin rejected communism because it "vividly demonstrated its ineptitude for sound self-development, dooming our country to a steady lag behind economically advanced countries...."

Enumerating the major threat to Russia, he said, "Be it under communist, national-patriotic, or radical-liberal slogans, our country, our people will not withstand a new radical break-up...Twice in the outgoing century has Russia found itself in such a state: after October 1917 and in the '90s...."

As to solutions, Putin declared that "I am against the restoration of an official state ideology in Russia in any form..." and that "another foothold for the unity of Russian society is what can be called the traditional values of Russians. Patriotism is a source of the courage, staunchness, and strength of our people. If we lose patriotism and national pride and dignity, which are connected with it, we will lose ourselves as a nation capable of great achievements..." concluding that "Russia was and will remain a great power. It is preconditioned by the inseparable characteristics of its geopolitical, economic, and cultural existence reliably protecting its security and upholding its national interests in the international arena, than in its military strength."

In conclusion, Putin recognized that "the main threat to human rights and freedoms, to democracy as such emanates from the executive authority. And poverty has reached a mind-boggling scale in Russia.... For the first time in the past two to three hundred years, it is facing a real threat of sliding to the second, and possibly even third, echelon of world states."

THE TRANSFORMATION OF PUTIN AND PUTINISM

In 2001, Putin met newly elected president George W. Bush. Bush was initially taken with Putin ("I looked into his eyes..."). Putin apparently played to his religious conversion, presenting Bush with a crucifix allegedly belonging to his mother—one of many Putin would present to other leaders. Bush claimed this story was untrue.

Bush's abrogation of the ABM Treaty was regarded by Moscow as a serious retrenchment, eliminating a strategic centerpiece of the Cold War. September 11 disrupted international politics overnight. Although Putin offered Bush assistance and advice on Afghanistan based on the Soviet Union's unhappy experience, it was rejected. Putin took this as a personal rebuke that reflected American unilateralism, triumphalism, and disrespect for Russia.

Putin argued vociferously against the invasion of Iraq in 2003, accurately forecasting that a war would spread chaos beyond the Middle East and to Russia. Russia had reason to fear the backlash. Its population included significant numbers of Muslim minorities, and it had waged a bloody war against Muslim Chechen rebels. Russian intelligence also doubted Saddam had weapons of mass destruction

(WMD), believing that "Curve Ball," the so-called confirming Iraqi source of WMD, was passing on misinformation.

With the launch of Operation Iraqi Freedom and the catastrophe that followed, Putin became convinced that the US was not only untrustworthy. Its actions were also a danger to world order and stability. To Putin, America was overly arrogant and unprepared to respect Russia or treat it with proper seriousness. And America listened to no one. The expansion of NATO was another Russian bête noire.

After the Soviet Union imploded, Russians remained neuralgic about the expansion of NATO while often moderating its opposition as the alliance spread eastward. The creation of the Collective Security Treaty Organization (CSTO) and Eurasian Economic Union were attempts to offset NATO. The fear and paranoia of being surrounded and isolated had been firmly implanted deep into Russian culture by history. Putin signaled all this at the Munich Security Conference in early 2007. But who was listening?

Putin's concerns and warnings would reach a critical point at the 2008 NATO Bucharest summit regarding the newly independent states of Georgia and Ukraine that had been part of Russia and the Soviet Union for centuries.

In Munich, Putin railed against a unipolar world with reference to the United States, inferring that the interventions in Afghanistan and Iraq were disastrous uses of what he called "hyper force."

Putin asked:

> What is a unipolar world?....It is a world in which there is one master, one sovereign. And at the end of the day this is pernicious not only for all those within this system, but also for the sovereign itself because it destroys itself from within....
>
> I consider that the unipolar model is not only unacceptable but also impossible in today's world....

What is even more important is that the model itself is flawed because at its basis there is and can be no moral foundations for modern civilization....

Unilateral and frequently illegitimate actions have not resolved any problems. Moreover, they have caused new human tragedies and created new centers of tension. Judge for yourselves: wars as well as local and regional conflicts have not diminished....

Today we are witnessing an almost unconstrained hyper use of force—military force—in international relations, force that is plunging the world into an abyss of permanent conflicts. One state and, of course, first and foremost the United States, has overstepped its national borders in every way. This is visible in the economic, political, cultural, and educational policies it imposes on other nations. Well, who likes this? Who is happy about this?

About NATO, Putin said:

I think it is obvious that NATO expansion does not have any relation with the modernization of the Alliance itself or with ensuring security in Europe. On the contrary, it represents a serious provocation that reduces the level of mutual trust. And we have the right to ask: Against whom is this expansion intended?

And what happened to the assurances our western partners made after the dissolution of the Warsaw Pact? Where are those declarations today? No one even remembers them. But I will allow myself to remind this audience what was said.

> I would like to quote the speech of NATO General
> Secretary Mr. Manfred Wörner in Brussels on 17 May
> 1990. He said at the time that: "The fact that we are
> ready not to place a NATO army outside of German
> territory gives the Soviet Union a firm security
> guarantee." Where are these guarantees?

From these speeches and his questions and answers in Munich, Putin's intent was clear. After becoming acting president in 2000, his first priority was to maintain Russian integrity and prevent it from exploding and fragmenting as the USSR had. The West dismissed these realities. NATO expansion was anathema to three Russian leaders—Gorbachev, Yeltsin, and Putin—but likewise was largely ignored or downplayed.

Russia's sense of insecurity and vulnerability to outside forces, bordering on paranoia, was dismissed on the grounds that NATO was a defensive alliance. To Putin, Russia—and that meant him too—was being taken for granted. And Russia's psychological need for recognition and respect as a major or even great power was not appreciated by Washington. That gnawed at Putin.

Warning signals were unmistakable. Putin announced Russia was suspending participation in the Treaty on Conventional Armed Forces in Europe (CFE) in July 2007. CFE limited the number and deployments of conventional forces in Europe among the signatories. CFE was signed by NATO's then sixteen members and the Warsaw Pact's six members on November 19, 1990.

CFE entered into force in July 1992 after the Soviet Union and the Warsaw Pact had dissolved. That the Soviet Union and Warsaw Pact, the treaty signatories, no longer existed provided Putin the rationale (or excuse) for suspending CFE participation. The West did little in response.

Putin had other reasons for disagreeing with the West beyond NATO expansion. After abrogating the ABM Treaty, the Bush decision to station antiballistic missile defenses in Europe to counter Iranian intercontinental missiles raised alarms in Moscow. Just as Iraq had no weapons of mass destruction, Iran had no ICBMs or nuclear weapons.

The Russian military saw those defenses as capable of striking Russian shorter-range missiles that were vital to offset what the General Staff perceived as NATO's conventional military superiority. Hence, Russia raised a number of technical violations of the Intermediate Nuclear Force (INF) Treaty in objecting to the stationing of antiballistic missiles in Europe. President Trump would later leave the treaty.

These allegations were rejected by Washington as trivial, even though, technically, Russia was correct in terms of missile testing and the Aegis Ashore system that could be upgraded to fire Tomahawk missiles. Each of these technical treaty violations was easily corrected by the United States but, for whatever reasons, the US took no action.

None of Putin's reactions are excuses for subsequent Russian behavior. However, the failure of Washington to anticipate Russian responses to NATO expansion and unilateral American actions, given traditional Russian paranoia, contributed to the worsening relations. The NATO Bucharest summit in 2008 was a turning point and a further deterioration of relations.

Despite profound Russian objections, Georgia and Ukraine sought NATO membership. Both states had become independent in 1991. Russia still viewed them as partner states within Russia's sphere of influence. Indeed, Stalin was Georgian. Khrushchev was Ukrainian, as was one of Putin's parents.

Because many NATO members did not wish to antagonize Russia over further alliance expansion, Georgia and Ukraine were not offered entry into NATO's Military Assistance Program (MAP). But that concession to Russia was negated by George Bush.

For reasons that remain vague, as a consolation prize for being denied MAP, Bush gratuitously offered Georgia and Ukraine NATO membership at some future stage at the NATO Bucharest summit. NATO's North Atlantic Council (NAC) put this on its official communique. Putin was understandably furious, as this was a "red line" for Russia.

Putin confronted Bush and, using Bush's father's language after Saddam Hussein invaded Kuwait, told the president, "This will not stand." Bush tried to dismiss the pledge as politics and downgraded its importance. It did not work. This was a transformational moment in Russian-US relations. Putin was determined to make it impossible for Georgia and Ukraine ever to join NATO.

Several months later, Russia laid a trap for Georgia. South Ossetians who favored merging with Russia were directed by Moscow to attack local Georgian troops. Despite strong warnings from Washington and other capitals not to take the bait, Georgian president Mikheil Saakashvili launched military operations into South Ossetia. The Russians quickly intervened, routing the Georgian Army and declaring Abkhazia and South Ossetia as independent states.

The meaning and strategy were clear. According to the NATO treaty, states with contested borders were not eligible for membership. Russian occupation of eastern Ukraine and the annexation of Crimea in 2014 would follow. Georgia and Ukraine would not join NATO. That tension persists as both states still favor NATO membership. And many in the US Congress of both parties strongly support that initiative.

WHY RUSSIA AND PUTIN ARE MAD ABOUT MAD

The onset of the Fifth Horseman and the new MAD have favored and have been exploited and accelerated by Putin. Russia is far from the superpower the Soviet Union once was, but it is more than what the late Senator John McCain described as a "gas station with nuclear weapons."

Russia has huge economic constraints in its dependence on oil, an unhealthy and shrinking population of about 130 million, growing unhappiness with Putin and his autocratic government, the pandemic, and a shaky economy. That aside, Putin is playing a weak hand quite well in advancing Russian influence in Europe and the near abroad (its term for former Soviet republics and client states) while sowing dissent in NATO.

President Obama's caution in "leading from behind" in the 2011 attacks on Libya nominally to protect citizens in Benghazi from harm that led to civil war, and setting "red lines" against Syrian use of chemical weapons in 2012 it would ignore in 2015, convinced Putin of America's weakness and the continued danger posed by its policies under another administration. Putin may have also demeaned Obama due to his inexperience and perhaps even his color.

The end of the old rules-based Westphalian system and the influence of social media provided Russia with newer means to attack NATO coherence. Russia has also done well in convincing or coercing other states, usually American friends or allies in Europe, to support Moscow's policies that clash with Washington's priorities. The Nord Stream 2 gas pipeline is a prime example, no longer contested by Washington.

Germany was in strong favor of constructing the pipeline to assure the flow of energy. The Trump administration was adamantly opposed to the pipeline. This clash of wills led Trump to "punish" Berlin by redeploying ten thousand American troops from Germany, without any strategic or operational basis other than pique. But Chancellor Angela Merkel crossed Trump. The consequence was a further erosion of NATO solidarity and the increasing influence of Russia and Putin.

Moscow also employs quasi-alliances in the Middle East with Syria and the Libyan rebel government to counter US and NATO influence and increase its own. Putin intervened to save the Assad regime in Syria in 2015 with minimum military force and resources in stark contrast with the large and unsuccessful deployments of US and Western forces to Afghanistan and Iraq. Moscow also effectively employs private security companies such as the Wagner Group as surrogates to supply contract mercenaries and weapons, giving Moscow a thin measure of plausible deniability.

In retrospect, growing fissures between Russia and Western democracies were inevitable, as were fissures with China. Missteps, misperceptions, and wrong assumptions too often were inflamed and intensified by failures of knowledge and understanding on all sides of the US-Soviet/Russia-China relationships—tragically reminiscent of how World War I started. But the United States shared part of that responsibility and culpability for the decline of the US-Russia-China triangle. Indeed, under the Biden administration, the US now faces greater dual challenges from Russia and China.

Too often, American leaders dating back to Franklin Roosevelt assumed that by force of personality or close interpersonal relationships with other heads of government, divergent national interests could be overcome. As George W. Bush recorded in his memoir *Decision Points*, from the first meeting in Slovenia in 2001 to the Georgian intervention in 2008, Putin underwent a metamorphosis from ally and colleague to critic and then adversary.

At the end of 2020, Putin had brokered a peace agreement between Armenia and Azerbaijan over Nagorno-Karabakh that so far has ended the quarter-century dispute over sovereignty. But to solidify the peace, Russian peacemakers will be stationed in Nagorno-Karabakh, placing those troops at some risk. Putin is also making the Black Sea a Russian mare nostrum by virtue of his clever use of military diplomacy.

Flirtation with China, too, is an important means to break out of geographic isolation and NATO expansion surrounding Russia. Membership in the Shanghai Cooperation Organization (SCO) represents this move east. The creation of the Collective Security Treaty Organization (CSTO) in 1994 (Armenia, Belarus, Kazakhstan, Kyrgyzstan, Russia, and Tajikistan) and the Eurasian Economic Union (Armenia, Belarus, Kazakhstan, Kyrgyzstan, and Russia) in 2015 were efforts to assure both Russian security and economic relationships as counters to NATO and the EU. Azerbaijan, Georgia, and Uzbekistan withdrew from the CSTO after its inception, and the utility of both organizations is questionable.

Putin has emulated the most successful Russian tsars and the Soviet Union's most successful general secretaries, fortunately with less brutality, except for the occasional murders and poisonings of opponents inside and outside Russia. None of Putin's march from nominal friend of the United States and the West to adversary happened by accident. The cultures of societies, states, nonstate groups, and cults are usually deeply ingrained and driven by history. This is true of Russia and its (possibly for life) president certainly through 2036, when he may have to step down at age eighty-three.

THE AMERICAN AND WESTERN THREAT

The last US National Security and National Defense Strategies issued by past Presidents Barack Obama and Donald Trump and now by President Biden declared Russia and China explicitly as military threats engaged in a great-power competition. Regarding Russia, the 2014 Ukrainian intervention was a major inflection and crisis point, provoking what many in the West have called Cold War 2.0 after Moscow used military force to alter the post–Cold War boundaries. In both Ukraine and Syria, the Russian military, as well as mercenary forces from the Wagner Group, was tactically adept in annexing Crimea, occupying part of the Donbass, and supporting Assad's political survival in Damascus. Ukraine, however, had a unique historic, economic, and cultural attachment to Russia and vice versa dating back to Peter and Catherine.

The bulk of Russia's rocket and helicopter engines are made in Ukraine. The colored revolutions in the former Warsaw Pact states confronted Moscow with the possibility that unrest could spread to Russia. The Maidan Square massacre in February 2104 in which about fifty Ukrainians were killed led to the flight of ex-President Viktor Yanukovych and the collapse of his pro-Russian government.

From Moscow's perspective, Ukraine's attempts to move closer to the EU and away from Russia were unacceptable, especially with a new government forming in Kyiv. The US was not helpful from a Russian perspective. Moscow wrongly believed Washington and the CIA had intervened to drive Yanukovych from power in another example of fomenting regime change that could spread to Russia.

This then was an exploitable opportunity for Putin by preventing Ukraine's accession to NATO, curtailing its westward bias and Western influence. So-called "little green men"—Russian soldiers without identifying insignia—deployed into Ukraine's eastern Russian-speaking areas in the Donbass that were always closer to Moscow than Kyiv. And Crimea—which Khrushchev returned to Ukraine in 1954, with some permanently stationed twenty thousand Russian troops, much of the Black Sea Fleet present, and a ninety-nine-year lease—was occupied bloodlessly and allegedly with the near unanimous consent of the Crimean residents.

Russia, no matter how heavy handed its tactics, believed it was legitimate in its actions in Georgia and Ukraine and more so than the United States' interventions in Kosovo, Afghanistan, and most significantly, Iraq. The US and West perceived Russian aggression as a declaration of hybrid war in which the Kremlin would use whatever methods it deemed necessary to divide and weaken the West. And Russian intervention in the 2016 and 2020 American elections exacerbated relations.

Russian interference in the 2016 presidential elections provoked President Obama to tell Mr. Putin "to cut it out." But Trump took a much softer line, accepting Putin's word given to him in Helsinki in 2018 that Russia did not intervene. Trump's high regard for Putin continued, raising legitimate questions about the reasons for the former president's fondness for autocrats, including President Xi of China and North Korea's Kim.

Yet in July 2020, Trump told an interviewer that he had authorized a cyberattack on Russia's Internet Research Agency in St. Petersburg, apparently an action President Obama declined to take. Still, the debate over Trump's relationship with Putin came into further question in mid-2020 after the *New York Times* released a story reporting the Russian Military Intelligence, the GRU, was paying $100,000 bounties to the Taliban for killing American and British troops in Afghanistan. Thus far, no evidence has been presented to confirm or deny that report beyond the US military expressing "skepticism" over its credibility.

Without evidence, however, some (especially on the Democratic side) believe that Putin had leverage over Trump in some form of compromising material. Republican supporters argued that by maintaining good personal relations with Putin and despite strong economic sanctions against Russia, Trump attempted a reverse Nixon by encouraging Moscow to move closer to Washington at the expense of China.

Russia remains the key disrupter. US policy under Trump was at best ambivalent. We await to see what President Biden intends.

On one hand, Russia is a strategic competitor and potential adversary. On the other, Presidents Trump and Putin had a good personal relationship. Russia will continue to use active measures to disrupt Western coherence while refusing to provoke a crisis that could lead to conflict or a crisis Moscow could not control or one that would stiffen Western resistance.

The first test for the West and for Washington is to ensure better understanding of Russia, Putin, and his motivations and interests. Recognizing how much history has affected Russia is important not as an excuse but as the foundation for forming future strategies and pursuing policy outcomes and not simply reacting to Moscow. A Brains-Based Approach is vital to this change in thought processes and is explained in Chapter 8 and the appendix.

Until a major change in US strategic thinking occurs, American and NATO policy toward Russia will remain adrift at best and divisive at worst. Putin will exploit that drift as Russia simultaneously confronts the seven disruptors.

RUSSIA, MAD, AND WHAT LIES AHEAD

Russia is not immune to the Fifth Horseman and the new MAD. Climate change is both opening the Arctic as ice caps recede and causing extreme environmental damage. Massive forest fires in Siberia to equally large oil leaks in the far north are plaguing Russia. The combination of cyber and social media so far is being used to great advantage by Moscow in its active measures to disrupt NATO and other individual states and strengthen political control at home. So far, the response by the US and its allies has been tepid.

Terrorism cuts two ways. The threat of Islamic extremism in Russia is real and reflects the often-racist bias by Russians against the Muslim culture. The real danger of Chechen terrorism (such as the Beslan school shooting and the Moscow Opera siege) has been neutralized by awarding President Ramzan Kadyrov virtually absolute power in Chechnya. Kadyrov has exercised that power ruthlessly and often mercilessly. From Putin's view, while Islamic extremism remains a major threat, Chechen nationalism has been cynically repressed.

Control of the state and the public makes the impact of drones less disruptive inside Russia. However, the Russian military is exploiting this technology possibly well ahead of the West. But it is debt and a failed and failing government that are among the most disruptive dangers to Putin's regime and his presidency.

Russia has huge economic problems resulting from low energy prices, the pandemic, sanctions, and the absence of a vibrant, free enterprise system. The latter has always been a Russian and Soviet Achilles' heel. Providing basic needs for the public and raising standards of living has been elusive under Putin and his government. The July and August 2020 protests in Khabarovsk in Siberia over the firing of the local governor on murder charges are not good news for Putin. Failed government could be the cause of Putin's eventual downfall or forced retirement.

Where are Russia and Putin headed? Putin is hostile toward and suspicious of the US and the West because in his view, American interventions into Afghanistan, Iraq, Syria, and Libya have made the world more dangerous. Whether trust and confidence can be reestablished in a MAD-driven world is a formidable challenge for Putin and the Biden presidency. But areas for cooperation over arms control, climate change, confidence building measures, de-escalation and crisis management, COVID-19, and counterterrorism exist.

Despite Putin's claim, Russia is not and never will be a democracy in the Western sense. That aside, peaceful coexistence persisted between Khrushchev and Eisenhower in the midst of the Cold War and an ideological dispute. That history offers a glimmer of hope in reducing hostility and seeking a mutually beneficial modus operandi.

Further, the Russian people have a long history of suffering and surviving dismal conditions, whether from invasion or other privations of drought, winter, and disease, and have a high tolerance for pain.

Whether Russian patience will continue to tolerate diminishment of standards of living remains a crucial focal point for Putin's legitimacy. In a MAD-driven world, it is not clear how long that patience will persist.

What does this mean for Putin and the next few years?

During the Cold War, Georgi Arbatov, then head of Moscow's leading think tank, the Institute for the Study of the USA and Canada, would remind his Western interlocutors of a certain geostrategic reality in the form of this question. Suppose there were eight hundred million Mexicans armed with nuclear weapons wanting Texas back. What would the US do? Clearly, Arbatov was referring to China.

Putin would put this question in current terms. Suppose Mexico, Central America, and Canada, armed with nuclear weapons, formed a military alliance against the United States claiming lost territories back—over which America had suffered millions killed in seizing— and imposed sanctions to force a return. America's view of its security would be very different. While the analogy is incomplete, it is suggestive of how others might have different views of providing for the common defense.

First, Putin believes that under his leadership, Russia is on the right course. His major political and legitimacy challenges are to maintain marginal improvements in standards of living or achieve sufficient external successes that play to and placate the Russian psychological yearning for respect. Thus far, Putin has maintained this balance.

But, like Khrushchev, a future Cuban Missile Crisis for Putin could prove politically fatal in this high-wire act. And like Stalin, Khrushchev, Brezhnev, and Gorbachev, Putin is pragmatic. Each, in their own way, dealt on that basis with the West.

Second, Putin regards disrupting the cohesion of NATO and the West as an important but not vital interest worth risking war or even a limited military conflict. Following this logic, Russia will continue to employ active measures as a primary tool to advance and protect its interests with limits. Interference in and disruption of politics and elections will continue unabated in the United States as well as in NATO countries. One goal will be to prevent the US from continuing what Russia perceives as destabilizing the international environment and creating unnecessary crises through its overly militarized foreign policy.

The UK House of Commons Select Committee on Intelligence and Security released a searing report in July 2020 on Russian interference in British elections and Brexit on the leave side. The accusations were made more damaging by disclosure of the extent of financial contributions made to the Leave Campaign by Russian billionaires, many residing in Britain. Russian money was hard at work.

Russia is fully exploiting the internet and social media as enablers for campaigns of misinformation, disinformation, propaganda, and false allegations. Given the sophistication of "deep fakes" that can create lifelike images of anyone and everyone in the most compromising of situations, it would be naive not to anticipate the increased use of this malign yet effective form of propaganda. The Internet Research Agency (IRA) is a primary arm of not only hacking but influence-building operations as part of active measures. In August 2020, the US Department of State's Global Engagement Center released a seventy-seven-page report called *Russian Pillars* that was an extraordinarily comprehensive compendium of these activities.

Third, Putin will continue to engage aggressively in regional politics in the near abroad, the Persian Gulf, and the Middle East. The use of the Wagner Group will increase as a surrogate. Putin's aims are corollaries of his first priority to disrupt NATO and the US and gain more regional access to increase both influence and penetration of foreign markets largely for arms sales and energy-related deals. As noted, Russia will also attempt to make the Black and Baltic Seas Russian lakes by flexing its military might through deployments, exercises, and implied threats of coercion and intimidation.

Fourth, Putin will focus domestically on a troubled economy and increasing public discontent because of declining standards of living and of health exacerbated by coronavirus/COVID-19. It is clear that Russians have substantial tolerance and endurance when it comes to accepting harsh conditions. Yet Putin's options are limited.

Russia exports outside energy are de minimus. It produces little else. Ukraine was once the breadbasket and heavy manufacturing center for the Soviet Union. While Russia has a very well-educated and technical cohort, free enterprise has never taken hold. Hence, the economy remains a key weakness and vulnerability.

Fifth, Putin has modernized his military at the conventional, unconventional, and nuclear levels. The Gerasimov Doctrine, named for the long-serving chief of defense, has declared information warfare is dominant. Conflicts in Georgia, Syria, Ukraine, and Nagorno-Karabakh have honed this form of war in which Russia may be ahead of the West intellectually.

Russia is fielding new-generation submarines, ballistic and hypersonic missiles, and a long-range, high-speed autonomous underwater nuclear delivery system called Poseidon. Poseidon is reported to be eighty feet in length, is transoceanic with speeds possibly in excess of one hundred knots, and is armed with a thermonuclear warhead. Interestingly, the first Soviet nuclear retaliatory weapons were submarine-launched torpedoes designed to explode in harbors of coastal cities and ports.

Putin will use his modernized military and emphasis on information warfare as diplomatic leverage to intimidate and coerce NATO members and thus disrupt alliance cohesion even further.

Sixth, Putin will continue to attempt to improve relations with China and has signed a multibillion-dollar energy deal with Beijing. Russia is also a member of the Shanghai Cooperative Organization created by China in 2001. And Russia will use its military to increase its access and influence in Africa, the near abroad, and Southwest Asia.

Seventh, Putin will continue to use disruption as a key political policy tool to advance Russian interests and neutralize or defeat counteractions and strategies on the part of the United States and others.

Eighth, Putin will continue to exploit sound strategic thinking and planning to maximize use of scarce resources across government. The Soviet/Russian military and intellectual community has always required an intellectual and theoretical foundation for its thinking. The limiting factor was the irrational nature of the Soviet system.

Ninth, Putin's State of the Nation address in April 2021 laid out his priorities. The first was to deal with COVID. Second was to improve the economy and standards of living in part by improving educational resources. Third, Putin promised to raise life expectancy to eighty-two from the current mid-sixties.

Only in the last part of his speech did Putin discuss "red lines" crossed by other states that would be answered by an immediate response. Western reporting did not focus on the bulk of his speech. Instead, "red lines" and inferred threats made the headlines, exposing the continued failure to have sufficient knowledge and understanding of Russia and Putin.

Tenth, on July 12, 2021, Putin published a five-thousand-word essay on Ukraine declaring it and the Russian people were one. The implication was clear based on the past record of Putin signaling future actions. Putin no doubt will use such means to show his intentions. By the time this book is published, it would not be surprising to see a major Russian initiative to draw Ukraine closer, very likely using military force to intimidate Kyiv to make concessions.

The answer as to what Lenin would recommend is straightforward: Attack the legitimacy of the Russian regime by attempting to affect, influence, and even control its will and perception as fits Western and not the Kremlin's interests. This includes reverse engineering active measures to work against Putin. Despite tight control of the media and internet, Russia is still a very porous society. Reinvigorating the

Voice of America and Radio Free Europe with more social media content is certainly needed.

Second, allies count. Building coalitions to oppose Russian policies, particularly those that attempt to disrupt political coherence in the West, are vital. NATO would be an obvious starting point. Bringing friends and partners in Asia such as Australia, New Zealand, Japan, and South Korea closer to NATO would send a signal.

Third, counter Putin's military strategy by reversing the cost-exchange ratio so that Russia pays an exorbitant amount to keep pace. That means shaping Russian will and perception to recognize that all forms of aggression will exact a price in conditions of peace, "gray zone" operations that are neither peace nor war, and in actual conflict. The Porcupine Defense strategy described in detail in Chapter 9 is designed for these purposes. And do not overstate the so-called Russian threat. In many ways, the better psychological ploy is to downplay and ignore.

Fourth, use diplomatic psychology skillfully. The Montreux Convention of 1936 is a good example. The convention limits non-riparian states in sending warships into the Black Sea. But one of the signatories, the USSR, no longer exists, and two, Georgia and Ukraine, did not exist when the treaty was signed. Even the suggestion of a review will sound alarm bells in Moscow. Further, as the USSR was neuralgic about America's use of human rights to criticize the regime, there is no reason this practice could not be repeated.

Reality, however, has been far different in practice. The United States has consistently been reactive in policy responses that reflected its thinking and not how the other side reasoned. That predictable outcome has almost always been a failure in the past. Einstein was correct: Insanity is constantly repeating the same action and expecting a different outcome.

A Brains-Based Approach can rectify this failing if properly utilized. Later chapters discuss specific recommendations, beginning with defining the outcomes in this relationship with Russia that will become our strategic objectives that rely on a better understanding of how Russia thinks, acts, and deals with providing for its common defense.

Chapter Four

DRAGONS AND BEARS II: CHINA ON A MAD COLLISION COURSE

Suppose America lost the Revolution against Great Britain, fought multiple civil wars, was partitioned for a century by foreign powers, lost tens of millions in these conflicts, and was not unified until 1949. How would that have affected American policies and politics today?

For good or ill, America and China are on a collision course. The image of the unsinkable giant ocean liner *Titanic* and the massive iceberg comes to mind, with two exceptions. The first is that America or China could represent either the *Titanic* or the iceberg. The second is that if this collision occurs, both the giant ship and the iceberg could figuratively sink, the ultimate disruption.

How both powers arrived at this precarious condition and what happens next are highly relevant questions. In hindsight, history shows that this impasse was not inevitable if rationality and common sense prevailed. But if both are not present, the future is safe only if the two giants can establish some form of peaceful coexistence or at least agree on an off-ramp for this great-power competition.

As with the Soviet Union, the failure to garner sufficient knowledge and understanding invariably leads to failure. A case study of the first months of the Korean War (1950–1953) illuminates this unvarnished truth and serves as a further warning as the United States pursues a great power rivalry with China.

In the immediate aftermath of World War II in September 1945, the occupation of Korea after Japan's surrender was set by future secretary of state and then lieutenant colonel Dean Rusk. To ease the logistic burdens of occupation, Rusk arbitrarily divided Korea at the thirty-eighth parallel. The Soviets were assigned the north and the allies the south.

Five years later, in a speech in early 1950, Secretary of State Dean Acheson inadvertently omitted Korea from the nations the US would defend against communist expansion. Seizing what appeared to be an opportunity, Stalin convinced or coerced North Korea's leader Kim Il-sung to attack the south and unify the peninsula.

With the tacit support of the PRC, on June 25, 1950, North Korean troops poured across the thirty-eighth parallel. The suddenness of the attack and the unreadiness of American forces resulted in US and UN forces being driven back and trapped inside the Pusan Perimeter on Korea's southeast coast.

President Harry Truman responded to this unprovoked invasion with what would be called a "police action." Because the Soviet Union began a boycott of the UN Security Council in January over its refusal to expel Nationalist China and replace it with the PRC, it was not present at the Security Council vote on the resolution to authorize force in Korea. Without Soviet presence and veto, the vote was unanimously approved as required by the UN Charter. The police action became a UN military operation led by the United States that would last three years until a truce was finally signed at Panmunjom in mid-1953.

Under the command of General of the Army Douglas MacArthur, an audacious amphibious landing at Inchon, the port of Seoul on Korea's west coast some thirty miles from the DMZ, was launched in September 1950. The landing surprised, cut off, and trapped the North Korean Army in the south just as US forces had been cornered in Pusan. A massive retreat followed as North Korean forces fled northward to avoid complete destruction. UN forces raced north chasing the defeated North Korean Army. Crossing the thirty-eighth parallel in hot pursuit, by November, UN forces closed in on the Yalu River marking the Chinese border with North Korea.

UN forces occupying the whole of the peninsula meant a unified Korea, an unacceptable and thus intolerable outcome for the newly unified People's Republic of China. Purposely signaling its intent to intervene, the People's Liberation Army (PLA) made three successive major armed probes, attacking and then withdrawing after each.

The threat and signaling of a massive Chinese intervention should have been unmistakable. It was ignored. UN forces continued the march north to the Yalu despite these signals. Washington issued further warnings to MacArthur that the PRC was mobilizing for a major offensive.

MacArthur refused to listen. He believed China would not cross the Yalu and face annihilation by his superior firepower and that nuclear weapons would also prove a deterrent. Because UN forces had not attacked Chinese forces based north of the Yalu in Manchuria, MacArthur concluded restraint would convince Beijing that the UN had no territorial designs on China.

On a subzero Thanksgiving Day 1950, hundreds of thousands of PLA troops ended MacArthur's myopia by swarming into Korea. UN forces were overwhelmed by the onslaught, eventually retreating to the thirty-eighth parallel. A bloody stalemate persisted until the June

1953 truce halted hostilities. The lesson: When the PRC shows serious intent, forgetting or ignoring that history could lead to a future MacArthur-like failure.

Fifty years later, the same lack of knowledge fueled the persistent and bipartisan erroneous belief that Saddam Hussein possessed weapons of mass destruction that turned the second Iraq War into America's worst strategic disaster since the Civil War. A series of presidents wrongly assumed that, over time, Russia under Putin and China under Xi would move closer to the West and its liberal values. That did not happen.

Similarly, to honor a campaign promise to end "endless wars" in the waning months of his presidency, Donald Trump ordered significant drawdowns in Afghanistan and Iraq. These were opposed by the then-secretary of defense, Mark Esper, who Trump promptly fired, replacing him with the inexperienced and accommodating Chris Miller.

The reason for all these failures was identical and predictable: lack of knowledge and understanding compounded by hubris displayed by both Republican and Democratic administrations. Further evidence of this repeated failure was the inability of American presidential administrations to take seriously major speeches and statements made by the leaders of both Russia and China.

What Putin and Xi said in advance turned out to be the policies and actions that were undertaken and followed. Ignorance of the other side is no excuse for mistakes made by Washington. The conclusion was self-evident. American political leaders need to bear this history in mind regarding how policies are developed vis-à-vis China, intensified by this great-power competition in a 51 percent nation.

Putin's Russia was summarized in a sentence by Senator McCain. In a similar shorthand, he wrote, "China is a 21st century version of the Qing Dynasty (1644–1911) with an advanced economy, leading edge technology, nuclear and modern conventional weapons, and

Middle Kingdom attitudes regarding its neighbors if not as vassal states than certainly within Beijing's orbit of influence. China also has rekindled nationalism as a means of rallying the public under near total party control."

Further, many in America believe that the old-world liberal order of a rules-based regime is being disrupted by China. In seeking to displace the West and the US as "a or the" global leader in economics, technologies, and influence, Beijing is imposing its "rules" through Belt and Road, Regional Comprehensive Economic Partnership (RCEP), and promiscuous amounts of money for investment or loans. Applying new security laws to Hong Kong in what amounts to abrogating the 1997 agreement with Britain and virtual annexation, China is aggressively suppressing dissent. A major reason is the Chinese Communist Party's (CCP) fear of blowback into the mainland by Hong Kong's protest movements.

Unfortunately, in Western capitals, particularly Washington for the last decade, assessment of Chinese actions and intent often exaggerated actual capabilities, underestimated limitations, and, most dangerously, failed to create comprehensive strategies in concert with allies. A strong dose of Western hypocrisy is also at play in dismissing the negative effects of the tariff war and the great-power competition that has emphasized the military aspects and blamed China for the buildup of its forces.

China fortified a series of tiny islets in its coastal seas and extended its geographical claims well into international waters. Ironically, China is pursuing what two hundred years ago America proclaimed as the Monroe Doctrine, declaring that outside intervention into the Western Hemisphere was unacceptable and not to be tolerated. Has China adopted its own version of a Monroe or applied a Middle Kingdom doctrine to this expansion?

Deeper understanding of China begins with appreciation of its history and the recognition that despite the authority of the CCP, China is not a monolithic superpower. It has weaknesses.

From about 1600 BC until the Opium Wars beginning in the 1840s—over three millennia—China was dominated by the Middle Kingdom and heavenly mandate complexes and presumptions of cultural, intellectual, societal, and technological superiority. This hubris regarded outsiders to the Middle Kingdom and its fiefdoms as barbarians. This history and Middle Kingdom complex loom large in the psychology of China's leaders and the CCP. One vignette makes this point.

The former head Chinese spy in Washington, the defense attaché, was a good friend. He was well connected. His wife was the equivalent of China's deputy attorney general. After two long tours in Washington, he was headed back to China and probably retirement, which meant transitioning to a civilian intelligence assignment. With all the luxuries here of a big house in McLean, a car and driver, and an expense account, I asked how he would make do with a humbler existence in Beijing without all these comforts. His answer was stunning yet not readily understandable by Americans.

"I am going back to a truly civilized country." And he meant it. The Middle Kingdom view was very real in the twenty-first century. Too often, history and culture are forgotten.

For the century following the Opium Wars, called the period of "humiliation" by the Chinese, China was torn by massive internal and external disruptions, including peasant revolutions, foreign occupation, civil wars, and in 1937 the Japanese invasion prior to World War II. Following the war, Mao and the CCP fought and ultimately defeated Chiang Kai-shek in 1949, forcing the KMT (Nationalist Party) to retreat to Taiwan. While history does not excuse China's current policies, attitudes, and behavior, ignoring that past will ensure future American policies are partially or largely ill-informed and thus could fail.

From those contexts, a thoughtful evaluation of China's strengths, weaknesses, and political, social, and economic constraints is essential. Just as Putin was clear in announcing Russia's aims and intentions from his first days in power, China and Xi have been explicit in stating objectives and the means for achieving those aims.

While both China and America bear significant responsibility for the dramatic decline in relations and increase in tensions, actions trigger reactions and vice versa. None of China's policies and intentions are secret or hidden. One barrier is that most, but not all, of China's public statements and websites are in Mandarin. Yet sufficient English translations are available to provide the foundation for a better understanding of China's aims and policies.

Thorough comprehension of China requires more than relying solely on analysis provided by sources external to China. And that comprehension must not fall prey to exaggerating China's intentions, motivations, and what is perceived in the West as malign actions. Constraints on China are real.

China's huge underclass may approach half a billion people. Government neglect of the needs of its citizens, magnified by massive corruption, fomented major protests, riots, and civil unrest that reportedly reach a hundred thousand a year in number. Belt and Road have consumed trillions of renminbi that could have been spent domestically and is a further aggravation to many of its citizens.

China has a huge debt and a shadow banking system that is potentially vulnerable should financial markets be further disrupted by the pandemic or other shocks. China has potential real estate bubbles generated by over-construction of buildings that lay vacant. It is dependent on supply chains to foreign suppliers for vital components needed in manufacture of its computer, information, and high-tech products.

Although the CCP is in firm control and has implemented a government- and public sector-wide series of integrated national strategies, execution is always an issue. The best of strategies will fail if not put into effective practice. Having the CCP as a disciplinary tool is dual-edged. Integration can be mandated. At the same time, discipline can produce inflexibility and brittleness in the chain of political command that is destructive to productivity.

While China's foreign policies have become more aggressive and militarized over the past decade, from a historical perspective, the last war it fought, aside from border skirmishes with India, was an expensive incursion into Vietnam in 1979 when its army was badly bloodied and forced to withdraw. China still claims it will abide by no first use of nuclear weapons and will not employ them against nonnuclear states. And, so far, China has not chosen to deploy large numbers of strategic nuclear weapons, conforming with Mao's view that a few atom bombs are enough.

That could change. The backlash China has created in Asia by its more aggressive policies and demands, particularly regarding territorial claims, could be a powerful counterweight if properly exploited. Trade and economic issues fall into this category as China, likewise, moves to increase its influence and regional authority. Unfortunately, both Republicans and Democrats seem oblivious to the prospect of Chinese actions generating resistance by other states in the region.

Beyond Belt and Road, China established the fifteen-nation RCEP that included a number of American Pacific allies and friends in late 2020. The explicit aim was to establish a free trade zone. One implicit consequence was that China exploited the retraction of America under the Trump administration in part because of its withdrawal from the Trans-Pacific Partnership (TPP). A second more obvious consequence is China's increasing influence in the region.

Understanding how China is dealing with the seven major disruptors of MAD—climate change, cyber, social media, terrorism, massive

debt, drones, and failed and failing government—likewise is important, especially to determine which of these China fears, is fighting, or
is friending. The pandemic heightens the importance of how MAD
is also affecting China. The Trump administration accused China
of spreading the coronavirus/COVID-19 pandemic, calling it the
Wuhan Flu and China Flu. This question resurfaced in 2021 and so
far, has not been resolved. However, while China's release of the virus
DNA was critical in producing vaccines, the source of the coronavirus
has led to further suspicions about China's role and accountability.

A corollary question arises over the consistent use of the term
"rise of China" as a peer or near-peer competitor by American officials. Does this phrase reflect a deep-seated cultural and psychological
antipathy to and fear of ceding peer status to a rival as occurred in
the 1980s when Washington feared Japan was overtaking the United
States as the leading economic superpower? Or is this term simply
patronizing and demeaning, as China believes?

Greater insight into China and Chinese society can be gained from
three specific vantage points. The first is China's innovative "tri," not
just dual, use of technologies that seek to improve the standard of
living of its citizens by facilitating the buying, selling, and paying for
virtually all items; concurrently empowering population control of the
public by the CCP; and enhancing military modernization.

The Chinese Great Firewall; facial and electronic forms of recognition, including digital collection to keep nearly instantaneous track
of citizens; and "social credits" that will be defined below are examples of how the party is increasing its control and surveillance of its
population. Multiple uses of technology are also applied to improving
healthcare and education. And Military-Civil Fusion is the key mech-
anism for technology applicable to both sectors.

Second is China's venture capital market and what K. F. Lee
terms in *AI Superpowers: China, Silicon Valley, and the New World Order* the

"coliseum," a metaphor to underscore the life-and-death environment permeating competition among start-up companies in China. This conduct reflects what these Chinese companies consider "normal" business practices from corporate cannibalism; theft of intellectual property; and highly unscrupulous means to destroy the competition reminiscent of American "robber barons" of the late nineteenth and early twentieth centuries and, more recently, corporate raiders and "vulture capitalists."

One consequence of the "coliseum" is the intense pressure for generating even greater creativity in innovation and technology. That pressure breeds the requirement for large numbers of technically qualified personnel. To that end, Lee runs several courses a year training AI engineers.

Ironically, many of the instructors are Americans. In a good year, seven hundred Chinese students graduate from these courses. The curriculum of the course is shown later so that the reader can better understand how far ahead China leads the US in AI development and creative thinking. All this is available in the open press.

Third is the impact of *Unrestricted Warfare*, published in 1999. The book analyzed the nature of war past, present, and future and applied the findings to how China must fashion its national security and defense. While the US military asserts that China (and Russia) is fielding an anti-access, area denial (A2AD) to defend the nation from external attack, that is a simplistic conclusion. In the view of the author, future war will be waged far beyond the military domain in which "information" will determine winners and losers. That explains why China is focused on three "great power strategies" for maritime, space, and cyber and informationalization, the last to be defined shortly.

FROM EMPEROR TO TIANANMEN

China's history has suffered tragic disruptions and failures. China dates its origins as far as five thousand years ago, although 1600–1300 BC may be more accurate. That perspective is still a very long time ago compared with 1776 and 1789 for America. Since the thirteenth-century Mongols and, later, the Ming/Qin Dynasties that reigned from 1644 until 1911, China embraced the "Middle Kingdom" philosophy of cultural superiority and the "heavenly mandate" to rule and dominate what constituted the then-known world.

Marco Polo's travels in the latter part of the thirteenth century recorded the grandeur of China and the riches to be found in Asia. More than a century later, Admiral Zheng He, in the first decades of the fifteenth century, took his fleet on several expeditions to Southeast Asia, the subcontinent, the Indian Ocean, the east coast of Africa, and Arabia, representing China's strength and scope of influence.

When Lord McCartney was sent by King George III to China in 1793, the Qianlong Emperor kept him waiting for months. During the one meeting granted to the visitor, the emperor told McCartney that nothing the "barbarians" could offer in tribute was needed by China. The arrogance of this heavenly mandate complex would prove fatal as China, compared to the West, was technologically primitive. Despite having invented gunpowder and cannons in the thirteenth century, the emperor and his advisors could not comprehend that China's technology was vastly inferior in every category to the West's.

The century of humiliation began with the Opium Wars of the mid-nineteenth century. The cosmic arrogance of the Qing Dynasty refused to acknowledge China's military inferiority and would lead to the opening and later partitioning of China. The weakness of the dynasty compounded by Western imperialism and colonization of China's major coastal cities became the predicate and cause of riots and unrest, leading to civil war.

The Taiping Rebellion (1850–1864) was one of the bloodiest wars in history. The rebellion pitted the Qing Dynasty, aided by the French and British, against the Taiping Heavenly Kingdom established by Christian converts in the south and led by a mystic called Hong Xiuquan. Abetted by the Opium Wars and natural disaster, some twenty million Chinese perished.

During the second half of the nineteenth century, the United States had an Asian moment. Commodore Matthew Perry had "opened" Japan with the visit of his Black Ships in 1853. That visit and the obvious contrast of Western military technologies would lead to a revolution that in several decades would modernize Japan. In that modernization, Japan fielded a highly capable and technologically advanced military, defeating China in 1895 and bloodying Russia a decade later in the 1904–1905 war.

Trade was followed by American missionaries eager to convert heathen Chinese to Christianity. Toward the end of the nineteenth century, when China was being carved up by outside powers, the US proposed the "Open Door" policy to forestall and prevent that division. But China remained in turmoil, partitioned by Western powers and Japan.

A series of clan wars, revolts, and attempted revolutions followed. This nearly ubiquitous unrest was crushed at enormous cost in blood and treasure by the emperor. That draining of resources led to the fatal weakening of the Qing Dynasty and the authority of the central government that had reigned since 1644 and the rise of regional warlords. Attempts to modernize China's feudal technology, the Guangxu Emperor in 1898 with the Hundred Days of Reform program was thwarted by the Dowager Empress. And in 1900, a massive peasant uprising called the Boxer Rebellion would lead to the death knell for the Qing Dynasty.

Named for a Chinese secret society known as the Yihetuan, or Righteous and Harmonious Fists, the aim of the Boxers was to overthrow the Qing Dynasty and expel all foreigners from China. The rebellion was supported by the Dowager Empress to rid China of all foreign interference. The regime, opposed by the empress, was unable to defeat the Boxers.

An army of about nineteen thousand Western troops was mustered to protect and safeguard the foreign cantonments threatened by the rebellion. Beijing was captured in August 1900. The Dowager Empress was forced into exile in Xi'an, finally crushing the Boxer Rebellion in the process. But the dynasty was mortally wounded.

The subsequent peace treaty imposed impossible demands on the dynasty to assure the continuation and safety of Western presence. The one-sided treaty provoked the 1911 revolution and the abdication of the Last Emperor, the child Puyi. Thousands of years of dynastic rule ended when the Republic of China was declared on New Year's Day 1912. Sun Yat-sen, who was crucial in the reform and rebellion movements, was elected as the first president. The same year, the Chinese Nationalist Party (Kuomintang, or KMT) was formed.

Frustrated by inaction, Sun soon resigned and went into exile in Japan, replaced by Yuan Shikai. Yuan made the fatal error of abolishing national and provincial assemblies and the KMT, declaring himself the emperor of the Empire of China in 1915. That was also the year Japan imposed the infamous "21 Demands" on China that further weakened Yuan.

Facing rebellion over his incompetence and ego, Yuan soon abdicated and died in 1916. His death left a power vacuum in which the republican government was a facade. The chaos produced by the absence of a central government was replaced by the anarchy of the Warlord Era. Major parts of China became separate entities ruled by shifting coalitions of competing provincial military leaders without a central loyalty, causing further disunity. The common denominator was that the Chinese people bore the brunt of this violence and division. World War I exacerbated this chaos.

After World War I, the Treaty of Versailles awarded German holdings in <u>Shandong</u> Province to Japan. The cabinet was outraged and helpless; China refused to sign the treaty and the government fell. In 1919, the protest against the treaty provoked the May Fourth Student Movement. Formed in Beijing, it quickly spread nationwide.

Two years before, in 1917, Sun Yat-sen returned to China with the aim of unifying the country wracked by war and dominated by warlords. Sun set up a series of regional governments. He received critical support from the Soviet Union and advice from Comintern agent Gregory Voitinsky. Guided by Voitinsky, Sun forged an alliance with the fledgling Chinese Communist Party (CCP), formed in 1921, that would last until 1927.

Sun died of liver cancer in 1925. Chiang Kai-shek, a key lieutenant, seized control of the KMT. Through a series of military campaigns, Chiang finally defeated the warlords in south and central China and secured a nominal allegiance with the northern warlords. In 1927, based on his victories and pact with warlords and the CCP, Chiang established a national government provisionally in Wuhan and then permanently in Nanjing.

Having established a national government, Chiang turned on his erstwhile ally, the CCP, to cement his power and control of the country. The civil war between the Nationalists and Communists would continue until 1949 with a pause from 1937 to 1945 to contest Japan's invasion and occupation of much of China and its major coastal cities. During the CCP's famous long march in 1934 to escape Chiang's forces and prevent its elimination, Mao Zedong would emerge as the CCP leader.

With Japan's defeat and the end of World War II, civil war between the CCP and KMT consumed China. A series of American mediation missions failed to end the war. By late 1949, Mao and CCP forces drove the KMT from the mainland, retreating to Taiwan where it remains. On October 1, 1949, the People's Republic of China (PRC) was formally established, and the CCP faced a devastated, divided, and impoverished country.

After the Korean War, Mao ordered collectivization and seizure of land, leading to massive executions and imprisonment in forced labor camps. An estimated forty-five million Chinese died. Peasants were ordered to build smelters in backyards to produce steel and other nonsensical products. Famine persisted. And Mao's critics threatened to isolate and contain him.

In 1966, to regain power, Mao instituted the Great Proletarian Cultural Revolution meant to re-indoctrinate the Chinese to Mao's form of communism. The predictable result was a major upheaval in society. Many millions were "reeducated," families were separated, and China in Western views seemed bent on self-destruction. Manufactured newspaper photos of Mao swimming the Yangtze reinforced this skepticism.

Meanwhile, China's tensions with the Soviet Union were building. The Sino-Soviet rift was becoming apparent, although not to American political leaders, who still saw the threat as "godless, monolithic communism." In 1969, China's then defense minister, Lin Biao, warned of an imminent Soviet attack. Fighting broke out on the Ussuri River that bordered both countries. Sporadic fighting continued until 1971 when an agreement with Moscow was reached. By then Mao was prepared to view Washington as a potential ally against the Soviet Union, culminating with President Richard Nixon's historic 1972 visit to Beijing.

Following Mao's death in 1976, a power struggle over succession ensued. Ultimately, Deng Xiaoping emerged as the de facto leader from 1978 to 1992, although he never assumed the role of head of the party or of the state. Deng was a reformer, promising "capitalism with a Chinese face." The party loosened controls, communes were disbanded, and China was launched on an open market economy that would result in its current economic strength and breadth. Had Deng survived or had other like-minded leaders followed him, it is at least arguable that China might have remianed a more open society. Sadly, that would not happen.

In 1989, the death of former and pro-reform general secretary Hu Yaobang sparked the Tiananmen Square protests as many Chinese feared the end of this reform movement. For months, protestors railed publicly against the government, demanding an end to corruption and greater reforms for more individual freedom and especially for freer speech. On June 4, the protest reached a head in Beijing.

PLA troops were deployed to remove forcibly the protesters from the square. A large number of protesters were killed, wounded, or arrested. Famously, one protester was filmed heroically and physically blocking a PLA tank. But the forceful repression created worldwide condemnation and sanctions against China, setting relations back for some time.

Under General Secretary and President Jian Zemin, economic growth was double figured and perhaps two hundred million peasants were uplifted from poverty. In 1997 and 1999, the former territories of Hong Kong and Macau reverted to China. In 2001, China joined the World Trade Organization, supported by America.

THE RISE OF XI AND THE END OF COLLECTIVE LEADERSHIP

Following his rehabilitation, Xi quickly ascended the ladder of power in China's coastal provinces. He served as governor of Fujian from 1999 to 2002. He then moved and was promoted to governor and party secretary of neighboring Zhejiang Province until 2007. After the removal of Chen Liangyu as Shanghai party secretary, Xi briefly replaced him until his further promotion to the Politburo Standing Committee and Central Secretariat in October 2007. A year later at age fifty-five, Xi was designated as President Hu Jintao's successor as paramount leader and was made vice president of the PRC and vice chairman of the Central Military Committee, which he would chair in 2012.

In 2013, Xi became president of the PRC and currently holds the three top leadership positions of the government, party, and military. He is the first of a younger generation of leaders to rise to dominance. And Xi was quick to assert that domination from the very beginning of tenure as paramount leader.

After Mao's death, collective leadership in the Politburo Standing Committee, China's highest political and decision-making authority, steered the country. Two major objectives drove that process. The first was to maintain "stability," that is to prevent rebellions and revolts that had plagued China for centuries with violence and chaos. Indeed, the number one mission of the PLA is precisely that—maintain stability.

Second was economic growth. The collective leadership understood that without sustained and vibrant growth, China could not advance nor keep its population under control of the party. The underclass was too great in number. And hiding Chinese citizens from the outside world was virtually impossible despite internet restrictions.

By the time Xi became the dominant leader, China had created near miraculous annual economic double-digit growth. But money corrupted and prosperity bred an independence that was antithetical to party control. Xi immediately began to centralize power and authority in his hands. He assumed leadership, i.e., control, of the key committees overseeing economic reform, national security, and cyber.

Xi began anti-corruption campaigns to weed out opposition and to rein in the very rich who believed that wealth created a certain independence from the party and political control. The unstated message was that making money was fine, but the party would not tolerate loss of control or deviation from its overall policies. Further, corruption hampered entrepreneurism and innovation and hence hindered economic growth.

By the Nineteenth Party Congress held in October 2017, Xi was firmly in control. "Xi Jinping Thought on Socialism with Chinese Characteristics for a New Era" became part of the party's constitution that only had been accorded to Mao. Allies were added to the twenty-five-member Politburo and the seven-person Standing Committee of the Politburo. Xi continued to tighten control domestically, politically, and economically. Internationally, China has taken a much higher profile and aggressive foreign policy.

The Chinese have a comprehensive national strategy that combines "whole of government" with the whole of the population approach. The thesis is that what is best for the people should also be best for the party and vice versa, although the party must dominate. That philosophy leads to "dual use" policies that fit national and domestic needs.

Many in the West either do not understand this philosophy or believe it is riddled with fundamental flaws and contradictions alien to liberal democracies, considering it part of a neo-totalitarian form of population control. As viewed in the West, a free-market economy cannot flourish without accompanying freedoms and human rights. That is certainly true where democracy has a healthy and lengthy history.

But China never really experienced full democracy with basic rights, including the vote to elect leaders. The grand Chinese bargain is that citizens are free to enjoy economic and financial success provided the "rules" are followed and not challenged. As Deng believed capitalism could have a Chinese face, this philosophy could be called prosperity with a Chinese face and strict party control. This is one reason China has clamped down so hard on Hong Kong.

Hong Kong enjoyed large measures of prosperity and independence until the security law of 2020 incorporated the colony into China. Hong Kong residents took to the streets in protests. China imposed strict measures to quell the dissent that clearly were a direct challenge and threat to this philosophy of prosperity under party control. Similarly, as colored revolutions broke out on Russia's periphery, Putin was fearful that dissent would not be contained by borders and would infect the homeland. In both cases, China and Russia have a powerful neuralgia and fear of dissent that could challenge the authority and legitimacy of the leadership and, in Xi's case, the party.

Chapter Five

DRAGONS AND BEARS III: CHINA'S PLANS

*The best strategy is to defeat the enemy's strategy. The
best outcome is to win without fighting.*
—Sun Tzu
The Art of War
500 BC

*Beijing intends to dominate the U.S. and the rest of the
planet economically, militarily, and technologically.*
—John Ratcliffe
Director of National Intelligence
Wall Street Journal
December 4, 2020

China's planning efforts to coordinate strategy are impressive, comprehensive, and important to analyze and understand not from the perspective of the United States but Beijing. The most concrete example of this coordinated strategy is the multiuse philosophy central to the Military-Civil Fusion policy. In 2014 and then again in 2017, the party declared that all Chinese companies must collaborate in gathering intelligence. "Any organization or citizen," reads Article 7 of China's National Intelligence Law, "shall support, assist with, and collaborate with the state intelligence work in accordance with the law, and keep the secrets of the national intelligence work known to the public."

Military-Civil Fusion (MCF) is a prime example of how China is developing comprehensive whole of government and private sector integrated strategies for dual use technologies. Xi heads and personally oversees the strategy, which brings together IP and R&D from all sources to be used by China. The most comprehensive presentation of this dual-use strategy and the MCF policy comes from a 2020 Air Force University publication from its China Aerospace Institute, *China's Military-Fusion Strategy* by Alex Stone and Peter Wood. On page 38 is a diagram that links the six major systems of systems in the MCF with five national strategy objectives.

This diagram is a stunning visual piece of the comprehensive and integrative strategy China is pursuing.

The five military systems of systems (SOS) related to national strategies consist of these components: Regional Development Strategy, Manufacturing Great Power Strategy, Innovation-Driven Strategy, Talent Great Power Strategy, and Strategy of Integrating Science and Education. Interestingly, the Talent Great Power Strategy was derived from the millennia-old series of examinations that brought the best and brightest people from across China to Beijing to serve the emperor.

China's Unified Military-Civil System of Strategies*

MCF Components | National Strategies

Six Major Systems of Systems (SoS)
[六大体系]

- Basic Domain Resource Sharing SoS
  [基础领域资源共享体系]
- Defense S&T Industrial SoS With Chinese Characteristics
  [中国特色先进国防科技工业体系]
- Military-Civil S&T Coordinated Innovation SoS
  [军民科技协同创新体系]
- Military Personnel Cultivation SoS
  [军事人才培养体系]
- Socialized Military Support SoS
  [军队保障社会化体系]
- Defense Mobilization SoS
  [国防动员体系]

Regional Coordinated Development Strategy
[区域协调发展战略]

Manufacturing Great Power Strategy
[制造强国战略]

Innovation-driven Development Strategy
[创新驱动发展战略]

Talent Great Power Strategy
[人才强国战略]

Strategy of Invigorating China Through Science & Education
[科教兴国战略]

Major Security Domains
[重大安全领域]

- Maritime [海洋]
- Space [太空]
- Cyberspace Security & Informatization [网信]

Maritime Great Power Strategy
[海洋强国战略]

Space Great Power Strategy
[太空强国战略]

Cyberspace Great Power Strategy
[网络强国战略]

Economic & Military "Going Out"
[经济和军事"走出去"]

Belt and Road Initiative
[一带一路战略]

Nascent Technological Areas
[新领域]

- Bio-tech [生物技术]
- New Energy [新能源]
- A.I. [人工智能]

AI 2.0 Development Strategy
[人工智能2.0发展战略]

*: Chart represents the author's interpretation of reviewed materials

Immediately below, MCF components for Maritime, Space, Cyber and "Informationization," and Economic and Military "Going Out" are harmonized with Maritime Great Power Strategy, Space

Great Power Strategy, Cyberspace Great Power Strategy, and Belt and Road Initiative. "Informationization" is a Chinese term that in the West incorporates all forms of non-kinetic warfare embracing influence-gaining operations across the military and civil sectors. Note the use of "Great Power" strategies. And after studying the MCF not fully understanding China's defense priorities would be inexcusable.

Further, MCF requires Chinese state-owned and private entities to acquire a range of advanced technologies through acquisition, mergers, investments, and outright IP theft. The focus is on dual-use or tri-use technologies with civil, defense, and intelligence applications so that by 2050, China will become the undisputed technology leader in virtually every advanced sector from health, biology, quantum computing, and energy to computing, space, cyber, materials, propulsion, AI, and 3D manufacturing.

Of many examples, the Chinese drone manufacturer Dà-Jiāng Innovations (DJI) now controls more than 70 percent of the global commercial market. The PLA Navy is on a major expansion and modernization path. Since 2004, for example, beyond building an aircraft carrier and amphibious assault ships, the PLAN produced over eighty relatively small, stealth, twin-hulled catamaran Type 22 missile boats. Aside from a few experimental stealth boats, the US Navy has none. China is aiming to put astronauts on Mars, possibly within a decade, already having launched a probe to the red planet.

Just as Putin's Russia has exploited and accelerated the demise of Westphalia and relied on the use of MAD, China followed suit. By 2020, it was clear that China sought to influence and, where possible, dominate international norms and organizations using its economic, diplomatic, and increasingly powerful military capabilities as leverage. While many in the United States (and elsewhere) believe that China's priority is to disrupt, challenge, and change the so-called liberal rules-based order of the old Westphalian system, which it is, there is a better explanation for China's motives.

In 2014, Xi explicitly broadcast Chinese intent in a speech when almost playfully he predicted that China would be "constructing international playgrounds"—and "creating the rules" of the games played on them. However, China's strategy is far more geostrategic and geo-economic in character, with disruption as a tactic.

In a sense, Xi has poached the idea of a Monroe Doctrine for China. Just as the United States declared the Western Hemisphere to be its region of influence to prevent or reduce foreign interference in the early 1800s, China is constructing a similar concept. The "nine-dash line" so far marks the extension. But make no mistake: this is China's intent.

By militarizing islets in the coastal seas, China is expanding its borders as far as possible beyond the so-called first island chain that runs from Japan to Taiwan to Vietnam to the nine-dash line that is a further extension. Given the Obama/Trump defense strategy to "deter and defeat" in this case a would-be enemy China, Beijing has taken this threat seriously. China is enhancing what the US defines as an anti-access, area denial (A2AD) capability to prevent direct attacks against its homeland should conflict occur. However, these stationary islets are themselves very vulnerable targets in wartime.

Xi also knows that stability at home is very dependent on maintaining substantial annual economic growth as well as ending corruption that pervades the country. Three to five hundred million Chinese exist at or below the poverty line. Each year, China endures possibly hundreds of thousands of domestic demonstrations and riots protesting those conditions and the failure of government to provide a better life, sustaining that growth, well before the appearance of coronavirus/COVID-19. But these aims could not be accomplished internally. In 2013, Xi put in place the "One Belt, One Road" program, now the Belt and Road Initiative as an alternative to stimulate growth.

The unstated but actual aim is to increase Chinese influence by greater access to markets and resources. It is these markets that will be ripe for Chinese goods, trade, and services, hence engines for economic growth. Using the metaphor of the ancient Silk Road and accompanying sea routes, China has set up nearly one thousand projects in many dozens of states.

Projects are largely contracted to Chinese firms and extend beyond infrastructure for highways, dams, and electrical power plants and running at least seventy-five ports and terminals in three dozen countries from Sri Lanka (it foreclosed on its port because of defaulted loans) and Pakistan to Greece. In the process, however, China is generating negative reactions and hostile responses from its neighbors and states that are defaulting on Belt and Road loans and investments. These realities will be components of proposed policy recommendations for America and its relations with China.

THREE INSIGHTS

Three specific examples were cited that provide intimate insights into China, its society, and current and future policy trajectories. The first is "dual-use technologies" that both advance the individual and the economy and control by the party in the form of China's Social Credit System. The second is the "coliseum" of the venture capital world and the training of AI engineers. And third is the book *Unrestricted Warfare*.

The Social Credit System dates back centuries in more primitive forms of record keeping. A trial program was started by Paramount Leader Jiang Zemin in 2001 with regional testing in 2009. Xi began a national pilot in 2014 that became centralized under the People's Bank of China in 2018.

The purpose is to standardize and evaluate the credit worthiness and economic and social reputations of citizens and businesses to determine trustworthiness. Clearly, this is dual use that facilitates commerce and, more importantly, party control. The system is dependent on China's mass surveillance systems such as Skynet that integrates facial recognition, big data collection, and evaluation and positional location that can be tracked and stored.

Beyond exposing criminal and fraudulent financial conduct, social credits have expanded throughout greater Chinese society to affect and control citizens' behavior. Seemingly insignificant actions such as minor traffic violations for jaywalking or parking illegally and not honoring hotel, airline, or restaurant reservations have reduced one's social credits. Positive behavior for charitable work and donations increases credits.

The second area is China's venture capital markets and the earlier reference to K. F. Lee and his book on superpowers and AI. Lee cites many examples of the conduct of Chinese start-up companies that in the United States would be highly unethical if not illegal. This is important because China employs milder means of these tactics in competing beyond its borders. Chinese theft of IP and other data has been proven beyond any reasonable doubt. The use of Trojan Horse operatives also out to gain insights and information on overseas companies, universities, research institutes, and technologies is well documented. In addition, China demands that foreign companies operating in China follow not only Chinese rules and regulations but adhere to tight restrictions and censorship in even commenting about China's policies.

The tensions between exploiting highly profitable Chinese markets and these restrictions are growing and apply to virtually all business opportunities. When the National Basketball Association's Houston Rockets, which has a huge Chinese market, was critical of the repression of Hong Kong, China was prepared to cut off the scheduled games. This also affects manufacturers such as Nike and Adidas, with huge dependence on Chinese markets. And foreigners interested in investing are likewise constrained by this tension and to the big American investment houses who see great opportunity in providing financial management services for literally tens of millions of wealthy Chinese.

Lee also runs an AI school for software engineers that utilizes US instructors and trains upward of a thousand students a year. This is the curriculum:

Knowledge-Based

- Trends of Artificial Intelligence Industry
- AI: From Academic Teaching to Engineering Practices
- Deep Learning: Foundation, Challenges, and Engineering Practices
- Frontier Development and Engineering Practice of Machine Learning
- Machine Learning and Deep Neural Networks
- Safety Study and Key Challenges in Frontier AI Technology
- Visual Computing on Clouds, Ends, and Cores
- Natural Language Processing Foundation and Industrial Practice
- Frontier Development and Industrial Practice of Intelligent Robots
- Interpretation of Deep Learning Based Autonomous Driving Technical Roadmap
- Principles and Latest Development of Intelligent Voice Technology
- AI to B: Algorithms and Engineering
- TensorFlow Foundation and Practice
- Product Design for Engineers

Practical-Based

- Smart Vending Machine
- Delivery Robot-Men
- Automatic Sorting System by Using Mechanical Arm
- 3D Human Skeleton Detection
- Automatic Driving
- Trajectory and Motion Analysis of Pedestrians with Multi-Camera
- Automatic Lyric Writing & Music Composing
- Reinforcement Learning in Real-Time Strategy Gaming
- Offense and Defense Practice with Deep Learning
- AI Based Quantitative Finance
- Chatbot Designing
- Crop Pest Detection Based on AI
- Image Generation 2D
- Image Aesthetic Evaluation
- Behavior Recognition

Unfortunately, the United States has no comparable programs for training AI engineers as opposed to AI experts, and it is on the engineering side that many breakthroughs will occur.

Last is *Unrestricted Warfare* noted several times before. First, the book argues that in future conflict, there will be no boundaries between the military and other domains. Economics, law, social media, and technology will be engaged. Second, the book shows a thorough understanding of American military history with focus on the first Iraq War (1990–1991) and the preference of relying on technology to drive strategy, specifically with precision weapons, rather than strategy driving technology, which is the Chinese view.

Third, the book was prescient in using the term "hybrid" to describe future conflict and its multidimensional aspects decades before the Pentagon adopted the phrase. And in 1999, two years before September 11, it identified Osama bin Laden as a major threat representing the unrestricted aspects of war.

But a major error was in the book's high regard for Japanese Admiral Isoroku Yamamoto, the architect of the attack on Pearl Harbor. Yamamoto is often referred to in the book as an innovator, perhaps implying that in the future, China will rely on a twenty-first century "sneak attack," crippling an enemy by attacking and disrupting its dependency on networks. What the book fails to appreciate is that Yamamoto's plan to seize Midway in 1942 turned into the catastrophic and irreplaceable loss of four aircraft carriers and 250 aircraft and pilots.

China's current focus on great-power strategies for the maritime, space, and cyber-informationalization domains comes directly from this book, as does how China's national security strategy is fundamentally based on disrupting, confusing, misleading, and deceiving potential adversaries using all national assets. This book also anticipated the arrival of MAD and the necessity of integrating capabilities across government and the private sector and not merely confined to the Ministry of Defense.

As noted, A2AD seems to be the focal point for the countervailing US National Defense Strategy. Yet it is clear from *Unrestricted Warfare* that China's perspective is far broader than simply the military domain. As noted earlier, both the Cyberspace Solarium Commission and the secretary of the navy's report highlight the vulnerability of American networks to hacking and interference. Further, that China specifies only three great-power strategies, it would seem sensible if America's NDS reflected each. It does not. Nor does the NDS recognize that China's aim is to defeat the American strategy without fighting. Hence *unrestricted means* is the way to accomplish that.

WHERE IS THIS HEADED?

China and its president, Xi Jinping, have reacted predictably, interpreting these American policies as direct threats to China's physical and economic security since the last years of the Bush 43 administration and certainly by the Obama presidency. In fairness, if Chinese or Russian military doctrine were to deter and, if war came, defeat the US and its allies, the reaction in Washington would not be different. Despite Xi's promise to Obama that China would not militarize the islets in the various China seas, it has done that. And China's territorial claims extend to the so-called nine-dash line well outside the first island chain running from Japan in the north through Taiwan to Vietnam and the South and East China Seas.

Belt and Road programs are progressing to enhance China's access and influence to markets and resources. The fifteen-state RCEP reflected not only Beijing's growing influence and economic strength; it was also a clever diplomatic success. RCEP may not isolate the United States from Asia. But it was a powerful signal of Beijing's reach and ability to extend its influence that will complicate the Biden administration's agenda in how it will deal with China.

The propaganda war intensified over the coronavirus and the responsibility for causing the pandemic as well as blaming China for the failure to provide enough early warning about the disease to limit its spread. So-called wolf warrior diplomats, named for a Chinese movie made extolling that breed, are making increasingly aggressive declarations about Chinese foreign policy. The tariff war has not been resolved. And China is flexing its military muscles in its bordering seas while using its handling of the pandemic as a model to contrast with failures elsewhere, particularly in America.

Many factors have contributed to the current state of the tense and hardening US-China relationship. US concentration on the wars in Afghanistan and Iraq convinced the Obama administration that a "strategic pivot" to Asia was vital given China's rising influence and regional growing economic dominance. As noted, this sparked fear and uncertainty among allies and anger in Beijing. The 2008 financial crisis probably convinced Beijing that it needed to be more flexible in pursuing its financial interests.

Under Xi, politics and economics have become more controlled and disciplined by the party. And China has become more nationalistic and aggressive in responding to American policies and actions under both Obama and Trump. In essence, the post-1979 era of strategic engagement has been or is being replaced by a still undefined new era of rivalry, competition, and declining relations.

This has led to uneven and, many believe, chaotic American policies in response. Human rights have now become more central in the Biden administration's messaging as the United States is using Hong Kong, Taiwan, and Xinjiang and the Uighurs to criticize Beijing. In addition to the trade war, battles over technology, IP, cyber hacking and theft, and even talent, in denying China access to American universities are waging. In the South and East China Seas, American freedom of navigation operations are directly challenging Chinese claims of sovereignty and its militarization of various islets that could lead to a confrontation far more serious than the knockdown of a US Navy P-3 aircraft over Hainan in 2001.

The consequence is a struggle over regional influence and even dominance across the entire geostrategic, political, economic, diplomatic, military, technological, and public relations spectrum. Lost or made no longer relevant was the stability of the relationship that both sides took care to nurture prior to Obama's pivot to Asia. With the trade war and now the COVID-19 pandemic that exacerbate already tense relations, greater pressure has been placed on both Xi and Biden.

Xi's anti-corruption campaign, used in part to eliminate political opposition, is resented by many Chinese for its brutality and ruthlessness as well as deviation away from collective leadership. The massive military reorganization has alienated hundreds of thousands of veterans who lost benefits as well as standing and prestige in the community. And the large number of personnel changes Xi made in the national security sector writ large to bring in loyal supporters, culminating in the July 2020 "rectification campaign," suggested the extent of opposition to his leadership and authority.

Politics in America likewise drove US policy. Prior to the 2020 election, Trump's policy advisors for China were deeply divided with no clear-cut direction. Hard-liners such as economic advisor Peter Navarro and Lieutenant General H. R. McMaster, Trump's second national security advisor, called for tariffs and a tougher national security line toward China, as expressed in a December 2017 strategy document and a June 2020 *Foreign Affairs* piece by McMaster. Navarro was opposed by two former Goldman Sachs executives, former National Economic Council head Gary Cohn, and Secretary of the Treasury Steven Mnuchin.

By March 2020, as the pandemic swept through America, President Trump reversed his view of China and the "great work" President Xi was doing. Coronavirus became the China or Wuhan Virus, and China was going to pay for the spread.

After China implemented its draconian national security law for Hong Kong that criminalized dissent as terrorist or seditious, Washington responded with sanctions and, on July 14, the signing of the Hong Kong Autonomy Act that gave the president the authority to impose sanctions on "foreign persons" who undermine Hong Kong's autonomy to the benefit of the PRC. But the deterioration of Hong Kong could be a death knell to US-Chinese relations.

Taiwan is another geostrategic ticking time bomb. One of the subsets of US defense strategy is preventing a fait accompli scenario of the PRC invading or attacking Taiwan. China lacks the military capability for the foreseeable future of crossing the hundred-mile-wide strait to invade Taiwan, much as Hitler was never able to span the twenty-five miles separating England from the Pas-de-Calais.

The PRC could obliterate Taiwan with missiles or attempt to impose a naval and air blockade. The costs would be excessive for China, as it would no doubt be sanctioned and even cut off from international commerce or hurt financially, as Taiwanese have many billions and possibly trillions of dollars invested in the mainland. However, the preferred tactic is to work from within to ultimately persuade, convince, or compel the final integration of One China.

Taiwanese president and leader of the Democratic Progressive Party (DPP), Tsai Ing-wen, rejects China's understanding of the "1992 consensus" that there is only "one China," as both sides cannot agree on what that means. The Hong Kong crisis reinforces polls that indicate about 90 percent of Taiwanese regard themselves not as Chinese but Taiwanese. And the situation is complicated by the three communiques negotiated over the period 1979–1982 and the Taiwan Relations Act (TRA) of 1979.

That act states "the United States will make available to Taiwan such defense articles and defense services as may be necessary to enable Taiwan to maintain a sufficient self-defense capacity." The act also states that non-peaceful means to determine Taiwan's future such as boycotts, embargoes, and coercion with or without the use of force would be "of grave concern" to the United States, with Congress required to "maintain the capacity of the United States to resist any resort to force…that jeopardize the security…of the people on Taiwan."

The TRA is not a mutual defense treaty. For decades, however, the ambiguity has worked. And despite the protests of Beijing, which have been frequent, over American arms sales to Taiwan, the Trump administration provided new capabilities such as advanced F-16 fighters. China also protested the visit of Health and Human

Services Secretary Alex Azar in August 2020 to discuss the coronavirus/COVID-19 pandemic, underscoring again Beijing's neuralgia over Taiwan.

Although unlikely, if one recalls the PLA shelling of Matsu and Quemoy Islands in the early 1950s, China could provoke a crisis over Taiwan's Dongsha or Taiping Islands in the South China Sea or the Wuqiu Islands off Taiwan's coast. More likely, the South China Sea and the nine-dash line controversy could be the source of military confrontation or miscalculation. Seven states claim some form of jurisdiction in these waters: Brunei, China, Indonesia, Malaysia, the Philippines, Taiwan, and Vietnam. The 2016 ruling of the Permanent Court of Arbitration rejected the basis for China's claims of sovereignty over much of the South China Sea; that did not go down well in Beijing.

Since then, China has relied on its fishing fleet and its "maritime militia" to encroach on contested areas. Unfortunately, US protests relying on the UN Convention on the Law of the Sea are made less credible, as Washington has never ratified the treaty. Freedom of navigation exercises have been conducted in the Taiwan Straits and the various south China seas to challenge these claims.

The protocols negotiated by the Obama administration to prevent the risks of escalation and accidental mishaps between US and PLA forces have atrophied, given the deteriorating state of relations and greater tensions. Should an incident similar to the 2001 knockdown of a US Navy P-3 aircraft occur, including warships colliding with each other, how escalation could be prevented is not clear. The South China Sea holds potential for a further crisis not only between Beijing and Washington but with other claimants in the region.

The decline in American-Chinese relations could be measured by President Barack Obama's experiences beginning with his first of three state visits to China in late 2009, followed by his last as president in 2016.

Presidents Obama and Xi met a total of eleven times, lastly in 2017 after he left office. The first visit was civil, with some disagreement over the joint statement. The 2016 visit was decidedly uncivil. When Air Force One landed, no stairway was initially provided to allow the president to disembark. And Obama's meeting with students was heavily censored within China. What awaits President Biden remains to be seen.

THE SEVEN DISRUPTORS

How China regards MAD and its accompanying seven disruptors offers an important insight as to its future policies. Climate change and the threat of environmental catastrophe are well understood in Beijing. The coal-based energy sector will be replaced by new "green" technologies that constitute environmentally safe and sustainable solutions, but not until well into the second half of the twenty-first century. China also intends to lead in the electric car field.

Cyber has become a or the leading technology for China both to advance the well-being of its citizens and increase party control. In a defense and national security context, cyber is one of three great-power strategies. As claimed in *Unrestricted Warfare*, cyber is one of China's most potent weapons. Cyber will be used to disrupt, deceive, confuse, immobilize, and where possible, destroy civilian and military networks as discussed in Chapter 3. In a war, however remote, China will attempt to make US forces blind, dumb, and impotent by taking down networks as well as space-based systems, to be discussed shortly.

Cyberattacks against America's power grid, banking, transportation, communications, and other critical national infrastructure systems will be massive and catastrophically disruptive. Indeed, referencing Yamamoto's attack on Pearl Harbor, China will attempt to employ cyber as a means to defeat the United States non-kinetically by striking first. And America is not prepared.

Social media likewise is a dual-use technology to improve standards of life and to increase party control. There is a third role, much as Huawei and its 5G technology is playing. Social media provides access to many countries and billions of people. Just as Russia is brilliantly manipulating social media, China is using it as a means of access not merely to individuals but to data and IP.

As the "coliseum" is the metaphor for the zero-sum nature of the domestic venture capital sector, social media is being used to advantage by China for the potential it has to collect and harvest data and thus impose greater political control on its citizens. With quantum computing, machine learning, and AI, this data will provide actionable means for exploiting access and control.

Terrorism is less of a direct threat to China because of population control. However, terror is useful when it is applied to opponents of the party such as the Uighurs and non-Han Chinese and in Tibet, where independence from Beijing is unacceptable. Terror will be used to empower the party to minimize and eliminate dissent.

Debt remains a huge burden. The only solution is economic growth. That growth is dependent on the success or failure of Belt and Road, which is premised on gaining access to foreign resources and, more importantly, foreign markets for Chinese goods and services. If Belt and Road succeeds, then sufficient economic growth can be sustained to continue to move millions out of poverty. If it fails, a massive problem will be created for the party and for Xi that could lead to widespread internal unrest, riots, and even revolts that would challenge political control.

Regarding drones, China's DJI is the world's largest manufacturer. Drones fit this tri-use category. Their employment can revolutionize standards of living in terms of real-time delivery and access to unprecedented amounts of goods, products, and services. Drones likewise reinforce party control and surveillance. Finally, in a military application, drones, better defined as autonomous vehicles in all dimensions, will increase the effectiveness and efficiency of operations and lethality, especially when used in conjunction with space and cyber.

Finally, the major issue is failed and failing government and possibly Xi's greatest potential weakness and liability. In consolidating power across all key sectors, Xi has great autocratic control. By eliminating opposition and placing loyal subordinates, that control increases. However, the downsides are real.

Many Chinese inside the party and with influence resent this realignment. Loyalty is not synonymous with competence. If the party cannot govern and fill the needs of its citizens, as occurred in past regimes, dissent eventually feeds some form of backlash and even rebellion. That happened to Mao in the mid-1960s.

In summary, China has become a twenty-first century variant of the Middle Kingdom, with major and obvious stunning differences. Instead of an emperor, China has the Party and its leader. The party maintains a "heavenly mandate" perspective unconstrained by borders and supported by the mythology of cultural superiority and self-sufficiency. It recognizes the need for global access and it enjoys exploiting the most advanced technologies as its economy is on track to become the world's largest.

That said, here is a further possibility to ponder. Has President Xi become a Chinese version of Mikhail Gorbachev? Like Gorbachev, Xi understands the profound and underlying potential weaknesses that could become crises for China, its government, and its coherence. Unlike Gorbachev, Xi has not put in place either glasnost or perestroika that ultimately imploded the Soviet Union.

But Xi has imposed greater discipline and control from the center and from his office. He has relied on technology to provide some options to resolve economic shortfalls and moved aggressively to kill corruption that is a cancer to any state. On his success will rest much of China's future as well as if he fails.

The so-called rise of China is not a zero-sum game for the West and the US. However, unless or until the US appreciates what motivates China and its leaders and learns how to resolve the major policy disputes and differences through coalitions and international bodies rather than unilateral and often misguided action, tensions will continue and possibly increase. Likewise, understanding China's growing sense of "nationalism" to rally the public and, more importantly, increase party control is essential. The rise of diplomatic wolf warriors is an example of this nationalism and growing aggressiveness in a more Middle Kingdom–like view of the world.

What would Mao advise? Mao won the revolution by "swimming among the people," meaning avoiding a direct battle that would be lost while converting the public to his side. That is what Mao would counsel today. Avoid a direct confrontation with China. Subtlety works. Abandoning the TPP is a case in point. The Trump administration lost any chance to influence China by withdrawing from the TPP where leverage could have been applied.

Chinese leaders understand that collective opposition is far more difficult to counter than the actions of individual states, particularly the United States. China has significant vulnerabilities: an aging population, the need for substantial annual economic growth, a huge underclass, a fragile infrastructure, dependence on outside markets and resources, and potential geographic isolation. The leakage of democracy and dissent from Hong Kong is likewise a potential weakness.

Mao would also argue that an effective military strategy must be indirect. Sun Tzu would add: attack the enemy's strategy. China's strategy is defensive. Instead of attacking, contain it, Mao would advise. And framing the competition as a contest of "values" will not work because China regards these so-called values of a liberal, rules-based order incendiary means of repressing Chinese interests.

As the Fifth Horseman and MAD need not always be feared and can be contained or, better, can be embraced, the same logic extends to China. The aim of strategy should be to turn the adversarial relationship into a respectful rivalry. Specific recommendations follow in Chapters 8, 9, and 10, employing the Brains-Based Approach to affect, influence, and possibly control will and perception of the leadership in Beijing—precisely what Sun Tzu would recommend.

Chapter Six

FROM PANDEMIC
TO PANDEMIC

*President Woodrow Wilson downplayed the presence of the
Spanish flu. President Donald Trump purposely downplayed
the seriousness of coronavirus/COVID-19. After the Spanish
flu dissipated, America embarked on its greatest economic boom.
Will history repeat itself?*

Comparing the 1918–1920 Spanish flu and the 2020 coronavirus/COVID-19 pandemics is instructive, as is comparing the
extraordinary transformation of American (and all) society over that
century. What can be learned from these comparisons? Several observations are particularly relevant.

The postwar years 1918 to 1920 was a far more disruptive time
than today. A world war, a pandemic, the threat of a "Red Scare,"
and terrorist letter bombings led to draconian laws muting not only
criticism of the government but even acknowledging the extent of the
Spanish flu. A century later, little was remembered or learned when

COVID-19 struck. Information about the extent of COVID and its impact was readily available. But as occurred in 1918, then President Trump emulated Woodrow Wilson by downplaying the pandemic.

To understand how deadly pandemics are, compare the weekly loss of life with World Wars I and II and the Vietnam War.

Some 670,000 Americans, or about 1,500 a week, died from the Spanish flu in 1918–1920. That is five times more than those who died on French battlefields per week. In the forty-five months of World War II, some 300,000 Americans were killed, on average 1,750 a week. In the ten years of the Vietnam War (1964–1974), 58,000 American died in action, or about 125 a week. Thus far, about 620,000 Americans have died from COVID-19. In its deadliest days in mid-2020, on a weekly basis, COVID resulted in more than five times the death rate of World War II and eighty times Vietnam's.

In 1918–1920, the world was still operating under the old Westphalian system of state-centric politics. By 2020, the old system was gone. In 1918–1920, government was much smaller. In 2020, government was one of the problems with a profoundly divided Congress, an undermanned executive branch, and a president who put his own political priorities about reelection above scientific and medical advice, keeping the economy (and later schools) open on the grounds that a continued shutdown would prove more costly to America than the pandemic's effect on public health.

In 1918–1920, society was still substantially rural and agrarian, with full industrialization underway powered by transportation (railroads and automobiles), raw materials (rubber, steel, oil), electrification, and communication technology. By 2020, the information age had long since overtaken the industrial age. The composition of the companies listed on the Dow Jones Industrial Average encapsulates how much the disruption caused by the information technology industry has indeed changed America for the better.

In 1920, the Dow consisted of twenty companies in railroads; automobile raw materials, to include rubber, copper, oil, and steel; electrification; technology; and only one in consumer products (Central Leather). Here is the full list:

- American Can
- American Car and Foundry
- American Locomotive
- American Smelting and Refining
- American Sugar Refining
- American Telephone and Telegraph
- Anaconda Copper Mining
- B.F. Goodrich
- Baldwin Locomotive Works
- Central Leather
- Corn Products and Refining
- General Electric
- Republic Iron and Steel
- Studebaker
- The Texas Company
- United States Rubber
- United States Steel
- Utah Copper
- Western Union
- Westinghouse Electric

The makeup of the current Dow Jones Industrial Average consists of thirty companies in technology/IT, healthcare, finance, heavy industry, energy, entertainment, and food/consumer goods. The list:

- 3M
- American Express

- Amgen
- Apple
- Boeing
- Caterpillar
- Chevron
- Cisco
- Coca-Cola
- Dow
- Goldman Sachs
- Home Depot
- Honeywell
- IBM
- Intel
- Johnson & Johnson
- JPMorgan Chase
- McDonald's
- Merck
- Microsoft
- Nike
- Procter & Gamble
- Salesforce
- Travelers
- UnitedHealth
- Verizon
- Visa
- Walgreens Boots Alliance
- Walmart
- Walt Disney

What this comparison shows are the positive effects of disruption. Transportation shifted from locomotives and automobiles to aviation; technology from telephones and telegraph to the internet, social media, and information technologies; and electrification to IT and computers. No financial companies were listed in 1920. Most were privately held. Aside from Central Leather, no consumer products were on the Dow in 1920.

The 2020 (and current) Dow was heavy on consumer products, and one, Apple, had a $2 trillion valuation, or about 10 percent of the current GDP. No company has ever had that valuation or percent of GDP. The equivalent then was US Steel, the first company to be valued at a billion dollars (1901). When Carnegie Steel, the precursor of US Steel, was purchased from Andrew Carnegie that year, J. P. Morgan paid $480 million and the GDP was then $22 billion. When Morgan bought out what was US Steel in 1912, he paid $1.4 billion, and GDP was $37 billion.

In 1920, international business was a tiny slice of the Dow-listed companies. In 2020, international business is vital in some cases, and each of today's Dow is dependent on access to foreign markets, products, and supply chains.

The healthcare sector was not even in its infancy in 1920. Yet despite all the medical advances since, it is too soon to tell if the COVID-19 pandemic will prove less deadly and disruptive than the Spanish flu, if indeed it does not return in waves. Logic would suggest this pandemic should be more controlled and controllable given all the medical advances. Still, past pandemics have generally run their own course.

The crucial difference from 1920 is that the 2020 pandemic was the first deadly and indisputable evidence of the arrival of the Fifth Horseman and the new MAD. This nation, and much of the rest of the world, was entirely unprepared for the Spanish flu pandemic. Asian states that had suffered from SARS were better prepared for the second. But the United States was not.

The responses of the Trump administration, at least according to more than two-thirds of Americans, failed to halt the spread of

COVID-19. Former Trump administration officials strongly object, arguing they had performed admirably even though record numbers of Americans were still dying of COVID as 2021 approached.

Of course, no administration since Woodrow Wilson's had to deal with a real pandemic. HIV/AIDS affected a relatively small proportion of the population and was completely preventable by safe sex practices or abstinence. It took billions of dollars and more than a decade, but therapeutics were finally invented. H1N1 and other flus did not turn into pandemics. Ebola was primarily confined to Africa.

The George W. Bush and Obama administrations coped well with these relatively milder pandemics. How those or any administration would have coped with COVID-19 is debatable. There is little question that earlier action from the Trump administration, including mandating the wearing of masks and social distancing, would have saved tens of thousands of lives.

By the end of 2020, the United States, with about 4 percent of the world population, accounted for just under one-quarter of both the total cases and total global deaths. Of nearly two hundred states and territories confronting COVID-19, the United States, the world's largest and most modern economy, ranked sixth worst, with a morbidity rate of 656 per 100,000. How could that have happened?

Disruption-caused crises always have surprised presidents and administrations, and the responses have not always worked well. Woodrow Wilson downplayed the existence of the Spanish flu so as not to panic the public and detract from the war effort in 1918. But what is forgotten is that in addition to World War I and the Spanish flu, the nation panicked over the "Red Scare" of anarchy and socialism taking hold and a handful of letter bombs that were set off in 1919–1920, further terrorizing Americans. Finally, sufficient social immunity was able to dissipate the Spanish flu virus globally.

Fortunately, no world war, panic over terror, or existential external ideological threats existed in 2020 equivalent to 1918. While China,

Russia, North Korea, and Iran were cast as adversaries and even enemies, during the 2020 presidential election, the major domestic danger, before homegrown terrorism took that role, was the "other" political party. While politics had often been divisive, partisanship was rarely more bitter and hostile.

Republicans painted Democrats as socialist threats to the nation. Donald Trump asserted that under a Biden administration, the nation "would not be safe." Democrats returned the favor, arguing that Trump was the worst president in history, had miserably failed in dealing with the pandemic, and had to be defeated at all costs.

Despite assertions to the contrary, the Trump administration never created and implemented a national strategy to deal with COVID-19. The administration emulated Wilson for a different reason. In 2020, it was the economy and "law and order," not the Great War, that shaped White House arguments and its reelection strategy.

The economy was Trump's best case for reelection. The longer it was shut down, the more the economy would be damaged along with his chances for a second term. And protests in cities with Democratic mayors over police shootings of black citizens that led to violence and looting were exaggerated and used to frighten voters that under a Biden administration the mayhem would spread to the suburbs.

Trump repeatedly downplayed the pandemic, arguing that failing to reopen the economy would impose far greater costs than allowing even partial shutdowns to continue to control and limit or end infections. A similar argument extended to the administration's demands to reopen all schools, citing that children were less susceptible to infection and thus it was safe and socially necessary for education to resume. The White House left many of the preventive and remediation efforts to the states, relying on federal guidelines that were not mandatory.

The president's reluctance, indeed refusal, to wear a protective mask until months into the pandemic and ignore social distancing provided a conflicting message to the public. At his appearances at rallies in Oklahoma, Nevada, and Mount Rushmore for the July 4, 2020 holiday, many of the attendees did not wear masks or practice social distancing. Herman Cain, once a Republic presidential hopeful, contracted COVID at one of those rallies and died. The same disregard was evident at numerous White House press briefings and the Republican National Convention.

While the Trump administration used the Defense Production Act to procure vitally needed ventilators and personal protective equipment and embarked on Project Warp Speed to develop vaccines and therapeutics, testing for the virus was viewed as a hindrance. Trump asserted that the more testing that took place, the more cases would arise, confusing or denying that only through testing could the number of detected instances of COVID-19 be established as the basis for effective contact tracing. However, COVID-19 was bad for the economy. And the economy was essential to the president's reelection.

At the August 2020 nominating conventions, COVID-19 was a central Democratic theme. Former vice president Joe Biden promised that if elected, he would implement a national strategy to defeat the virus, of which testing would be crucial. At the Republican convention a week later, reference to the pandemic was missing in action. Pointedly perhaps, only the First Lady, Melania Trump, made full reference to the pandemic and used it as her first talking point.

Indeed, with the White House as a convenient prop, Trump accepted his party's nomination with some 1,500 attendees closely seated side by side in the Rose Garden. Few wore masks. And several weeks later, the event became a "super spreader" of the disease.

Similar to how Wilson downplayed the existence of Spanish flu, Trump initially argued that the disease was a hoax. He claimed it would dissipate in the summer, it would not infect many Americans, and children would only suffer sniffles at worst. Trump would claim nonsensical cures such as injecting disinfectant, promote hydroxychloroquine as a preventive when his FDA said otherwise, and refuse to wear masks and socially distance, defying science, safety, and fact. Still, comparing the impacts of the two pandemics and how the Wilson and Trump administrations responded is instructive to show the effects of disruption on the nation and what has changed and not changed over the course of a century.

The Spanish flu came in the midst of America's preoccupation with fighting World War I. The Espionage and Sedition Acts imposed severe restrictions on civil rights guaranteed by the Constitution. Censorship aimed against the enemy was also used promiscuously to restrict news and reporting on the Spanish flu.

In 2020, the coronavirus and its accompanying disease COVID-19 ravaged the globe. Fortunately, the world is not at war even though large swaths are unstable, dangerous, and suffer from violence. COVID-19 has intensified many of these tragedies and crises through the disruption it has and will continue to cause. And Americans by and large were more comfortable and less alarmed over the pandemic than the 1918–1920 generation were to the Spanish flu.

Comparison of these two pandemic disruptions provides important insights into what has changed and what has not over the past century and why disease has made MAD so relevant. Few know of the repression of civil liberties a century ago or of the extraordinary economic recovery that occurred in the immediate aftermath, bringing in the Roaring Twenties. However, the end of World War I left so much unfinished business that another world war would erupt twenty years later. Whether another economic boom will follow in 2021 and beyond remains to be seen but is still quite likely.

Finally, was the 1918–1920 Spanish flu or the 2020 COVID-19 pandemic more virulent and disruptive? Thus far, the Spanish flu was more deadly by a goodly number. However, the lack of healthcare facilities a century ago could have accounted for the differences, and statistics then were fewer.

A substantial number of COVID-19 victims, for example, were asymptomatic or had mild complications. During the first pandemic, no such data existed. As we will see, the 1918–1920 environment was far more disruptive—so far. Yet the impact was mostly short term and now is largely forgotten.

THEN AND NOW

According to the 1920 Census, the total American population was 106 million, despite the Spanish flu, up about three million from 1918. It was the first year that the urban population of the country reached 50 percent. The federal budget, in surplus, was $6.3 billion, down from the wartime high of $18 billion the year before. Using the CPI adjuster, $6.3 billion 1920 dollars equates in buying power to about $85 billion 2020 dollars. However, over a century, that figure does not take into account the changing economic conditions that probably increased that buying power substantially.

Today, there are about 330 million Americans, with about 81 percent living in urban regions. Last year's federal budget outlays were about $4.7 trillion. In calendar year 2021, the annual deficit due to COVID-19 will reach as high as $7 trillion.

Here is a summary of the major societal differences between 1918–1920 and today:

- Infrastructure was far less developed a century ago. There was no national electrical grid, national highway system, or means of connecting the nation more closely. Neighborhoods and local clusters of people had fewer outside interactions.
- There was less dependence on just-in-time delivery of key resources and materials or overseas sources and supply chains.

- There were more natural firewalls of space and distance between cities and communities.
- Americans were not dependent upon foreign oil. Today, while energy independence is asserted, the US imports about nine million barrels of oil every day.
- Food distribution was wider spread due to the lack of refrigeration and transport.
- Communities were more self-sufficient and more insulated from each other.
- Trains, with a top speed of about 40 mph, were the most rapid form of transportation compared with air travel today. Airplanes were used largely by the military and had short range. While automobiles would soon be mass produced, roads, gas stations, hospitality, and restaurants were still in their infancy. Few Americans traveled cross country or sailed to foreign countries other than for the war.
- As opposed to the internet, telephone, television, and cell phones today that are global in reach, telegraphs and trans-oceanic cables were rapid communications a century ago, as less than a third of homes had the relatively new telephone technology.
- The population was for the first time almost equally divided between urban and rural.
- The news cycle was dominated by daily newspapers, many of which had several editions during the day, unlike the 24/7 environment of today. Print and written sources for news were preferred, as radio was just coming online.
- Public understanding of civil and constitutional rights and privacy was different, making the Espionage and Sedition Acts more acceptable for a nation at war, especially as mandatory civics courses in elementary and high schools probably

encouraged greater civilian tolerance to accommodate these wartime restrictions.

- Medical facilities and pharmaceuticals were far less plentiful and sophisticated then. No serious anti-vaccine movements had formed. Indeed, by comparison, healthcare and medicine were still very primitive, although masks and social distancing were used as basic precautions.

- Daily life was far different: no supermarkets or widespread refrigeration existed. Preserved food was limited. Local grocers and butchers were the main sources of food. Milk was home delivered (and continued for many decades later).

- Credit cards and personal checking accounts (as opposed to letters of credit for the affluent) had not been invented. Commerce was a cash economy, and federal bank insurance did not exist.

- Banks and saloons were the last to close due to the pandemic in 1918–1920. In 2020 and 2021, the tension between the need to reopen the economy and to check the spread of the coronavirus was far greater than a century ago given the huge structural changes in the respective economies and the disruptive impact of the industrial and information revolutions.

TIMELINES FOR THE PANDEMIC

The Spanish flu arrived in four waves. The first diagnosis was attributed to a US Army cook, Albert Gitchell, at Camp Funston, near Fort Riley, Kansas, on March 4, 1918, although a physician in Maine had recorded a case in January. Within a week, the infection had spread to the East Coast. Because Camp Funston was a major training post for US troops headed to the war in Europe, the Spanish flu quickly spread, reaching epidemic proportions in the eastern half of America.

By April, US troops arriving in France brought the disease with them. Within weeks, the flu had spread from Europe to Asia. By July, it was global. However, the disease began to dissipate. At first, the pandemic was relatively mild, with mortality rates that were most substantially higher than normal. About 75,000 flu-related deaths were reported in the first half of July compared to about 60,000 during the same time period in 1915.

Military operations, however, were severely disrupted, something that was not widely reported or remembered. German Field Marshal Paul von Hindenburg blamed the flu and nearly a million infected soldiers as one of the causes for losing the war. Likewise, about three-quarters of French and about half the British forces contracted the disease. However, how many troops were actually disabled and too ill to fight, and for how long, has never been calculated.

Just as the COVID pandemic was not moderated by warm weather as former President Trump initially asserted would happen, the second and more deadly wave of the Spanish flu struck in the latter half of August. It spread throughout all of North America and then south to Latin America. From Freetown in Sierra Leone, the pandemic moved to West Africa and then to the rest of that continent. Russia and then Asia were reinfected.

The second wave, lasting until the winter, was more vicious and deadly. Nearly 300,000 Americans died of all causes between September and December 1918. Global deaths likewise climbed.

The third wave hit Australia in January 1919 and would persist in the United States through June. A fourth wave hit in late 1919. By 1920, the Spanish flu had abated. Of a world population of 1.8 to 1.9 billion, an estimated half a billion were infected and at least fifty million died. In the United States, between a quarter and a third of the population of about 105 million were infected and about 670,000 died.

In December 2019, the coronavirus infected a Chinese man in Wuhan. It was reported that the cause may have been a bat purchased at a "wet market." Bats are known carriers of many viruses. Two of China's major infectious disease laboratories were also located in Wuhan, arousing suspicions that the virus could have somehow been released at one of them. The Biden administration tasked the Intelligence Community in May 2021 to determine within sixty days, whether or not the virus originated from the Wuhan Virology Laboratory.

The following is a timeline for the spread of the pandemic as well as other significant events:

January 7, 2020: China formally identifies disease as
    coronavirus/COVID-19
January 11: First death reported in Wuhan
January 20: First US case reported in Washington State
January 23: China announces quarantine
January 30: World Health Organization declares
    health emergency
January 31: US announces partial travel ban on foreign visitors
February/March: COVID cases spikes, with Italy being
    hit massively
March 4: First US death reported
March 11: WHO declares COVID-19 a pandemic
March 13: US declares pandemic a national emergency
March 31: About one-third of the global population
    "locked down"
April 14: US withholds payments to WHO
April–mid-June: Five million cases reported globally
April: Total of 2,850 US deaths
May: Total of 55,337 US deaths

June: Total of 102,640 US deaths

July: Total of 126, 573 deaths

July 28: Ten million global cases; 500,000 deaths

August 1: Total of 126,573 US deaths

September 1: Total of 182,182 US deaths

October 1: Total of 206,642 US deaths

November 1: Total of 228,165 US deaths

December 1: Total of 264,808 US deaths

January 1, 2021: Total of 339,400 US deaths

January 14, 2021: Total of US deaths reaches 400,000

February 26, 2021: Total of US deaths reaches 500,000

March-May 2021: Pandemic begins to dissipate

June 1, 2021: Total US deaths approach 600,000

(Note: There are minor accounting differences in numbers depending on sources recording total deaths but these are de minimus.)

HOW THE 1918–1920 PANDEMIC AND THE 2020 PANDEMIC AFFECTED THE AMERICAN ECONOMY AND SOCIETY

Military operations in World War I were severely disrupted, something that was not widely reported or remembered. Likewise, the constraints imposed on the US public through the Espionage and Sedition Acts along with the uncertainty of how the disease might be contracted generated great anxiety and even panic throughout the nation.

To enforce the laws, the Justice Department deputized the quasi-official American Protective League (APL) that Attorney General A. Mitchell Palmer stated had 200,000 members operating across the nation. Other vigilante-type groups flourished to hunt down seditious activities, targeting the International Workers of the World in

Chicago. In Arizona, some 1,200 IWW members were loaded onto locked boxcars and sent out of the state.

American Vigilance Patrol vigilantes literally spied on neighbors for seditious activities, including hoarding food and other goods and not buying war bonds. For Americans who found the Nazi SS and Soviet KGB to be onerous and threatening, this did happen here. And it was exacerbated by the letter bombs in 1919 and 1920 amidst the "Red Scare" when many Americans genuinely feared America going socialist.

During the war, some states banned teaching German as "un-American." The *Providence Journal* in Rhode Island warned that "every German or Austrian in the United States…should be treated as a spy." And the government relied on the Committee for Public Information (CPI) for issuing much of its anti-German wartime propaganda to energize the public in the war effort.

The committee actually argued that "it matters very little if information is true or false" as long as it contributed to the ends. In essence, patriotism trumped truth. While Donald Trump may not have been aware of the CPI's activities, he certainly seemed to have purloined its tactics. Years later, Winston Churchill put this matter of propaganda in a proper context. "Truth," he argued, "must be protected by a bodyguard of lies."

One of Wilson's allies, newspaperman George Creel, organized the "Four-Minute Men," a virtual army of about 150,000 volunteers who would issue propaganda for "four minutes" prior to any public gathering. A cynic could observe that Mr. Creel was the future model for Roger Ailes and Fox News. The upshot was an unprecedented use of intimidation and propaganda to rally the nation for the war.

A collision between the pandemic and the propaganda machine was inevitable. The war effort had claimed an estimated quarter of all of America's doctors and nurses into service, obviously reducing the numbers available for public health. For many reasons, officials at all levels from local to national government played down the pandemic in large measure to keep the war effort primary and morale high. Cognitive dissonance had run amuck, as in dealing with the pandemic. Dissenting newspapers were closed down. And the message was "don't get scared."

But Americans were scared. Rumors and conspiracies abound. Many Americans were afraid of leaving home or having any social interactions. Questions were raised about allowing soldiers to return home, bringing the pandemic back. Community intimacy became a first casualty. And the federal government did little to confront the pandemic. The Public Health Service returned much of the money granted for pandemic relief to the Treasury.

Some charitable organizations, what would be called nongovernmental organizations today, were engaged. The American Red Cross was among the most prominent. Liberty Loans groups were organized around local communities to provide financial aid. Other similar groups were also established to help the public.

Absenteeism at work was very high, often in excess of 50 percent of employees. That included many of the nation's shipyards crucial to the war effort. Fear and panic of the Spanish flu led some to conclude that across much of the nation, the terror was akin to that of the Black Plague in medieval Europe that killed at least a third of the total population.

Movies were becoming popular. But many or most theaters were closed down. Likewise, schools, churches, and dance halls in cities across the country were also shut. Cities such as Kansas banned weddings and funerals with more than twenty participants. To reduce rush hour commuter traffic and crowds, cities such as New York ordered staggered work hours. In some locales but not nationally, masks were ordered. In San Francisco, protests against wearing masks broke out, a harbinger of today. Seeking safety, people chose to stay at home.

How cities responded to the pandemic reflected both extremes. As well reported in the literature, Philadelphia was a hot spot for the Spanish flu. Super spreader events were common. For example, in late September 1918, Philadelphia launched a war bond parade. The parade caused a major outbreak of the Spanish flu, and reportedly twelve thousand people died.

Basic preventive actions of wearing masks and social distancing took too long to implement. St. Louis, however, took immediate action, unlike Philadelphia.

The conclusion was clear: the sooner precautions were taken, the greater likelihood that the Spanish flu could be contained and infections reduced.

DOW JONES

The stock market is not necessarily a good indicator of the state of the economy. As of this writing, the NASDAQ and S&P 500 indices are at record highs. These are snapshots of the Dow Jones Industrial Average for 1918 and the following few years:

January 1918: 74.4
December 1918: 75.3
July 1919: 100.3
September 1919: 110.6
January 1920: 91.7
December 1920: 71.9
July 1921: (low point) 65.8
January 1922: 82.2

For 2020, the Dow Jones was:

    February 4: 28,807

    March 2: 26,703

    April 1: 20,949

    April 23: (low point) 18,591

    May 1: 23,723

    June 1: 25,475

    July 1: 25,375

    August 1: 26,664

    September 1: 28,439

    October 1: 27,940

    November 2: 26,691

    December 1: 30,083

For 2021, Dow Jones was:

    January 4: 30,417

    February 1: 30,054

    March 1: 31,065

    April 1: 33,054

    May 3: 33,904

    June 1: 34,558

HOW DID THE WILSON AND TRUMP ADMINISTRATIONS RESPOND TO THESE PANDEMIC-CAUSED DISRUPTIONS?

Woodrow Wilson ignored the pandemic, never mentioning it. He allowed or tolerated the use of the Espionage and Sedition Acts to censor news and reports of the Spanish flu. Ironically, the reason for the flu's name was that Spain was one of the first countries to report on the pandemic. Not being a belligerent in World War I, censorship was not in place in Spain. Otherwise, the disease could have easily been called the American or Army or Fort Riley flu, much as Donald Trump labeled corona the "Kung flu" and the "China flu."

Wilson had suffered from a series of strokes. His second wife, Edith, had taken on many of the presidential responsibilities. During the war, Wilson would not recognize the pandemic, as he thought it would detract from fighting it. After the November 1918 armistice, Wilson would spend about half of 1919 in Paris at the peace conference. Hence, illness and distance were further contributors to his silence. Still, with the war over and the pandemic raging, there was no excuse for the president to continue to ignore its existence unless he lacked the mental capacity to understand fully how serious the Spanish flu was.

A century later, that failure to acknowledge the pandemic would prove contagious. The reasons why Donald Trump underplayed COVID and then exaggerated the cures were discussed earlier. The Sunday prior to the Republican National Convention, the president held a press conference to report a major achievement.

The president triumphantly announced that convalescent plasma from donors who had been infected with COVID-19 proved effective in saving the lives of 35 percent of the patients receiving it. As Dr. Stephen Hahn, the director of the Federal Drug Administration who was present at the briefing would have to retract later, the data did not confirm that success rate. That made little difference to the president or his continued willingness to misrepresent information and make assertions that were false and misleading.

At best, Wilson believed the war effort superseded admitting the presence of the disease. Later, however, his physical condition and absence from the United States probably accounted for his refusal to recognize the Spanish flu. In the case of Donald Trump, the reasons for his handling of COVID-19 were more complicated.

That the economy was central to Trump's reelection no doubt led to underplaying the pandemic certainly from January through March 2020. As the pandemic grew worse and the economy suffered, reversing that contraction became more important. Perhaps refusing to wear a mask and not supporting social distancing was part of the case to make the economy the top priority and not let additional pandemic responses force further shutdowns.

The former president used the pandemic for daily briefings at which he held forth along with the Coronavirus Task Force headed by

Vice President Mike Pence. Then in May, the briefings stopped as the pandemic spread.

By midsummer 2020, it had become impossible for the president to dissent any longer with his key medical advisors on the Coronavirus Task Force, Dr. Anthony Fauci and Dr. Deborah Birx. Fauci, head of infectious diseases at the National Institutes of Health, and Birx, one of the key researchers in combating the AIDS epidemic, continually called for masks and social distancing. Both were criticized by the White House and president. By late August, Fauci and Birx were missing persons at briefs.

In the septic political environment infecting Washington, the last president was far from truthful, providing misleading and often factually wrong information to the public. The refusal to mandate masks and social distancing and to allow and encourage attendees at rallies and other events continued through the election. These superspreader events were estimated to have caused at least fifty thousand more cases and thousands more deaths. And promise for therapeutics, cures, and vaccines went unfilled.

WHAT EMPOWERED THE ECONOMIC BOOM FOLLOWING THE 1918–1920 PANDEMIC?

Comparison of these two once-in-a-century disruptions provides important insights into what has changed and what has not over the past century.

How and when will America and Americans fully emerge from the COVID-19 pandemic and its consequences? The 1918–1920 Spanish flu offers several insights both encouraging and cautionary. First, perhaps surprisingly, that period was far more violent, turbulent, and disruptive than 2020–2021, both inside and beyond America's shores.

Second, despite that upheaval, the post-pandemic recovery led to an unprecedented American economic boom.

Third, while an actively engaged president was essential for the economic recovery, the boom ended abruptly with the 1929 stock market crash, and the failure to confront the crises in postwar Europe would lead to an even more calamitous global conflict.

As the pandemic hit in early 1918, World War I was still raging. By the November armistice, the warring states in Europe were exhausted, depleted by four years of war. Germany, crippled by debt, was a petri dish for extremists and radicals from which the seeds for another world war were sown. The Soviet Union was ravaged by a civil war following its 1917 revolution. China too was in chaos.

Woodrow Wilson was an absentee and then incapacitated president. He spent half of 1919 out of America in Paris negotiating the Treaty of Versailles, to be rejected by the Republican-held Senate. Contracting the Spanish flu while in France, Wilson refused to acknowledge the pandemic or his illness. In October 1919, Wilson suffered a stroke, making him unable to carry out the duties of president for the rest of his term.

In America, labor unrest and riots wracked the nation. Letter bombs in 1919 and 1920 panicked the public far more than al-Qaeda's September 11 attacks would do in 2001. The so-called Palmer Raids to catch the perpetrators, named for Attorney General A. Mitchell Palmer, arrested tens of thousands of suspected anarchists, deporting many without due process. The bombers were never found. Prohibition and women's right to vote likewise were highly divisive political issues, often ending in violence.

Economic recessions in 1919 and 1920 struck Europe and America hard. In 1920, US unemployment reached 14 percent. Approximately fifty million people died from the flu—about 650,000 in America, equivalent to over two million US deaths today. Fortunately, the Spanish flu ran its course by 1920, a hopeful harbinger for today. By 1922, America's economic boom was well underway, stoking the

Roaring Twenties until upended by the 1929 stock market crash and the Great Depression.

In November 1920, Ohio senator Warren G. Harding and his running mate, Calvin Coolidge, won in a landslide over James Cox and his running mate Eugene V. Debs, in jail for opposing the war. President Harding's election brought a needed measure of confidence and competence that reassured the public. Relief for the agricultural sector and tax cuts helped. But Harding knew it would take a combination of technology and pent-up capital to produce an economic renaissance.

Electrification of America sparked this boom. Consumer demand for cars exploded and was a second economic recovery engine. Massive highway construction was empowered by the Federal Highway Act of 1921 (more than three decades before President Eisenhower created the Interstate Highway System).

The rubber, steel, oil, and construction industries flourished as hotels, gas stations, and restaurants became essential to accommodate Americans made mobile by Henry Ford and Walter Chrysler. Radio linked the nation, and movies provided mass entertainment.

Economic growth in the 1920s was impressive. Ownership of cars, new household appliances, and housing was spread widely through the population. New products and the processes for producing them drove this growth. The widening use of electricity in production and the growing adoption of the assembly line in manufacturing combined to create a continuing rise in the productivity of labor and capital.

Though the average workweek in most manufacturing fields remained essentially constant throughout the 1920s, in a few industries, such as railroads and coal production, it declined. New products and services created new markets for lighting and radios as well as for iceboxes, irons, fans, vacuum cleaners, and other labor-saving household appliances.

The electricity to power these products was distributed by the growing electric utilities. The stocks of those companies helped create the stock market boom of the late 1920s. RCA, one of the glamour stocks of the era, paid no dividends. But its value appreciated because of great expectations for the new company's future prospects. Like the internet boom of the late 1990s, the electricity boom of the 1920s fed a rapid expansion in the stock market.

By 1923 and the recovery underway, American unemployment was down to 4 percent. Harding would die that October of a heart attack, never receiving full credit for his brief but important presidency. Who, then, and what are today's Henry Ford and the technological equivalents of electricity?

Beyond vaccines and treatments to render COVID-19 impotent, the parallel to electrification is expanding internet, broadband, and 5G access throughout all America that will lift economic productivity possibly by an order of magnitude.

Broadband and internet access must be part of the larger solution: massive infrastructure spending through a national private-public investment fund capitalized to around $3 trillion. The Biden administration however has taken a different approach with its Rescue, Jobs, and Family bills that did not rely on public-private partnerships. As of mid-2021, it is unclear and uncertain what Congress will pass or reject.

The purposes of this fund are to modernize and repair the nation's failing infrastructure, from airports to bridges, dams, medical facilities, power grids, roads, and schools, while reducing unemployment. Neither of President Biden's Jobs and Family Bills have been passed so far. And even with what seemed the new COVID-19 Delta variant wave, bipartisan support for passing any infrastructure law remains elusive, raising the limited prospect for an alternative such as the 1923 Fund.

No matter how grim today's crises may seem, the 1920s America made an extraordinary economic recovery at a far more troubled and violent time. The key question is whether America will seize the opportunity for another dramatic economic renaissance. A second question is if Joe Biden is capable of becoming another Harding to lead this boom while avoiding future unintended and unforeseen disasters.

WHAT LESSONS SHOULD BE LEARNED?

Applying what happened in 1918–1920 and now in 2020 provides historical perspective that is critical for deriving plans for today. One of the saddest lessons is that handbooks for dealing with pandemics in the form of results from war games and other exercises were readily available. In late fall 2019, the US Naval War College conducted a pandemic war game. If the published results and recommendations had been read and consulted, a clear-cut strategy and action plan could have been immediately drawn from the war game's conclusions. This did not happen. Nonetheless, here are the lessons that should be learned from historical perspective.

First, the earlier the preventive actions, the greater is the likelihood of arresting the spread of the pandemic. Otherwise, as was experienced in nursing homes in Washington State and in New York, medical resources are quickly overwhelmed. Perhaps in 1918, the war effort was an overriding if not sufficiently compelling reason for downplaying the Spanish flu. There was no overriding national reason for downplaying the coronavirus in 2020 except incompetence or, worse, the demands for reelection based on a strong economy that could not be jeopardized by a pandemic.

Creating a national strategic response must be the government's first duty. Part of the strategy should be setting priorities to be achieved and timelines to achieve them. For example, shortages of medical equipment from masks and protective gowns to swabs and ventilators must be corrected. That means it is vital to implement the earliest use of the Defense Production Act.

Testing is the next priority. Former President Trump's antipathy to testing was not sufficient grounds for failing to ramp up production and to mobilize private university and veterinary laboratories, many of which remained unused for testing.

Obviously, developing vaccines and therapeutics is vital. The Trump administration authorized Operation Warp Speed, resulting in the creation of a number of vaccines in record time. And no other country was better organized or more advanced in these efforts.

Second, the organization of government is critical but only if properly mobilized and led. Coordinating the Health and Human Services Department with the National Institutes of Health, the Food and Drug Administration, the Centers for Disease Control and Prevention, the Defense Department, the Department of Veterans Affairs, and the myriad other agencies is inherently difficult simply because of the size of these federal bureaucracies. Add fifty states, a half-dozen territories, and the extensive private sector health facilities and infrastructure, as well as coordinating with other nations, and organizing becomes monumentally complicated and often unworkable.

Creating "czars" to lead has always been problematic, as the various wars on drugs, poverty, and inequality have shown. Frequent reference to the Manhattan Project that developed nuclear weapons or the space program to put a man on the moon is made. However, regardless of the Herculean efforts that built the bomb and landed men on the moon, no matter how technically challenging, both took time. Pandemics do not allow the luxury of time once they strike and cut across too much of society to make establishing a czar the best solution.

The Pentagon was made the lead agency for Operation Warp Speed. Given the vast capacity, resources, and strength in planning it brought to bear, the military option was a sound one. In this case, the path for success not only for future pandemics is not another task force. Instead, anticipation and response should be best served through an expanded National Security Council.

The president has an assistant for national security. A permanent position of a second assistant or deputy for the new MAD should be created. The purpose for this person and directorate would be to begin contingency planning for all manner of disruptions short of war. That would include the seven disruptors and potential pandemics. Coordination with responsible departments is essential, and this office would not dilute the responsibility for the respective secretaries.

When the current pandemic struck, there was no plan in place. While the government has gotten better at planning for hurricanes, other potential environmental disasters have not received the same attention. More on this follows including annual war games to evaluate the progress in planning for MAD.

Third, while this sounds jejune and naive, science and medical fact and advice count. If a president is unprepared to take that advice, the question is how to reverse that view. That requires cabinet secretaries and members of Congress of the same party to be heard. How many resignations occurred as secretaries and chiefs of staff stepped down over disagreements with then President Trump pertaining to the pandemic? The answer is none although Dr. Anthony Fauci, one of the nation's leading epidemiologists, and Dr. Birx were eventually sidelined by Trump for their candor and refusal to accept his obvious falsehoods and misrepresentations about the pandemic.

Whether or not to resign has always been a question usually but not always answered by concluding that it is more effective to remain inside an administration than to complain or protest from the outside. In fairness, very few resignations other than during the Watergate affair have had impact. However, this should be a question asked of every nominee for a confirmed position about principle and expediency and under what circumstances resignation is the only option.

Fourth, preparation is always critical. The question is, however, how much planning and preparation can go into contingencies that never occur? Put another way, is it possible to forecast and handicap with some certainty which possible crises are most likely? With a national security assistant focusing on these disruptive possibilities, preparation should improve.

Fifth, truth and its dissemination are vital. In 1918–1920, truth was withheld. As a result, people died. Today, in a deeply politically polarized nation, dis- and misinformation appear regularly on social media and the internet. Knowing who and what to believe is no longer a trivial matter.

A substantial portion of the public will refuse to accept truth and fact if both contradict what those individuals believe. The strong backlash to vaccinations is one example. A second is, as the former president suggests, to downplay basic precautions in attending outdoor rallies where few masks are seen and social distancing is not practiced. Allowing this form of cognitive dissonance to persist can only lead to possible super-spreader events.

Sixth, plans for opening the economy and schools have to be based on science and expert advice. Further, the choices are exquisitely diabolical. How are risks and the need for livelihoods and education balanced? A working family with young children in which either both parents or a single parent must work poses unsolvable dilemmas. Staying at home can lead to losing a job. Day care may be unavailable or unaffordable. While children are less susceptible to contracting COVID in school or day care, they can still spread it. All are bad options.

Seventh, mobilizing all laboratories from universities to animal husbandry facilities is essential. These resources were never fully utilized. If testing is to be available to all who need it to improve contact tracing, these additional facilities must be used.

Eighth, the government needs a single, accurate message that is repeatable and replicable. Even slight variations confuse the public. Today, messaging, along with the pandemic, has become polarized. When one side refuses to listen or two competing messages on the pandemic are broadcast, at best confusion is inevitable. At worst, societal divisions will become even greater.

If only one conclusion can be drawn, it is this. The new MAD is upon us. Coronavirus/COVID-19 is perhaps a final warning that massive disruptions must be central in this nation's national security thinking and planning processes. If they are not, the nation will be unprepared and unsuited for the next disruption. The question is not if the next one will strike; the question is when.

The other infection beyond coronavirus may be more serious and even deadlier: the politicization of a pandemic. The former president chose to listen to advice that conformed with his instincts rather than to science. The FDA and CDC were used to present the message the president and the administration wanted. At one stage, the public was told masks did not work. At another point, they were told cures such as hydroxychloroquine worked. The same wrong advice applied to convalescent plasma, which the head of the FDA had to correct after he supported the false assertion that deaths were reduced by 34 percent.

By late November 2020, two vaccines had proven 95 percent effective in preventing COVID-19. While the Trump administration's Warp Speed was impressive, its planning for distribution was missing in action. Vaccinations were to begin in January 2021. At least seven hundred million doses were required as both the Pfizer and Moderna vaccines required two injections for 330 million Americans. With the emergency approval of the Johnson and Johnson vaccine, only one inoculation was required reducing the need for the total number of doses.

The first priority of the Biden administration was to vaccinate Americans as quickly as possible. Here the administration excelled.

By the end of May 2021, more than 60 percent received at least one shot and the goal of inoculating about 70 percent by July 4th was set. Of course, the problem is no longer production and distribution. The problem is the size of the population refusing to be inoculated.

While by summer 2021, it appeared that COVID-19 was dissipating, the arrival of mutant strains, the probable need for booster shots and not achieving population-wide immunity were grounds for concern. Hope is not a strategy. But perhaps by the time this book is published in late 2021, better answers to these questions will have emerged.

This book argues that the Constitution is under assault for reasons noted before. This assault was exacerbated by the pandemic. At the end of 2020, nearly 350,000 Americans died. By June 2021, that number swelled to nearly 600,000. The economic recovery has been "K" shaped. The upper arm refers to the stock markets returning to pre-corona levels. The lower arm reflects the majority of Americans whose economic future has been imperiled.

No more compelling evidence of the arrival of the Fifth Horseman and MAD exists than this pandemic. It is understandable that governments cannot be prepared for every contingency. But the threat of pandemics has been raised, studied, and war-gamed many, many times. Why, then, was no contingency plan immediately available?

One reason rests in perhaps the most major and significant disruptor: failed and failing government. The vulnerability and fragility of societies are increasing as globalization, the diffusion of all forms of power and technology have a Janus-like effect. Disruption has positive and negative consequences. Every advance creates a weakness. For example, as financial services provide consumers with many new options, each is subject to hacking, intrusion, and possible criminal activity. Chapter 2 outlined a few of the more distressing scenarios.

The 1918–1920 pandemic passed and was largely forgotten. The "Roaring Twenties" followed with an economic boom. It is too soon to know how this pandemic will evolve, for better or for ill. Yet if this warning of the arrival of the Fifth Horseman and the new MAD is dismissed as the Spanish flu was, one outcome is unavoidable: the nation will be worse off. And for the first time since the Civil War, the prospects for a new and different form of an uncivil political war are no longer an academic question.

Chapter Seven

1914, 1939, 2001 OR
1918, 1945, 1989?

Do we learn from history? Perhaps not. What happened in 1914, 1939, and 2001 and in 1918, 1945, and 1989 is instructive. But will we notice? And will we learn or act?

The years 1914, 1939, and 2001 marked the start of two world wars and the global war on terror. Meanwhile, 1918, 1945, and 1989 marked the end of two world wars and a cold one. Does 2021 more closely resemble the first or second set of inflection points? Or is there another possibility in a MAD age? This chapter addresses these comparisons.

Here are chilling linkages to consider: The Trump US National Security Strategy (NSS) was based on waging a global power competition against two peer or near-peer competitors. In simple terms, this is a great-power rivalry. Lest we forget, great-power rivalries were one of the causes of World War I. What makes 2021 different from 1914? One hopes a great deal!

In 1939, Europe had continued to ignore Nazi Germany's rearmament and territorial expansion. While China's current increases in military power and control of proximate seas has been anything but ignored by Washington, are there limits to Beijing's military and territorial ambitions? And is future great-power conflict inevitable as it was in 1939?

In 2001, despite possessing an extraordinarily complex national security organization and spending billions of dollars on intelligence, the US was incapable of detecting or preventing the attacks of September 11. If 2020 was indicative, aside from a handful of states largely in Asia, no other countries were prepared for the onslaught of the coronavirus. What was learned, if anything, from this first dose of the new MAD that was orders of magnitude more deadly than September 11?

1914

In 1914, before the guns of August set the world on fire, Europe enjoyed the benefits of a century of relative stability and prosperity empowered by technological revolutions. The major disruptors in 1914 were growing great-power rivalry, globalization, industrialization, military technological revolutions, terrorism, immigration, consumerism, and a perceived collapse of moral values. Indeed, a sampling of the interesting "firsts" provides context for the period.

In January 1914, the first commercial airline, the Saint Petersburg–Tampa Airboat Line in Florida, opened for business. Henry Ford declared an eight-hour workweek and guaranteed a five-dollar weekly paycheck. Charlie Chaplin made his first movie, and Babe Ruth played his first baseball game as a professional for the Boston Red Sox. The first electric traffic light was installed in Cleveland. The US Navy's first super-dreadnought, USS *Nevada*, was launched.

In March, the first successful indirect blood transfusion was made. In April, Congress approved President Woodrow Wilson's request to use force against Mexico over the so-called Tampico Incident, and the Navy and Marines occupied Vera Cruz. The Panama and Cape Cod Canals were opened. Assassins tried to kill the villainous monk Rasputin in Moscow, and a plot to blow up John D. Rockefeller in New York literally exploded in the faces of the anarchists who accidentally ignited the bomb.

Meanwhile, Europe was edging toward war. Few realized how dangerous conditions were growing. Despite the close ties among the royal families of Britain, Germany, and Russia linked by blood and marriage and ruled by monarchs whose grandmother was Queen Victoria, great-power rivalries permeated Europe. Cousins Georgie (King George V), Nicky (Tsar Nicholas II), and Willy (Kaiser Wilhelm II) referred to each other by nicknames. Those seeming friendships did not diminish; however, great-power rivalries clashed over influence, foreign colonies, and strategic and economic interests and status.

Britain, isolated by its failure in the Boer War (1898–1902), Russia, and, in due course, France, embittered by the disastrous 1870–1871 Franco-Prussian War and threatened by the formal unification of Germany in 1871, would form an entente against Germany and her allies—the Austro-Hungarian Empire, Turkey, and, until 1915, Italy. Both sides put in place secret agreements and treaties that would inadvertently doom any incident to escalate possibly out of control. London had guaranteed by treaty Belgium's neutrality in the event of war. And Russia would aid Serbia in a crisis.

From 1800 to 1914, globalization expanded trade from about one-thirtieth to one-third of global production. Global investment soared by about twentyfold from the mid-1800s. Europe accounted for the bulk of foreign investment and trade. Foreign-born laborers flocked to industrial facilities in Europe, raising issues over immigration.

Industrialization, with the advent of the steam and internal combustion engines, electricity, telephone, telegraph and wireless communications, and increasing productivity, was a major disruptor. On one hand, standards of living greatly improved. On the other, the disruption caused by industrialization led to political unrest as wealth was unevenly spread across society. Globalization accelerated industrialization as world markets not only opened but were connected by speedy steamships and transoceanic underwater telegraph cables.

The proliferation of military technologies and the lessons from the American Civil War and Franco-Prussian War fueled arms races and war plans that would be based on mobilizing and mounting a rapid offensive before any enemy could react. The two wars demonstrated the strategic importance of railroads for timely delivery of supplies essential to sustaining large armies in the field. Advances in armaments with rapid-firing machine guns, breech-loading artillery, and rifled barrels made battlefields both more lethal and vastly larger in scale as weapons had much longer killing ranges. By 1914, aviation and submarines were becoming militarily important.

The naval arms race pitted Britain's Royal Navy, shifting from coal to oil for power and building highly armored super-dreadnoughts with fifteen-inch guns, against the Kaiser's High Seas Fleet. Their lordships in Whitehall saw this naval competition as a mortal threat to England's centuries-old command of the oceans. A military revolution was on, and it was not limited to navies, armies, and fledgling air forces. Poison gas was being developed by both sides.

In 1870, Prussia overwhelmed France on the battlefield because of its ability to mobilize quickly. Just as nuclear weapons in the latter half of the twentieth century came to dominate strategy, in 1914, the theory was that the first side to mobilize had the one advantage almost certain to bring victory. The fatal flaw was that once one side started to mobilize, it was impossible to stop, making diplomacy and other potentially peaceful resolutions useless.

Germany found itself geographically trapped between Russia to the east and Britain and France to the west. The German General Staff chose to resolve this strategic dilemma with the Schlieffen Plan. To win a two-front war, France had to be defeated quickly, possibly within six weeks, and faster than in 1870.

To achieve a swift victory, the offensive had to roll through neutral Belgium to outflank French defenses. German planners doubted Britain would honor its agreement to guarantee Belgium's neutrality. Regardless, before the British Expeditionary Force could mobilize and sail across the channel, the German Army would have defeated France. Germany then could turn east on Russia. A quarter of a century later, Adolf Hitler would find this a compelling strategy to fight a two-front war in similar geographic circumstances after he had defeated France in June 1940.

According to newspapers and reports of the time, terrorism was perceived as a greater threat in 1914 than it is today despite the potential of WMD-armed terrorists, possibly home grown. The revolutions of 1848 sparked violent revolts and protests in which terror was a most effective and persistent weapon to attack the establishment. Alfred Nobel's invention of dynamite in 1867 gave terrorists the limited equivalent then of nuclear weapons today.

In 1886, dynamite was used in the infamous Haymarket bombing in Chicago. The Iron Workers Union, seeking to break the power of US Steel, detonated more than one hundred bombs at industrial plants between 1906 and 1911, peaking in 1910 when two union organizers dynamited the offices of the pro-management *Los Angeles Times*, killing twenty-one.

Assassinations were common. Russia's Tsar Alexander II was murdered in 1881. Two years before, President James Garfield was shot by a disgruntled diplomat, Charles Guiteau, at the Baltimore and Potomac Railroad Station. The president died seventy-nine days later. In 1901, President William McKinley was assassinated by Leon

Czolgosz. And in 1912, former President Theodore Roosevelt survived an attempt assassination, shot in the chest.

Of today's seven major disruptors, climate change, debt, and drones did not exist then. Cyber and social media took different forms. Code breaking was the cyber of the day. Social media was confined to printed material. But pamphlets and books had the equivalent force of Facebook, deep fakes, and fake news spreading propaganda. For example, the infamous Zimmerman telegram that promised a return of Texas to Mexico by Germany was used, unsuccessfully, by British intelligence as leverage to induce the US to enter the war in 1916.

Before 1914, debt was not an issue. Indeed, US budgets often ran a surplus. Programs such as Social Security and the Great Society had not been invented yet. However, failed and failing government was a major factor and a major cause of the First World War.

That failure was manifested in the great-power rivalry that became the explosive ingredient, making World War I inevitable. The parallels with today are interesting, if not disconcerting. Seven major powers were arrayed against each other in 1914—Britain, France, and Russia opposed Germany, Austria-Hungary, Turkey, and briefly, Italy. Serbia too was an important power. While Asia was secondary, in the coming war, Japan was a formidable power. China was in disarray with major coastal cities occupied and partitioned among foreign powers.

The June 28, 1914 assassination of Austria-Hungary's Grand Duke Franz Ferdinand and his wife, Sophie, in Sarajevo ignited the fuse starting World War I. Today, what disruptors akin to June 28 could precipitate conflict among the three main powers? Many scenarios are suggestive. The likely cause is a future massive attack of disruption.

As the imaginary President Bennett outlined in her first address to the nation, environmental catastrophe, cyber, social media, terrorism, debt, drones, and failed and failing government each had the seeds for potential future conflict. If any lesson is relevant, it is that great-power rivalries are not stabilizing. The Cold War was not fought in the context of a broad great-power rivalry. It was geostrategic and ideological in character, as the Soviet Union was never an economic superpower. Deterrence and containment succeeded in that last conflict.

But will we learn in time to prevent the next conflict?

1939

In 1939, the world was still in the grip of the Great Depression and the devastation of World War I that claimed the lives of many of that younger generation in the trenches of that horrible conflict. Despite New Deals and social legislation in the United States, some economic conditions were actually worse than in 1929. Similar crises persisted throughout Europe. Major disruptors were a function of failed and failing government that ignored growing threats in Germany and Japan and persistent debt from the Great Depression.

The most vibrant economy was Nazi Germany's. Hitler and National Socialism had rebuilt much of the country and attracted well-known converts such as Charles Lindbergh. The Soviet Union, recognized by the United States in 1933, propagandized itself as a worker's paradise. Italy too under Benito Mussolini was seen as a modernizing state where the railroads were said to run on time.

Isolationism had taken hold in America after World War I. Republican isolationists led by Senate Foreign Relations chairman Henry Cabot Lodge rejected the Versailles Treaty and Wilson's League of Nations. "America firsters" exemplified this mood and the depth of resentment to foreign entanglements. In many ways, the United States was far from what Ronald Reagan would call "Morning in America" four decades later.

The year 1939 began with temperatures in Sydney, Australia, reaching a record 113 degrees Fahrenheit and the massive Black

Friday bush fire destroying twenty million acres. In America, the 1939 World's Fair opened in Flushing Meadows, New York, as an effort to boost national morale still suffering from the Depression. The first FM radio station began transmitting in Connecticut.

Batman comics appeared for the first time. On July 4, Yankee great Lou Gehrig announced his retirement from baseball, afflicted with ALS that would become known as Lou Gehrig's disease. In August, Albert Einstein and Leo Szilard sent a letter to FDR on the likelihood of fission that would evolve into the Manhattan Project and the atom bomb. In Europe, Pius XII was elected pope.

Francisco Franco won the Spanish Civil War and was anointed *caudillo*, or leader. Nazi Germany and Italy signed the "Pact of Steel" and Mussolini invaded Abyssinia. The Molotov-Ribbentrop Pact was signed between the Soviet Union and Nazi Germany, clearing the way for the Nazi invasion of Poland on September 1 and its partitions as spoils for Moscow. On the same day Hitler invaded Poland, General George Marshall became US Army Chief of Staff.

The assault on Poland started World War II. Britain and France declared war on Nazi Germany and Italy. Two months later in November, Hitler barely escaped an assassination attempt and the Soviet Union invaded Finland. But a so-called phony war with no significant military operations would persist until April 1940 when Germany launched Case Yellow into France. Six weeks later, France capitulated.

The fundamental causes of that war rested in the failure to achieve an equitable peace after World War I and are covered shortly in the section on 1918. The Allies mandated a draconian peace, forcing the newly formed Weimar Republic to accept massive reparations and agree to limiting its military to one hundred thousand troops. From that disruptive and violent period within Germany, Hitler would be appointed chancellor in 1933.

The victorious powers were not unaware of German rearmament under Hitler, his consolidation of power, and his later annexation of Austria and the Sudetenland in 1938. But the Great War had drained Europe of blood and treasure, and few political leaders had an appetite for deploying force to stop Hitler. Further, the harsh nature of the Versailles Treaty and the view that Nazism was a counterweight to Soviet communism caused second thoughts. When he returned to Great Britain from the Munich Conference at the end of September 1938, Prime Minister Neville Chamberlain confidently stated that this piece of paper "brought peace in our time."

Hence, appeasement of Germany, Italy in Abyssinia, and Japan's intervention in China was an understandable and undesirable outcome. Only a few, namely Winston Churchill wandering in a political wilderness, sounded the alarm. It went unheeded.

In 1939, the United States still had not recovered from the Great Depression. President Roosevelt was considering running for a third term in 1940, breaking tradition with George Washington's decision to retire after eight years in office. While isolationism ran deep in the Republican Party, not all Americans were oblivious to the threats growing in Asia from fascist Japan and from Hitler in Europe.

In 1934, Congress had passed and FDR signed the Vinson-Trammell Naval Construction Act cosponsored by Georgia representative and chairman of the Naval Affairs Committee Carl Vinson and Florida senator Park Trammell. The law was written after Japan abandoned the Naval Arms Limitation Treaty authorizing 102 warships to be built for the US Navy over the next eight years to regain parity with Japan. In 1938, a second Vinson-Trammell Act was passed with further naval increases after Japan expanded the war in China and Hitler annexed Austria and the Sudetenland.

Without both laws, it would have taken years after the Pearl Harbor attack to build a powerful navy, a stunning example of strategic farsightedness. A question to ponder is what in a Westphalian II era, when MAD is the main threat, might be the equivalent of a 2021 Vinson-Trammell Act? Chapter 8 proposes several ideas.

Of the disruptors then, the heat wave and fire in Australia were distant precursors of climate change well in advance of the accumulation of and damage caused by greenhouse gases. Propaganda using the social media of the day—paper and radio—was a key part of the war effort. Lord Haw-Haw, Germany's English language spokesman, began his first propaganda broadcasts in late 1939. Terrorism would become engrained in the bombing campaigns on both sides to destroy civilian will.

Debt had been one of the main causes of the rise of Hitler as Germany could not afford reparation payments. Debt was also a reason why the Allies did not rearm. There was no money.

A key disruptor was failed and failing government. Between 1918 and 1940, France had thirty-six changes of governments and prime ministers, or one every eight months. Britain, more stable, had nine changes of government. The United States had five presidents, as one, Warren G. Harding, died after just over two years in office. Germany had sixteen chancellors. Hitler, like Roosevelt, came into power in 1933.

The Soviet Union had only one leader once Stalin consolidated power after Lenin's death in 1924. Japan had twenty-one prime ministers until Hideki Tojo assumed power in late 1941. But in Japan, the fascist military was in control so the prime ministership until Tojo was weak, and the godlike status of the emperor provided continuity. Italy had five prime ministers before Mussolini seized power in 1922 until he was overthrown in 1943.

Clearly, while the democracies faced a series of failed governments, the continuity of leadership and government in Germany, Italy, and Japan did not win World War II. In 2021, the seeming decline in the legitimacy and effectiveness of liberal democracies may be suggestive of 1939 as autocratic governments increased in number and influence. Hungary, Austria, and Turkey were the more prominent examples in Europe. One of the problems is perhaps an over-reliance of the Western democracies on the power and attraction of the so-called liberal rules-based order in a MAD-driven world, especially when in the past, pragmatism took precedence over principle.

The alliance with Soviet Russia in World War II and the embrace of non-democracies during the Cold War in NATO or the proximity of relations and commitments to keep oil flowing from the Middle East despite Saudi Arabia's autocracy should not be forgotten. Of course, if states break international law and norms, recourses are available. But if the comparisons of past inflection points are relevant, another assessment of the primacy of the liberal rules-based order is needed.

2001

After eight good years of relative economic improvement and international stability once the Kosovo bombing campaign ended in 1999, the Clinton administration left office in January 2000 following one of the most contested elections in US history. Vice President Al Gore won the popular vote, and had the Supreme Court not stopped the Florida recount, he might have won the only vote that counted in the Electoral College. The United States regarded Russia and China as friends and potential partners. Clinton's National Security Strategy (NSS) reflected this absence of major adversaries or rivals. It declared:

> National interests…do not affect our national
> survival, but…do affect our national well-being and
> the character of the world in which we live. Important
> national interests include, for example, regions in which
> we have a sizable economic stake or commitments
> to allies, protecting the global environment from

severe harm, and crises with a potential to generate substantial and highly destabilizing refugee flows.

There are cases we will intervene because our values demand it. Examples include responding to natural and man-made disasters; promoting human rights and seeking to halt gross violations of those rights; supporting democratization, adherence to the rule of law, and civilian control of the military; assisting humanitarian de-mining; and promoting sustainable development and environmental protection.

Clinton's NSS also declared that "vital interests" provide the United States the right to intervene militarily and to ensure "uninhibited access to key markets, energy supplies, and strategic resources." However, no mention was made of specific enemies or adversaries.

On January 20, 2001, despite losing the popular vote, George W. Bush took the oath of office. Bush entered office promising to "transform" the American military for the twenty-first century. However, transformation was ill-defined beyond focusing on space, missile defense, and new weapons technology. Because the ABM Treaty restricted ballistic missile defenses, Bush gave the required one-year notice that the US would withdraw from the agreement. Moscow was not pleased. This was the first of many strategic and foreign policy missteps that his administration would make.

At the beginning of the year, earthquakes hit El Salvador twice, killing nearly a thousand. Shortly after, Gujarat, India, was destroyed by a massive earthquake, killing an estimated twenty thousand. NATO responded with a rescue mission. And for the first time, the entire human genome sequence was published.

In April, Bush faced his first crisis. A US Navy P-3 antisubmarine patrol aircraft was forced to land on China's Hainan Island after being disabled by a PLA F-8 fighter that struck the American plane. That crisis was resolved peacefully and the P-3 was returned.

In May, for the first time, the United States did not hold a seat on the UN Human Rights Commission. Tropical Storm Allison hit the Texas coast and inflicted the costliest damage of any storm up until that time. In the Middle East, John Paul II became the first pope to visit a mosque during a visit to Syria.

That summer was full of disruption in the Pentagon. The required Quadrennial Defense Review was in its final stages of completion. But the senior military leadership were disquieted by the new secretary of defense, serving in that post for the second time, Donald Rumsfeld. Possessing a dominating personality, having thrust transformation on the Pentagon, Rumsfeld directed the services to define what that meant. Without guidance, the brass was frustrated. Reports that Rumsfeld would be the first casualty of the administration circulated.

September changed the world. After the September 11 attacks in Washington and New York, the next day and for the first time in its history, NATO, led by former UK defense minister and NATO secretary George Robertson, invoked Article 5—an attack against one was an attack against all. In a few weeks, NATO would find itself fighting in Afghanistan alongside the US to bring Osama bin Laden and al-Qaeda to justice.

Intended to deter a Soviet assault into West Germany during the Cold War, NATO's founding fathers would have been aghast to learn the alliance was at war for the first time in the graveyard of empires in Afghanistan. Several weeks before the Afghan operation began in October, letters that were believed to contain deadly anthrax were mailed to certain government addresses in Washington, heightening the terrorist threat. Fortunately, unlike 1918–1920 letter bombs that were in fact dangerous, no anthrax was present.

In response to September 11, Congress took two major legislative national security actions in October. The first was creating the Department of Homeland Security to integrate a dozen and a half agencies and offices under one roof. The rush, however, gave no time for a more rational and thoughtful approach. In retrospect, it is not clear that creating a new department was a good idea. And Congress passed the PATRIOT Act, giving the government additional power to execute the war on terror.

In November, as the Afghan Taliban were being routed and planning for the Iraqi invasion was underway, the Convention on Cybercrime was signed in Budapest. In December, the former energy giant Enron filed for bankruptcy, beginning an enormous scandal about how that company's greed had led to gross criminal activities to cover up its financial misdeeds. Terrorists attacked the Indian Parliament in New Delhi, and China was granted permanent trade status. Richard Reeves, the infamous shoe bomber, tried to bring down an airliner with explosives in his sneakers that failed to detonate.

Despite the enormous resources put into national security, bin Laden was able to launch his attack. The 9/11 Commission issued a scathing report in 2004 with thirty-nine recommendations, some of which still have not been implemented. The fundamental flaw was the failure of government and its organization to use the available intelligence to conclude attacks were imminent. Again, the absence of knowledge and understanding of the other was at fault. Congress was not spared from harsh criticism either. Because of the overlapping committee system, the Department of Homeland Security still reports to about two dozen committees and subcommittees in both Houses.

The years 1914, 1939, and 2001 described both international and domestic conditions in the US at the start of wars and historic inflection points. What happened in 1918, 1945, and 1987 after the end of two world wars and the Cold War is equally instructive.

1918

On the eleventh hour of the eleventh day of the eleventh month of 1918, battlefields in Europe stood silent for the first time in more than four years. The armistice came into force with a formal signing at Le Francport near Compiègne between the warring Central and Allied powers. In fact, French Field Marshal Ferdinand Foch had signed the document much earlier at 5:45 a.m. Tragically, over 2,700 soldiers were killed in the intervening five hours and fifteen minutes before the armistice took hold. While the armistice was a victory for the Allies, Germany never formally surrendered.

The original terms of the armistice were dictated by Foch that would later be turned into French demands at the future Paris Peace Conference. These included cessation of hostilities, withdrawal of German forces east of the Rhine, surrender of its arms, release of Allied prisoners of war, eventual reparations, and no relaxation of the naval blockade of Germany. The armistice had to be extended three times until the Treaty of Versailles was signed on June 28, 1919, the anniversary of the archduke's assassination, taking effect on January 10, 1920.

Twenty-seven states sent delegates to the Paris Peace Conference that began in January 1919. The conference was dominated by the "Big Four": US president Woodrow Wilson, British prime minister Lloyd George, French prime minister Georges Clemenceau, and Italian prime minister Vittorio Emanuele Orlando. Complicating the negotiations was Wilson's insistence on making his Fourteen Points the centerpiece of the peace to come. In January 1918, Wilson issued his Fourteen Points outlining the postwar goals of free trade, open agreements, and democracy.

Wilson's Fourteen Points called for a negotiated end to the war, disarmament, withdrawal of the Central Powers from occupied territories, rebuilding the European economy, establishing mandates for prior colonies, dealing with ethnic issues in the Middle East and elsewhere, creating a Polish state, and most importantly, establishing a League of Nations to assure political independence and territorial integrity.

Wilson failed to include any Republican senators on the delegation. The only Republican commissioner to accompany Wilson was the diplomat, Henry White. This failure practically guaranteed the Republican Senate's rejection of both the Versailles Treaty and the League of Nations. Not until 1921 would Republican president Warren Harding sign a peace treaty with Germany.

The British, French, and Italian governments (Italy had changed sides in 1915) strongly dissented with Wilson's Fourteen Points, regarding them as clever American propaganda to undermine the morale of the Central Powers and place the blame for the war on German political parties rather than the German Army. The Fourteen Points were dismissed as vague and unworkable.

The French wanted revenge. France lost about 1.3 million dead along with massive destruction of much of the country in the war, some still in evidence today. Prime Minister Clemenceau's aim was to ensure Germany would never threaten France again. Having lived through the 1870–1871 Franco-Prussian War, Clemenceau wanted the conference to ensure a weakened and even crippled Germany would result. He also wanted guarantees from Britain and the US to prevent any future German aggression.

British prime minister Lloyd George had more focused goals that would ensure the security of France, end the naval threat of the German High Seas Fleet, settle territorial claims particularly over former colonies, and support the League of Nation. Seated between Wilson and Clemenceau, in frustration, Lloyd George would quip that to his right was Jesus Christ (Wilson) and to his left Napoleon (Clemenceau). Unfortunately, Wilson as Christ had not brought enough of the proper apostles with him, and he was weakened by the absence of political support at home.

Given these realities, and with no primus inter pares on the Allied side, fashioning a durable peace was simply not possible. The idealism of Wilson collided with the cynicism of Clemenceau. That the war ended with an armistice and not a surrender by Germany meant that the only threat the Allies could muster was to resume the war. Regardless, Clemenceau's position won out.

Germany was crippled with reparations. It was limited to a 100,000-man army, largely a self-defense force denied offensive weapons. The Alsace-Lorraine region was returned to France and the Brest-Litovsk Treaty of 1918 was negated, with Belarus and Ukraine returned to what would become the USSR, which had come into existence five years after the 1917 Russian Revolution. The Baltic states and Poland became independent.

The treaty was infected with profound flaws that, left uncorrected, would inevitably provoke another war. Germany was put in a desperate economic condition with hyperinflation and unemployment running rampant. Fear of both communists and socialists disrupting society and even gaining power likewise was palpable in Germany. Radical groups formed across the political spectrum. From a beer hall in Munich, the Nazi Party would metastasize and twenty years later, the world would be at war again.

Could that war have been avoided? The answer is no. The Paris Peace Conference simply was incapable of producing a fair, just, and lasting peace. The main reason was that the most important participants could not and would not agree to such an arrangement. And no countervailing forces emerged to change the course to war.

The lesson was not learned in 1945 when the Second World War ended in Europe. The Allies initially imposed a draconian peace on Germany. The same was not quite true in Japan because of the vision of Douglas MacArthur.

1945

Germany surrendered on May 8, 1945. Two atom bombs dropped in August eviscerating Hiroshima and Nagasaki persuaded Japan's emperor to support peace and surrender. On September 2, the war in the Pacific ended. After signing the instrument of unconditional surrender on the main deck of the battleship USS *Missouri*, General of the Army Douglas MacArthur declared "these proceedings are closed." And then he watched as thousands of US warplanes flew overhead as a warning to the Japanese government as to who was in charge.

FDR had put in place a vision for a postwar world with a United Nations organization and economic and monetary framework to ensure stability and growth. However, the Axis Powers were not part of that framework. A Carthaginian peace was to be imposed on Germany.

The United States would rehabilitate the defeated Axis powers. But that was not the original intent or plan. What finally convinced America and the Allies to change that view and not to exact the same harsh penalties of the Versailles Treaty on Germany? The seemingly contradictory answer was Joe Stalin.

The Nazis killed at least six million Jews and countless other "gypsies" and non-Aryans. Hitler's regime was evil incarnate beyond its racial policies. The Japanese were brutal overseers of POWs, believing in Bushido that surrender was cowardice. And Americans would not soon forget the "sneak attack" on Pearl Harbor.

In 1943, the State Department began planning for the postwar world. The plan developed by Secretary of the Treasury Henry Morgenthau was to turn Germany into an agrarian state without an army or a capacity to reconstitute one by preventing the rebuilding of an industrial base. His memorandum was titled a "Suggested

Post-Surrender Program for Germany." That plan was approved by Roosevelt in August 1944, noting:

> Too many people here and in England hold the view that the German people as a whole are not responsible for what has taken place—that only a few Nazis are responsible....The German people must have it driven home to them that the whole nation has been engaged in a lawless conspiracy against the decencies of modern civilization.

The Joint Chiefs of Staff issued a directive, JCS 1067, to implement that plan. The US military government of occupation in Germany was to "take no steps looking toward the economic rehabilitation of Germany [or] designed to maintain or strengthen the German economy." And the military government was to keep starvation, disease, and civil unrest below such levels so as to pose no danger to the Allied occupying force. Germany was divided into four occupation zones controlled by the United States, United Kingdom, the Provisional Government of the French Republic, and the USSR assuming "supreme authority...including all the powers possessed by the German government."

From all appearances, the peace in Europe was a modern version of the Versailles Treaty a quarter of a century before. Fortunately, Stalin disrupted that plan and inadvertently caused the democratization of Germany. By 1947, it was clear that the Soviet Union had abandoned all pretenses of friendship with its wartime allies.

Europe was struggling economically. Realizing the territorial ambitions and ideological threat emanating from the USSR, a perpetually weakened Europe could be a geostrategic calamity. In January 1947, Harry Truman appointed George Marshall as secretary of state. Led by William Clayton and George Kennan, the State Department had been developing a European Recovery Plan. In June at a Harvard

University address, General Marshall announced the plan that would bear his name.

The act's long title was "(T)o promote world peace and the general welfare, national interest and foreign policy of the United States through economic, financial and other measures necessary to the maintenance of conditions abroad in which free institutions can survive and consistent with the maintenance of the strength and stability of the United States."

The noble aims were to rebuild and modernize the damaged states, remove trade barriers and improve prosperity, prevent the spread of communism, reduce interstate barriers and regulations, and increase productivity through modern business practices. Initially, $5 billion was appropriated and applied to sixteen states (about $200 billion in 2020 dollars), followed by another $17 billion in grants and loans ($700 billion today, the size of the TARP). General Lucius Clay, once the youngest brigadier general in the US Army, served as Military Governor in the US-occupied zone of Germany from 1947 to 1949 to administer the plan.

In Japan, MacArthur brilliantly organized the transition of that country with a textbook case of how to create a viable democracy. MacArthur had read voraciously about Japan and its culture, politics, and history. He included on his staff several experts on Japan. This is a vivid instance of how knowledge and understanding contributed to a successful outcome. But the fact was that in Germany and Japan, the United States had two accomplished and highly competent officers in charge of the postwar rehabilitation.

Two conclusions are clear. The first is that Stalin's disruption and occupation of east European states inadvertently led to establishments of a democratic and economically viable Western Europe. He deserves no credit for that.

Second, knowledge and understanding count even if the United States did not get it right the first time in its post-war thinking about

Germany and it certainly would not more than half a century later in Afghanistan and Iraq.

1989

On January 20, 1989, George H. W. Bush became America's forty-first president. Earlier that month, Prince Akihito acceded to the Japanese throne following the death of his father, Emperor Hirohito. On February 15, General Boris Gromov was the last Soviet soldier to leave Afghanistan as the Fortieth Soviet Army crossed the Friendship Bridge. In March, "cold fusion" was announced as a possibility, and the *Exxon Valdez* went aground off the Alaskan coast, hemorrhaging millions of barrels of oil and creating a monumental environmental catastrophe.

In April, protests broke out in Tbilisi, Georgia, that would spread to Eastern Europe. Ali Khamenei became Iran's Supreme Leader following the death of Ayatollah Khomeini. The riots and protests in Tiananmen Square would turn into a massacre that was a huge setback for China's relations with the West. Two months later, the communist government collapsed in Hungary. Jiang Zemin replaced Zhao Ziyang as China's general secretary.

In July, Cornell student Robert Morris was the first person indicted over violating the 1986 Computer Fraud and Abuse Act for inserting worms into computers. Nolan Ryan became the first pitcher to strike out five thousand batters. On November 9, one of the greatest disruptions of the Cold War sent shock waves around the world: East Germany opened all its Berlin checkpoints. The infamous wall would come down the next day, signaling the beginning of the end of the Cold War. The Velvet Revolution took hold in Czechoslovakia.

In December, Presidents Bush and Gorbachev met on the Soviet cruise ship *Maksim Gorkiy* off Malta. The US invaded Panama to oust Manuel Noriega. Just prior to Christmas, Romanian strongman Nicolae Ceausescu was overthrown and with his wife later killed.

The massive and tectonic disruptions of the Berlin Wall coming down, the Soviet Union about to collapse, and the 1991 Iraq War created an unprecedented opportunity for what George Bush claimed was a "new world order." His focus was on Europe first to aid the democratization of the former Warsaw Pact states and assist in the stable and peaceful deconstruction of the Soviet Union with the emergence of Russia and other newly independent states that would form the new federation.

Bush had the perfect team and the perfect résumé: eight years as vice president, the first ambassador to China, director of the CIA, member of the House of Representatives, and US Navy World War II torpedo bomber pilot. All had served in the Reagan administration in senior capacities except Brent Scowcroft, who was President Gerald Ford's national security advisor. Scowcroft's PhD dissertation was written on the Balkans, and he had taught international politics at West Point and the Air Force Academy.

Bush called for a Europe "whole, free, and at peace." Russia was crucial to that agenda. It was financially and politically weak and even unstable. Gorbachev was highly unpopular as the massive disruptions of glasnost and perestroika had the unintended consequence of imploding the USSR. And the effects of 1989, of course, continued to play out over the next few years.

In 1991, Boris Yeltsin was elected president of the Russian Soviet Federative Socialist Republic. In December, he presided over the formal dissolution of the Soviet Union and the formation of the independent Russian Federation. The old Soviet Union covered about 8.6 million square miles with a population of about 290 million. Today, Russia occupies 6.6 million square miles with about half the population of the Soviet Union—147 million—that is shrinking and with much shorter life expectancies than throughout the rest of Europe.

The first decade of the Russian Federation could hardly have been more disruptive. Yeltsin shifted the centrally controlled socialist economy to a market economy through a mix of shock therapy, exchange rate control of the ruble, widespread privatization, and ending price controls. The disruption and corruption were massive.

Economic collapse and inflation ensued. A small number of oligarchs gained control of most of Russia's heavy production and energy industries. Only through loans from America did the economy survive, a shrewd and important lifesaving contribution of the Bush administration.

In 1993, Yeltsin provoked a constitutional crisis by illegally dissolving the Supreme Soviet parliament that in turn attempted to remove him. In October, troops loyal to him stopped an armed uprising outside the parliament building, known as the White House, which in turn was fired on. Yeltsin survived.

Russian secession movements provoked two Chechen wars and the War of Dagestan between 1994 and 1999 that proved costly and bloody. On New Year's Day 2000, Yeltsin chose Vladimir Putin to replace him. It is little wonder that Putin regarded the end of the Soviet Union as the greatest strategic catastrophe of the twentieth century, as that dissolution was a direct threat to the future of Russia as a coherent state.

Meanwhile, the Bush administration continued to manage the transition of former Soviet bloc states to democracies. But the administration only had a short time remaining in office. In November 1992, Bush lost the election to Bill Clinton.

The "what ifs" of history are unknowable. Had Bush won, would the trajectory of Russia be any different? How far might have the expansion of NATO gone? Would Russia have been brought in more closely with the West even given the NATO-Russia Council and the Founding Act of 1997?

While no answers are possible beyond speculation, it is reasonable to assume that the more experienced Bush team may not have made the same mistakes as the Clinton administration. Perhaps that is wishful thinking. But the major conclusions from examining 1918, 1945, and 1989 are relevant to today.

WHAT HAVE WE LEARNED (OR NOT) FROM THIS HISTORY?

In 1918, circumstances made it impossible for the Paris Peace Conference to establish a lasting peace. That it took two decades and not less for a second world war to break out may have been the only positive achievement of the conference. There were no others. And as much as it would prove a valuable lesson for future transitions, 1945 was not fully exploited to seize the opportunity for establishing a durable peace and lasting security.

The vision that established the UN and Bretton Woods Conference was highly commendable and important. A political, economic, and financial framework was provided for the international system that still remains in place. That alone was a significant achievement. But had it not been for Stalin, Germany might still be divided and a largely agrarian state. Only after these disruptions that began at the war's end with the annexation or absorption of Russia's neighbors into its orbit did the West rally to counter the Soviet Union.

Japan was different. MacArthur's skill, knowledge of Japan, preparation for the occupation, and patience were instrumental in what would be the extraordinary success of Japan becoming a full-fledged democracy. The lesson reinforces the message that knowledge and understanding count.

About 1914, 1939, and 2001, the analogies are more troubling. Great-power rivalries were one of the major causes of World War I, and a naval arms race exacerbated that competition. Those causes combined, with the failure of 1918 and of Britain and France in 1939 in not taking more forceful stands against Hitler, are eerily suggestive of today.

The global great-power competition with China and Russia has no apparent off-ramp. How far will this competition proceed politically, economically, militarily, and ideologically? Past failures as well as the lack of more complete knowledge and understanding of others are potent reminders of how events can unravel.

While the Fifth Horseman did not exist then, the new MAD further complicates these conundrums. The most instructive observation from 1945, at least at first, was that the US got it half right. But the half wrong could have had consequences not dissimilar to 1918 if the Morgenthau Plan had not been overridden.

In 1989, the Bush team was on the correct track. Clinton may not have derailed that progress, but NATO's expansion created a series of disruptions with Russia that were unhelpful and ultimately dangerous. George W. Bush would sadly assure a derailment with his policies that alienated Russia, ranging from pursuing missile defense, the Iraqi invasion, and the promise to admit Georgia and Ukraine to NATO. Had none of those events occurred, would relations with Russia be any better today? That too is unanswerable. Similarly, Bush did not put unnecessary stress on China. Nor did Obama.

The Obama administration made the 1914, 1939, and 2001 parallels more relevant. The ill-advised strategic "pivot" to Asia, even when repackaged into the less controversial phrase of "rebalancing," alarmed most of the regional states while provoking China. The continuation of Aegis Ashore missile defense in Europe likewise damaged relations with Russia's leaders, who regarded this system as a threat to its shorter-range ballistic missiles.

Under former President Trump, no opportunity as presented in 1918, 1945, and 1989 to construct a more stable world order appeared, with one exception. If the mutual recognition of Israel by the United

Arab Emirates, Bahrain, Morocco, and Sudan and the Abraham Accords could have been expanded to other Arab states, especially Saudi Arabia, that would have been a remarkable and highly positive disruptive achievement. However, the short Israeli-Hamas war in May 2021 probably has neutralized that prospect. No matter, China and Russia remain larger issues.

Handling of the coronavirus and COVID-19 was certain proof that the most disruptive of presidents was incapable of coping with disruptions, whether of his making or of acts of nature and other external forces. The combination of the pandemic, extreme partisanship, and polarization made the 2020 election a spectacle, fundamentally assaulting and challenging the constitutional process for choosing a president and for which no rulebook or guidelines existed.

In 2001, the nation was unprepared, not properly organized, and completely surprised by September 11. In 2020, aside from a handful of Asian states, despite years of studying and war-gaming potential pandemic scenarios, the United States was not alone in being totally unprepared for the arrival of the coronavirus. What has been learned? So far, the answer is very little.

Most importantly, the arrival of the corona pandemic should have been a final warning of the arrival of the Fifth Horseman and a new version of the old Cold War MAD: Massive Attacks of Disruption. Disruption—whether from environmental catastrophes caused by climate change, cyber and social media attacks against persons and governments, terrorism worse than September 11, debt that could break the collective bank, or failed and failing government that cannot fill the public's needs.

As the nation was unready for September 11 and the pandemic, it is still largely unprepared for the next wave of MAD scenarios that will strike unexpectedly and at times not of our choosing because of indifference, ignorance, or refusal to learn from the past.

Second, great-power rivalries over a century ago bore responsibility for World War I. Ignoring or dismissing history would be derelict. The obvious conclusion is that the nation must deeply reexamine a strategy based on a closely related cousin of great-power rivalry, namely a global power competition with peers or near peers. Left unchecked, a naval arms race between the US and China as China's naval power grows and America plans to build at least 355 ships could become a twenty-first century version of Great Britain and Germany's competition to outpace the other in building super-dreadnoughts.

To ensure 2021 or 2022 and beyond is not 1914, 1939, or 2001, the Biden administration must challenge and test both the assumptions on which national security strategy rests, emphasizing the arrival of a new MAD—Massive Acts of Disruption—and the failures of the current organization of government to prepare, make ready, and anticipate the next crisis whenever and wherever it strikes—which it will. Well into 2021, the Biden team has not done that. While the pandemic persists, relations with China and Russia are certainly not improving. The Biden administration has embraced the importance of maintaining the liberal, rules-based international order and has declared that this is a competition (or conflict) between it and the autocratic examples of Russia and China. In other words, as in the Cold War, is the Biden administration expanding the great power competition into the ideological sector?

If so, then the comparisons of 1918, 1945, and 1989 will not apply with a very worrisome prospect: 1914 or 1939 may prove frighteningly more relevant to the future of the great-power competition.

Chapter Eight

RESTORING AMERICA I:
A NATIONAL RENAISSANCE

Political termites are eating away the foundations of democracy.

America, as it entered 2021, was not in good condition, endangered, infected, and engulfed by MAD and COVID-19. The election and inauguration of Joe Biden as America's forty-sixth president ended the tenure of the nation's most disruptive and controversial chief executive in its history who still contests the results. However, three COVID-19 vaccines were approved for use. The Dow Jones broke the thirty thousand mark for the first time just before Thanksgiving 2020.

Yet COVID-19 was far from contained and defeated. At the end of 2020, about eight times as many Americans were dying of COVID on a weekly basis than were killed each week in World War II. Compared with the Vietnam War, about eighty times more Americans succumbed to COVID each week than died in Vietnam.

For most Americans, the economy was fragile. Thirty-million Americans, or nearly 10 percent of the total population, suffered from food shortages. Many more were at financial risk as COVID slashed jobs, created shortages in food and supply chains, and pushed hospitals and healthcare facilities to breaking points. Initial optimism over a relatively quick end to the pandemic was dispelled by exploding infections, followed by lengthy delays in production, distribution, and uncertainties over the timing of vaccinations.

Relations with China and Russia were hostile as the great-power competition continued unabated. If history matters, lest we forget, in 1914, great-power rivalry was one of the major causes of World War I. Is this where the United States was still headed?

American influence and standing abroad were in tatters. And worse, Democrats and Republicans were increasingly divided in what was a 51–49 percent nation on virtually every issue from wearing masks to climate change. On that basis, can a political system based on checks and balances function at all as well as respond to MAD?

A political MRI would detect two dangerous symptoms threatening American society that differentiate today from the past. First, public trust in government has probably never been lower since the depths of the Vietnam War. The reasons were repeated failures of government to meet public needs and expectations further magnified by the hypocrisy, deceit, and misinformation common to both parties, and the absence of truth too often emanating from the Trump White House during its four years in office.

Governments inevitably lie or are deceitful. Woodrow Wilson ignored the existence of the Spanish flu. JFK and Lyndon Johnson lied about the Vietnam War, Nixon about Watergate, and Clinton over an affair with a White House intern. But Trump was the declared champion when it came to lying. That produced a chilling, if not frightening, effect.

Many Republicans dismissed or ignored these lies and distortions as part of the former president's oversized personality, supporting his policies nonetheless despite the absence of truth and fact. Indeed, a majority of Republicans still believed the former president's "big lie" of a stolen election. Some supporters even accepted his declaration that he would be re-instituted as president in August 2021.

Yet, can any society or government survive this persistent assault on truth and fact and acceptance of hypocrisy as the cost of doing business without paying a greater price? History is littered with unhappy examples. On the current course, the US could be one of them.

The second symptom of danger is a corollary of the first: the complete absence of trust between the Republican and Democratic parties and members of Congress. That has led to extraordinary levels of hostility and animosity and eliminated civility and compromise across the nation. The 2020 presidential election was filled with enough hypocrisy and falsehoods to last for decades.

The death of Associate Supreme Court Justice Ruth Bader Ginsburg and the urgency to confirm her successor before the election, while constitutional, intensified the dominance of the pursuit of power in that winning was everything rather than abiding by principle, tradition or ethical values.

Without regard to truth and trust, American democracy is in peril, arguably more so than any time since the Civil War. Divided government cannot work in a 51 percent nation unless there is a unifying danger or compromise and civility to bridge these divides and respond to MAD.

Rarely have these conditions been as stark and solutions seemingly out of reach as long as the nation remains so divided and polarized. Perhaps the Biden administration will begin closing these dangerous and destructive divisions as the president has frequently promised. That prospect, however, is bleak and probably unachievable.

On the other more optimistic side of the ledger, what follows is a three-track solution for creating economic, national security, and foreign policy strategies that meld these dire political circumstances with the vital priority of responding to MAD even as the pandemic is being contained.

Whether or not America and Americans will muster the political courage, will, and strength to reverse the failures of government and the perils of an intractably divided nation is the question that will be answered in the coming months and years.

Or will the world of 2029 as described by President Bennett come to pass?

A central thesis of this book is that the combination of globalization and the diffusion of power has brought about the demise of the old Westphalian order. In its place, a Fifth Horseman of the Apocalypse, armed with the MAD of Massive Attacks of Disruption, has arisen to challenge, threaten, and profoundly alter the status quo. This inflection point, so far, has been largely unrecognized by countries and publics. And these disruptions will prove more formidable than any time in the nation's history.

Not recognizing this new MAD has led to a further failure to understand the consequences of the new disruptors that have become the major dangers and challenges compounding, and in some cases, superseding, traditional threats posed by rival states. The coronavirus/COVID-19 was irrevocable proof of the arrival of the new MAD.

The purposes of the last three chapters are to propose recommendations and actions, domestically, internationally, organizationally, and operationally, for a twenty-first century MAD-driven world using a three-pronged approach. To empower this recovery, an investment fund (called the 1923 Fund after the greatest economic boom in American history) is proposed and later described at length.

Obviously, the Biden administration has already put forward its economic proposals. The 1923 Fund is an alternative should those proposals fail or falter.

First, to deal with MAD, organizational reform of government and its institutions accompanied by creating the 1923 Fund (or passing the relevant infrastructure programs in the pending legislation) is critical. The combination, when or if properly implemented, could generate a national renaissance to restore and rejuvenate a society and economy well positioned and able to compete and flourish in the twenty-first century. But this requires powerful leadership and bipartisan understanding that without profound change, a nation so divided remains at grave risk.

Second, new National Security and Defense Strategies must be adopted.

Third, smart foreign policies to contain, mitigate, and prevent the ravages of MAD and to deal with traditional threats posed by state and nonstate actors must be put in place.

To these ends, a Brains-Based Approach to Strategic Thinking is offered as a guide. The full version appears in the appendix. In summary, this approach has three components:

1. First, a Brains-Based Approach must be sufficiently knowledgeable to allow and facilitate complete understanding of all aspects of strategy, from basic aims to intimate analysis of the adversary; various courses of actions and assumptions underlying each and the consequences, including the resource implications; and objective calculations of costs in blood and treasure.
2. Second, this approach must have a twenty-first century mindset based on understanding of the end of the Westphalian system of state-centric politics and the arrival of the Fifth Horseman and MAD.

3. Third, the aim of strategy and policy must be to affect, influence, and control the will and perception of the other side through the power of the intellect, employing innovation, ingenuity, and inventiveness, often called "out of the box" thinking.

Fundamental organizational changes to government will be required. A whole of government approach is invariably offered as the school solution for coordinating policy. In practice, given the extent of how government is divided organizationally and politically, that solution is aspirational. What is needed is discipline inside government to mandate, coordinate, oversee, and translate policy and strategy into effective action.

That leads to two choices: establishing a cabinet form of government or delegating a specific White House office and senior principal such as the vice president the authority to impose accountability across government to ensure those mandates are properly executed across the administration and coordinated with Congress.

What is needed in turn is a national security policy and strategy that embraces relevant civil and governmental sectors along with an organization to assure assiduous, effective, and efficient implementation. This chapter derives an analytic framework for establishing priorities and timetables to deal with MAD, focuses on the seven major disruptors, and proposes the means for achieving them.

NEEDED: AN ANALYTIC FRAMEWORK

In analyzing any issue of magnitude and particularly MAD, the wisdom of Dwight Eisenhower and Albert Einstein is highly relevant. Ike's solution to solve tough problems was to expand them to understand the "big picture." Einstein counseled that solutions to difficult problems must be made as simple as possible but "no simpler," assuming that any simplistic and easy solution would be neat, clever, and wrong.

In this effort of dealing with MAD, several analytical pieces are missing. No topology exists for ranking and prioritizing threats posed by MAD and other dangers. When every threat is a priority, there are no priorities. Triage is necessary. Hence, a typology to conduct that triage is crucial.

A conceptual and intellectual policy framework is essential. The Brains-Based Approach is used in which the thrust of policy must be to affect, influence, and control will and perception of the public, allies, friends, adversaries, and others. In other words, understanding which audiences are to be affected and how that can be done is crucial. This is particularly true for the National Security Strategy and National Defense Strategy and foreign policy.

Third, a hierarchy of MAD threats begins with those that are existential to society, those that are potentially massively destructive and disruptive but not existential to society at large, and those of a lower priority that can be deferred with minimal risk.

Only three threats populate the existential category of MAD: thermonuclear war; catastrophic climate change producing the equivalent of an ice age, and exogenous dangers to include the highly improbable case of huge meteors or small planets hitting Earth or the sun exploding into a supernova. Thermonuclear war has been and is clearly avoidable and preventable. The second will depend upon how seriously the threat of climate change is taken. And probability may preclude the last.

For the second category of MAD, the disruptors can be contained, mitigated, and prevented if and only if the dangers are recognized in advance and acted upon with requisite knowledge in a timely fashion with an effective strategy given sufficient resources.

While it can be argued that a future pandemic could be an existential threat to society, throughout human history, even during the Black Death of the Middle Ages, fortunately, that never occurred. If the coronavirus/COVID-19 pandemic replicates the Spanish flu in morbidity that killed about fifty million, that number would equate to about half a billion deaths from a global population of about eight billion—tragic but not existential.

The third category are disruptions that, while possibly significant, are of a lower priority and thus can be pursued on a less urgent basis. For each category, a timetable must be defined in which to implement corrective action. Failed and failing government, climate change, and debt cannot be fixed immediately. Corrective actions will take, in these cases, possibly a decade or more. That the time horizon is long is no reason to defer action, as delay will likely accelerate the arrival of a disaster, particularly from climate change.

On the other hand, actions regarding the coronavirus pandemic can be mandated immediately. The wearing of masks and social distancing to contain the virus are simple, obvious, and effective actions. The Biden administration made this a top priority.

Given this threat hierarchy, climate change, failed and failing government, and the coronavirus/COVID-19 pandemic are the most immediate dangers posed by MAD. These are followed by cyber, social media, exploding debt, drones, and terrorism that again has returned to its traditional domestic roots with the rise of homegrown and violent extremists largely of the right resembling neo-fascist movements. And, of course, China, Russia, and regional challenges cannot be ignored and must be integrated in the response.

The 1923 Fund would have been the engine empowering a national economic renaissance and providing the resources for corralling MAD and for underwriting the new National Security and Defense Strategies.

Chapter 9 proposes new National Security and Defense Strategies and the concept of a Porcupine and Mobile Maritime Defense. Chapter 10 concludes with specific foreign policies and strategies for MAD, Russia, China, and other competitors. In each case, the Brains-Based Approach is applied to determine how, what, and whose will and perceptions are of primary importance to strategy and policy.

Regarding MAD and the seven disruptors, annual war games must be played to determine how mitigating and preventive actions are progressing and to assess the respective priorities in order to make appropriate policy and resource changes. This effort must center in the White House with possibly a second Deputy National Security Advisor whose responsibility is to ensure requisite action is being taken by each department or agency. And if actions are not being taken with sufficient urgency, to rectify those shortcomings.

The dilemma, in parallel to the quandary of spending huge resources for defense capabilities and systems that may not be used in anger, is providing funds for MAD and other contingencies that may never arise. However, if these crises and disruptions arise and are unanticipated, each could prove orders of magnitude more costly than early preventive actions.

WHAT ELSE MUST BE RESTORED?

In blunt terms, in a MAD-driven world, America's strategies to assure and safeguard its security and prosperity at home and abroad with and for friends and allies are, like much of government, failing. The proof: Do Americans feel safer and more secure than five or ten years ago? Most polls say they do not.

Some of these past strategies possessed critical flaws. Some were missing, such as a national strategy to contain, mitigate, and prevent coronavirus/COVID-19; a strategy for governing; and a strategy for climate change and other disruptors. Whether the current concepts, strategies, and policies are incomplete, obsolete, incoherent, or simply wrong, major revisions are essential if the disruptors are to be contained and if their unintended consequences, including conflict, are to be avoided or mitigated. The same approach applies to the challenges posed by China and Russia.

This requires a first principles level of analysis: determine what is wrong and then correct it. Unfortunately, while identifying problems is relatively easy, the difficulty has always been taking effective corrective action.

Inside America, partisanship has rarely been more bitter. Gaps between the rich and all others continue to widen. Left and right extremists are turning to violence. The debt is exploding, in part—an understandable economic and financial response to the pandemic—to provide money to millions who have lost jobs and incomes.

Past policies to grow the economy out of the fiscal debt debacle by cutting taxes and regulations and figuratively printing more money failed. Biden's plans to spend America's way to economic prosperity will create literally tons of debt by printing tens of trillions of dollars, very likely bringing inflation and a rise in interest rates that will be financially crippling.

As will be shown, the current organization of the American government reflects an earlier era, unsuited for the twenty-first century MAD- and information-driven world operating at the speed of light. Revising or amending the Constitution, as Jefferson urged should be done every generation, is virtually impossible in normal times. In a gridlocked political environment, it cannot be done. Past attempts at reducing, merging, and reorganizing government inevitably have led to larger and not smaller bureaucracies.

Whether publics and politicians will accept these warnings about MAD and the need for comprehensive action, along with the threat to the political system and Constitution, may be among the most critical issues facing this nation over the near and long term. While other remaining disruptors are serious, any one of them could metastasize and in turn become a grave threat to the nation, made more so by the inability of government to confront them either beforehand or after damage has been done.

In developing strategies and policies, three past programs are instructive: the Marshall European Recovery Program, the Manhattan Project, and the Vinson-Trammell Naval Construction Acts of 1934 and 1938.

The European Recovery Program or Marshall Plan rebuilt many economies destroyed in World War II and today is applicable to America. Second, the Manhattan Project that built the first nuclear weapons is an often overused but surely an equivalent technological example in containing the major disruptors and guiding the 1923 Fund. Last, the Vinson-Trammell Naval Construction Acts offer a vision for long-range, innovative thinking by funding of the Navy that helped win World War II years before Pearl Harbor.

THE SEVEN DISRUPTORS

FAILED AND FAILING GOVERNMENT I:
THE CONSTITUTION

In proposing any recommendations, the three fundamental conundrums of MAD must be resolved. These paradoxes are repeated:

- As societies became more advanced, they became more vulnerable and susceptible to disruption and especially to MAD.
- Bounding MAD will require more and not less international cooperation at time when powerful centrifugal political forces are headed in the opposite direction, particularly in America.

- And last is whether and how to allocate substantial resources to anticipate disruptions and crises that may never occur while assuring traditional challenges are met.

Government is not organized for resolving these paradoxes nor for dealing with current, let alone, future issues, challenges, and of course, MAD. Can failure to govern ever be "fixed" in a political process that at best suffers from gridlock and from which civility and compromise have disappeared? For the United States, perhaps a broader existential and rhetorical question is whether a political system created by the best minds of the eighteenth century can weather the massive disruptions of the twenty-first century.

Compounding these failures, it is far from clear that the "best and brightest," if such people exist anymore, are eager to serve in government. Trump was correct in that Washington has "swamp-like" qualities. Disincentives to public service range from financial to reputational damage, the lack of "psychic" rewards for accomplishments, and the lack of freedom of any independent action beyond a tightly controlled political agenda at both ends of Pennsylvania Avenue.

MAD intensifies the limitations of a government not appropriately organized for the challenges and issues of the twenty-first century. Analysis of the legislative and executive branches brings into stark perspective how unprepared, unready, and unable government was for the last pandemic and, unless action is taken now, will be for the next one. Refer back to the National Security Strategy's aspirational aims for containing a future pandemic and how that was handled. While some argue that Article III of the Constitution on the judiciary needs reform, that is beyond the scope of this book.

Regarding the dangers to the Constitution posed by MAD and raised in the 2020 election, the US government is based on a separation of powers, checks and balances provided by the three branches, and powers that are delegated to the federal government with all others reserved for the states. A Bill of Rights served as protection for citizens against government infringement. But debate still rages over whether the Constitution should be interpreted as originally written or in line with contemporary times. For example, the Seventh Amendment still allows for a jury trial for any cases involving twenty dollars or more in value. Is that relevant to the twenty-first century?

As noted, checks and balances only work when one party has veto-proof majorities and controls both ends of Pennsylvania Avenue, a crisis forces consensus, or compromise and civility bridges partisan divides. None of these criteria is in place. And COVID surely has not hastened consensus.

In the intervening centuries, this tripartite structure of the Constitution has had to accommodate political parties; lengthy and very expensive campaigns for office that have led to money and fund-raising dominating politics and influence; and substantial demographic shifts in the size and composition of American society that have been manipulated for political ends and not necessarily for promoting good governance. Purposely, the role of political parties was unmentioned in the Constitution. In fact, many drafters regarded political parties as disruptive "factions" destructive to governing.

While many Americans consider this country a democracy, in fact its Constitution established a representative republic. Originally, only the House of Representatives was directly elected and then by white, male landowners of a certain age. States appointed senators and the Electoral College chose the president. The fundamental reason for the Senate, long since forgotten or ignored, was to give states the power to balance the federal government.

Until 1913, each state, regardless of size or population, was awarded two senators it, not the public, would select. After that, political parties nominated candidates for the Senate that the public would elect. In 1789, states were more or less equal in size and influence. Why then do these changes affect the Senate?

Today, the fifty states are far from equal in size, population, GDP, and most other measures. In this case, is the Senate "democratic and fair" when two Dakotas with a total of 1.6 million residents have the same number of senators as California and Texas with nearly 70 million and one party can control the Senate (53–47 for Republicans in the 116th Congress) while representing less than a third of the total population? Of course, the House was originally meant to represent the public. The question is if this unequal representation works in the twenty-first century, especially when government is divided and partisanship has reached radioactive levels.

Clearly, both chambers of Congress are equally affected by the control of and loyalty to party. However, because the Senate originally was created to represent the respective state and not the party, how damaging is this contradiction or ambivalence between loyalty to the state or to the party? The House is not similarly affected, as it was never intended to represent the state but to represent its individual citizens.

Since the last decades of the twentieth century, this ambivalence in the Senate has been largely replaced by greater loyalty to the party (and to the last president by Republicans). Hence, the role of the Senate under the Constitution has been challenged as members in many cases owe greater loyalty to the party (or a president) than to the state. What can be done, if anything, about this divided loyalty?

Under these circumstances of divided government and a divided nation, as long as the filibuster remains in the Senate, gridlock is ensured. Is it time to reconsider the need for a supermajority to bring legislation to the floor? Or will gridlock remain the default option?

A partial answer to this question is whether the GOP (Grand Old Party) will remain the TOP (Trump's Own Party) now that Trump has left office. Regardless, in a 51 percent nation, both parties have lurched much further to the left and right of center, exacerbating the public divides representing the views of a minority of citizens, as about two-thirds sit in the left or right of center category. This has led to even greater hypocrisy infecting politics, making citizens understandably more cynical about government.

Money is a large cause of this constitutional crisis. Members of both chambers of Congress are consumed by fundraising both for themselves and for their party. In too many cases, fundraising prowess is a quid pro quo for plum committee and subcommittee assignments, producing a vicious circle. Members want seats on committees to serve constituent needs. That in turn leads to constituents understandably sending money to representatives both for reelection and committee assignments.

Money now overly distorts and can corrupt the political system. With the Supreme Court ruling that money is tantamount to "free speech," to bypass limits on individual contributions, political action committees (PACs) have become essential to the election cycle. No limits are placed on PACs in campaign and issue funding.

As presidential authority has expanded with increasing congressional gridlock, elections are gamed to exploit the weaknesses, gaps, and ambiguities in the Constitution. While the Electoral College was designed to ensure states and not the popular vote would select a president and thus assure the balance between delegated and reserved powers, in 2000 and 2016, winners lost the popular vote—in the second case by three million votes.

In 2020, Trump lost by about seven million popular votes and 306–232 electoral votes. Nonetheless, he contested the election with five dozen lawsuits, all of which were rejected even by judges he appointed. Fortunately for the nation, although not for Trump supporters, the former president had no apparent strategy other than asserting he won and allowing a world-class team of incompetent as well as incoherent attorneys to represent him.

The only real strategy Trump had, and it was a long and impossible shot, was to bypass the Electoral College and take the election to the House of Representatives. There, states have only one vote decided by each delegation. In 2020, Republicans controlled twenty-six delegations and under the Twelfth Amendment would have reelected the president.

But claiming fraud, asserting that a dead Venezuelan dictator used dark money to help Democrats, China printed phony ballots, and other truly bizarre conspiracy theories literally were laughed out of court. The frightening conclusion, however, was that an obstinate and self-consumed president could shake the foundations of the electoral process while it was absolutely clear he had lost the election.

The January 6, 2021 riot led to the second Trump impeachment that raised critical constitutional issues. A Senate trial would have been held after Trump left office. Conviction would have led to removal from office. But the ex-president was out of office as of noon on January 20. Hence, while impeachment was a permanent stain on the ex-president, in reality conviction would have had little meaning. Yet how would any president be held accountability for misdeeds and even high crimes and misdemeanors?

What was so tragic and dangerous about the occupation of the Capitol was that millions of Americans believed Trump's outright falsehoods about the election being stolen; that he won a landslide victory; and that Vice President Mike Pence had the authority to reverse the Electoral College votes that were being confirmed by Congress on January 6. Some tens of thousands gathered on the Mall to protest and some eight hundred ransacked the Capitol. More shameful in the aftermath was the refusal of most Republicans in Congress to break with the ex-president.

Many Republicans were fearful of provoking his wrath and the threat of his backing a primary challenger to their seat and hence would not accept the reality of Trump's role in inciting the mob as well as promoting the "big lie" that he won the election—another alarming signal as to why the Constitution is in trouble. Only ten House Republicans voted to impeach and seven in the Senate to convict.

After crises and since America's earliest days, national commissions have been widely used to establish cause and responsibility, derive lessons learned, and provide corrective recommendations. Commissions have been convened to address alcohol (and the misguided decision to impose prohibition), crime, drugs, missile defense, poverty, race, education, and terrorism among others. Throughout history, a common denominator emerged: almost all were downplayed or ignored. The 9/11 Commission and the Cyberspace Solarium Commission were formidable efforts.

Of the 9/11 Commission's thirty-nine recommendations, many were not followed. Few were aware of the Solarium Commission's report and fewer read it. One more commission is needed, however, to revise the Constitution if government is to be fit for purpose in the twenty-first century. Rejection by Senate Republicans of the proposed January 6 Commission was not a good sign either for other efforts. And this will prove potentially disastrous for Republicans not wanting to re-legislate Trump's role in inciting the insurrection. The reason is that the House will create a select committee on an entirely partisan basis that will do its best to discredit and taint the Trump administration and Republicans that cannot benefit the nation much as the Benghazi hearings attempted to do the same to the Obama administration and its Secretary of State Hillary Clinton.

The basic questions are whether the current constitutional system can work in the future and how far reform can go if the first answer is no. Moving towards a parliamentary system will not happen. Thus, how might federalism and checks and balances be reformed?

To ensure organizational and institutional reforms take priority, should a Constitutional Commission be formed, the agenda must be narrowly focused on presidential succession. That means revising the Twelfth Amendment and removing the ambiguities from the Electoral

Count Act of 1887 and the Presidential Succession Act of 1947. The proposed constitutional amendments should direct that votes of each state in the Electoral College are divided proportionally between the candidates to reflect the popular vote.

This revision would force Republican presidential candidates to campaign in Democratic states such as population-heavy New York and California, where it is normally a waste of valuable time, and Democrats in Republican states in the South, Midwest, and West. This would allow more citizens to see those individuals in person and not on television or online.

That change would extend to the Twelfth Amendment so that if the presidential election were to go to the House, all members and not just states will vote to ensure majority rule. The Presidential Succession Act should be part of the Constitution as well. Other changes in the law would also be important, beginning with campaign financing to ensure that the Constitution will be suited for the twenty-first century. The idea of legislating congressional representation on the National Security Council (NSC) and establishing an NSC-like joint committee for Congress also should follow.

Finally, one option to break gridlock could be nonbinding national referenda. Many American states as well as foreign countries use this method to arrive at decisions when or if the government cannot. Brexit is an example, although a sobering one. If constitutional reform is impossible, the alternative can be national referenda.

FAILED AND FAILING GOVERNMENT II: THE LEGISLATURE

Article I of the Constitution is titled "The Legislature." The Founding Fathers believed Congress was the first among equals of the three branches. It would pass legislation that the executive branch would carry out. To check and balance presidential authority as commander-in-chief, only Congress can "provide for the common defense," appropriate money, declare war, raise and support an army, maintain and provide for a navy, confirm appointees, and approve treaties.

The president, of course, claimed authority over foreign policy with checks noted above. For well-understood reasons and the specter of a nuclear conflict that would not necessarily allow Congress time to declare war, presidents assumed greater authority as commander-in-chief. This authority extended to using force as well, although after the Vietnam War, the War Powers Act was passed over presidential veto in 1973 that applied several constraints. As Congress became increasingly dysfunctional and gridlocked over the past decades, presidents further expanded authority through executive orders and actions stretching the limits of their power. Ex-President Trump took this expansion of power further than any of his predecessors.

As the first article of the Constitution, Congress is the starting place for repairing a broken government. All members of both chambers of Congress swear or affirm allegiance to the Constitution and not a political party or other organization. But divided loyalty to party or to constituents and indeed to the nation remains an open question. In 2021, most members of both parties seem more loyal to their side and confrontational to the other.

Abraham Lincoln was correct: "A house divided against itself cannot stand." Lincoln's wisdom must also raise a warning about a 51 percent nation. MAD is widening these divides.

Congress, as with all of government, has grown overly bureaucratized and gridlocked. Failure to pass a budget on time and a second COVID relief act in 2020 or demand a COVID strategy are only a few examples of gridlock and failing government. With few exceptions, Congress has lost any measure of agility other than when political expediency drives action. The Senate's mad rush to confirm Judge Barrett to the high court prior to the election is a sad example.

In a MAD-driven information age operating at the speed of light, speed is often essential in decision-making. Congress is simply not organized to respond to MAD or in other crises when partisan interests are not driving factors. One reason: a plethora of congressional committees and subcommittees guarantees redundant and overlapping jurisdictional oversight.

Requiring executive agencies and departments to report to dozens of committees and subcommittees in Congress is extremely inefficient, time consuming, and counterproductive. As supporting professional staffs have grown younger and less experienced and fewer employees are staying for the longer term, Congress is losing vital expertise. And gerrymandering of districts ensures a near permanence of party control that does not always represent the demographics of the nation.

Trimming committees and subcommittees would make Congress more agile. The current budgetary process is redundant. A budget authorization and appropriation process run more or less concurrently. One result is that budgets are rarely approved before a new fiscal year begins, and continuing resolutions that allow temporary funding at prior years' levels guarantee inefficiencies and waste, as no department can plan accordingly or in advance without any fiscal certainty.

One fix is to merge this three-part process, giving the authorization committees principal responsibility for oversight, the budget committee for setting spending limits, and appropriations for approving expenditures.

To coordinate and align both chambers of Congress with the other and with the executive branch, a new joint committee should be established called the National Security and Governance Committee. It should be cochaired by the president of the Senate, who is the vice president, and the Speaker of the House and include the majority and minority leaders of the House, the majority and minority leaders of the Senate, and no more than three of the most respected and experienced members from both chambers—six in number—for a total of twelve. This joint committee should also have a de facto seat on the National Security Council, represented by one member from each party in addition to the vice president.

One vitally needed organizational change applies to the Armed Services Committees of both chambers of Congress. Both are still organized around twentieth-century divisions across sea, air, and land forces that are no longer relevant to the twenty-first century. This is a proposed reorganization that will permit more effective and efficient oversight and as a result encourage a Pentagon reorganization as well. Congressional subcommittees should become:

- *Strategy, threats, and budgets*: Oversight to ensure strategy, threats, and budgets are integrated and in alignment where to set priorities given tradeoffs. This may conform with the budget/authorization/appropriation process, with the strategy subcommittee performing the rule of the budget committee to look at the top lines and ensure that the right priorities have been set, funded, and followed by the Department of Defense.
- *Strategic forces, intelligence, space, and cyber*: In the twenty-first century information age, it is impossible to see how these can be separated operationally and in terms of budgetary oversight. While overlap with the Intelligence Committee may exist, the Armed Services Committees would focus on the military and defense consequences.
- *Office of the Secretary of Defense, Joint Chiefs of Staff, services, and defense agencies*: Direct oversight of OSD, services, and defense agencies fits, although the JCS could fit in the next category as well.
- *Combatant commands and the JCS/Joint Staff*: Oversight of operational commands, something that has not been done and I believe is critical to conform with Title X responsibilities of

"conducting prompt, sustained operations incident" to combat. And boy will JCS resist!

- *Defense industrial base, research and development, dual-use technology, and intellectual property*: Conceivably, if gotten right, this could be the subcommittee with the greatest future impact.
- *Alliances, treaties, and arms control*: This will be an unmistakable signal that the US is no longer on an "America first" track. To deal with possible overlap with the Foreign Relations Committee, this subcommittee would focus on defense/military consequences.
- *Personnel, education, and management*: Oversight of people to ensure the department is managed; that social issues of retention, morale, adherence to good order and discipline, gender, race, diversity, and extremism are covered; the right officers and enlisted are promoted; and the Pentagon seriously addresses education.

A further major action is essential to complement these changes in organization. Before voting on a bill, members must pledge or affirm that they have read and understand the piece of legislation under consideration. For example, the 2021 Defense Authorization Bill in the House was 3,468 pages in length and 1,824 in the Senate. No one read that bill in its entirety or knew what was in it.

The uproar will be deafening. But no sensible individual signs a legal agreement or contract without carefully reading it first. Why should Congress be different, especially when the law of the land is crucial to a functioning democracy and trillions of dollars are at stake? The workaround that should not be allowed is for Congress to pass a very short bill allowing the details to be set by each committee or in separate documents not requiring a vote. That probably would be rendered unconstitutional. And if members are not prepared to invest the time to read and understand what they legislate rather than spending the bulk of their day raising funds and campaigning, perhaps members should be seeking another line of work.

In the wake of the Enron and other corporate scandals and acts of malfeasance, Congress passed the Sarbanes–Oxley Act in 2002. The act required public company CEOs to certify that all data and information provided publicly in corporate documents was accurate and correct. Perhaps an equivalent act is needed across the whole of government and especially for Congress.

Because Congress has responsibility for oversight, the 116th Congress should have demanded from the Trump administration a plan and strategy for combating coronavirus/COVID-19. The absence of a strategy was inexcusable. Republicans and Democrats in Congress have the duty to require one from the executive branch. A top priority of the Biden administration was to present a COVID relief bill to Congress the day it took office, which it did shortly thereafter.

The Senate and its relevance is a difficult and imponderable issue. That in past Congresses a majority of senators could represent a small minority of the American population seems neither democratic nor fair. Yet how to modernize the Senate would require a constitutional amendment, almost certainly politically impossible. This dilemma could prove to be a major reason why the Constitution may no longer fit the twenty-first century.

With that recognition, what can be done? Is it time to end the supermajority rule of the Senate requiring sixty votes to bring a bill to the floor? The filibuster as it is called is relatively new. The internal check and balance unique to the Senate was meant to give power to the minority to filibuster and halt legislation. But supermajority rule is not specified in the Constitution other than for approval of treaties, constitutional amendments, and convictions and removals from office.

Because, in a civil and functioning Senate, the filibuster is a check and balance and ending it permanently is extremely unlikely, the sensible option is to sunset the filibuster, say to the end of President

Biden's first term, or until the end of the first term of this Congress in January 2023 after the 2022 bi-election. That would provide the opportunity to assess the consequences of eliminating the filibuster.

The House, the chief executive, and, after *Marbury v. Madison* in 1803, the Supreme Court, are the primary agents for checks and balances, not minority rule in the Senate. And if or when both ends of Pennsylvania Avenue are controlled by a single party expressing the will of the voters, that should constitute a mandate for action with the court as the final check and balance. In conditions of divided government, checks and balance must still work.

That should not apply to confirming lifetime appointments to the Supreme Court, where the supermajority rule should be reinstated unless justices are term limited to twenty or twenty-five years or until a certain age, say seventy-five. That would ensure bipartisan support and bind the selection of jurists to the more politically accepted left and right boundaries rather than of more extreme views. However, the difficulties of gaining passage cannot be overstated.

As with slashing committees and requiring members to read and understand legislation prior to voting, this proposal will create a political firestorm. Yet, omelets cannot be made without breaking eggs.

Since imposition of campaign spending limits has never worked, would it be sensible to remove all limits on campaign financing, provided complete transparency was guaranteed and applied to PACs? The penalty for violating full disclosure would be a lifetime ban on holding or being appointed to any federal government office. Ensuring safeguards so that nefarious groups or individuals could covertly contribute without the candidate's full knowledge, putting that person at jeopardy of a lifetime ban, would be essential.

Last, Congress should become the focal point for helping to educate the public on the dangers of MAD and the Fifth Horseman. Public education has not been a principal role or responsibility of Congress. That must change. Finding constituents for this message, however, will take time. But if another tragic surprise such as the arrival of the coronavirus occurs, it may be too late.

FAILED AND FAILING GOVERNMENT III:
THE EXECUTIVE

The presidency includes the executive branch and the Executive Office of the President, fifteen cabinet positions, and the multitude of agencies and offices that report to the president or his key staff and cabinet offices. It is a massive bureaucracy that, with consultants and contractors, probably numbers over two million people. Its organization represents times past and not the rigors of the twenty-first century. Perhaps the only significant change has been in its growth.

Even during the Vietnam War, the size of the National Security Council staff was several dozen principals and a handful of supporting administration personnel. During the Obama administration, the NSC staff ballooned to over four hundred principals. It was reduced, but not substantially, in the Trump administration. Still, the size of the NSC staff is illustrative of governmental bloat.

The newest department, Homeland Security (DHS), was created in the aftermath of September 11. It combined twenty-two other agencies with responsibilities to counter terrorism and other domestic threats; protect and safeguard borders; secure cyberspace and critical infrastructure; enhance preparedness and resilience, including response to natural disasters; and preserve and uphold national prosperity and economic security. DHS employs about half a million people and many tens of thousands of contractors. The test, however, is how DHS coordinates across government where many responsibilities are shared, such as for cyber and WMD attacks.

The Office of the Director of National Intelligence (ODNI) was signed into law on December 17, 2004, by President George W. Bush in response to September 11. Its principal responsibilities are to coordinate, integrate, and provide oversight for the intelligence community. ODNI is organized into two directorates (Mission Integration and Policy and Capabilities) and three mission centers (National Counterproliferation, National Counterintelligence and Security, and National Counterterrorism Center). However, the ODNI has no control over budgets, and the bulk of intelligence funding resides in the Department of Defense for procurement of collection systems.

It is questionable that either of these new organizations has made the nation any safer or more secure or that the responsibilities of both could not be better assigned to other departments and agencies. It took the gross failure of the response to Hurricane Katrina for DHS to become better prepared for storms and destructive weather. However, DHS has not been particularly agile in reacting to the intense fires burning on the West Coast or other non-storm-related environmental catastrophes. The spate of cyber hacks is another reflection of the weaknesses and shortcomings not only of DHS but government as a whole.

In reviewing the performance and role of the fifteen cabinet departments, determining relevance and redundancy is important. Many departments are legacies of the past. Agriculture was important when a substantial portion of the population worked in the agrarian sector. Today, the total population of private farmers is statistically not relevant, as giant agribusinesses have consolidated the industry.

The Commerce Department has not moved from the industrial to the information age. The Department of Education does not reflect the importance of knowledge, understanding, distance learning, and new technologies in an information age. Nor does it have a National Chief Learning Officer to deliver this message other than the secretary who may or may choose to fill that role.

Energy does not focus sufficiently on the environment and climate change. Its name should be expanded to Energy, Environment, and Climate Change and can be the base for presidential envoy John

Kerry's efforts in climate change. Health and Human Services was ill-prepared for the pandemic. That must be corrected.

Housing and Urban Development was a creature of the 1960s and surely is antiquated. Interior should focus more resources on infrastructure. Labor would be better focused on and renamed Human Resources, assuming relevant responsibilities from other departments and consolidated in a single agency.

Justice and Homeland Security have overlapping missions for law and order and cyber. Would the Department of Veterans Affairs be better managed if it were under the Department of Defense? What are the roles of the Transportation Department as critical infrastructure encompasses that sector and related protection responsibilities reside in DHS and other departments? And is not a rejuvenated State Department vital with broader diplomatic responsibilities including more aggressive support of US businesses in international markets?

What any president could have done (and if not, should do) is task his cabinet secretaries (and *not* the transition teams so as to preempt the incoming team) with an immediate review of the functions, responsibilities, and authorities of each department to determine which are relevant, obsolete, incomplete, and need to be reinforced in a MAD-driven world to best support the president. This is perhaps the most important action to be taken to redress the current weaknesses and organizational shortfalls in the executive branch.

It comes as no surprise that overlaying the seven disruptors—climate change, cyber, social media, terrorism, drones, debt, and failed and failing government in a MAD-driven age—with the responsibilities and authorities of these departments reveals organizational disarray. Who is in charge of each disruptor? The answer is everyone and no one.

While providing detailed reorganizational changes across all of government is not the principal purpose of this book, the government is not fully prepared nor sufficiently organized for the most daunting twenty-first century challenges. Nor is it good at anticipating crisis. Terrorism and September 11 are cases in point.

As September 11 and the coronavirus caught the United States unaware and unprepared, have prior organizational and policy changes made the nation safer or more secure? The answer, given before, is no. The Trump administration, for example, denied climate change and neutered the Environmental Protection Agency (EPA). The Department of Health and Human Services was unprepared for the pandemic.

Overseas, Abu Bakr al-Baghdadi was killed and ISIS smashed, at least for the time being. But the reasons and causes for domestic terrorism and for radical groups largely arising from rage, disenfranchisement, and desperation have not been eliminated and remain real. Which department or departments are the lead agencies not merely in preventing terror attacks but in addressing the causes especially for domestic extremism?

No matter the validity of successes against terrorists claimed with some justification by the Trump administration, the coalitions, policies, and programs for waging the war on terror date back to Bill Clinton and George W. Bush. Barack Obama created the coalition that ultimately defeated the ISIS caliphate in Iraq.

Regarding cyber, the DHS, FBI, and Department of Defense have many overlapping requirements and responsibilities. How much redundancy is useful and how much is wasteful? Regarding social media, who is responsible for setting policies that preserve freedom of speech and expression while protecting the nation and individual from damaging, libelous, and scurrilous tweets and posts?

Drone policy is in its infancy; it has no rules of the road to prevent interference and especially criminal and illegal use. No one seems to mind the soaring debt, now more than one and a half times the GDP, and how the principal and interest will be paid. As for correcting failed and failing government, no champion from either party has emerged to take up this cause.

One crisis that was well handled was the 2008 financial collapse. Treasury and the Federal Reserve took the lead. But it was the steady hands of Henry Paulson and Ben Bernanke, assisted by the regional bank presidents, that produced the Troubled Asset Relief Program (TARP), righting the system and ultimately returning to the government all the loaned funds plus interest. The personalities and competence of the responsible officials, using the authority of their offices and personal stature and not the organization, prevailed and succeeded in ending the crisis.

The nation cannot guarantee that it will always be so well served. The Biden appointees, so far, reflect people of intellect, stature, competence, and experience. How well the team works is of course the issue as many of these appointees are more skilled in policy than in operations or management. And the time it takes to recruit, select, and confirm the nearly 2,000 positions to be filled has sadly taken longer and longer. The administration may not be fully manned by the time this book is published in December 2021.

The major decision-making organizations inside the White House are nominally the National Security Council for national security, foreign policy, intelligence, and defense issues and the Domestic Policy Council for domestic issues. NSC membership is determined by each president differently. Normally the NSC is composed of the president and vice president; the secretaries of state, defense, and the Treasury; the national security advisor; the homeland security advisor; and other officials as needed or as observers to include the chief of staff, the director of national intelligence, and the chairman of the Joint Chiefs. President Biden has added the UN ambassador, following earlier precedent, and his envoy for climate change, John Kerry, to the NSC.

The current Domestic Policy Council consists of the president and vice president, all cabinet officers except the secretaries of state and defense, the chairman of the Council of Economic Advisors, the assistant for economic affairs and the directors of the Office of Management and Budget, Environmental Protection Agency, and Office of National Drug Control Policy. Normally, the chief of staff sits in on both.

The key question is whether separating national security and domestic issues makes sense in an era where distinctions between the two are often diaphanous and the relationships intimate. Note that Congress is absent in this process. Also, simply by virtue of being a cabinet officer does not necessarily imply expertise or particular knowledge in that field.

The fundamental organizational dilemma is that in dealing with virtually every major issue, a fully coordinated governmental approach is vital if policies and actions are to work. How, for example, are climate change, cyber, social media, terrorism, debt, drones, and failed government addressed with this bifurcated organization? The answer is that they are not.

One conclusion is the need for modernizing the White House organization for governing in which artificial boundaries cannot work. Yet no president so far has embarked on this form of reorganization. The last time it was attempted was during the first years of the Reagan administration, and little was achieved.

Two options are feasible. Both would be best served if the role of the vice president were expanded. The first is to have true cabinet government, as is the case in the UK and other parliamentary systems. The cabinet would function as a de facto board of directors to advise, recommend, and then implement decisions made by the chairman, in this case, the president. The vice president would be the principal directed to coordinate implementation.

The second is to designate the vice president as the chief management officer and direct him or her to serve as the president's number two in executing and providing oversight to ensure implementation.

The differences in the options are between coordination and execution and the role of the cabinet. But whichever option or other design is used, the purpose must be to coordinate and discipline responses, as each of the seven disruptors is not easily confined bureaucratically to one or even several departments.

THE PANDEMIC

About coronavirus and COVID-19, this is what the president's National Security Strategy, issued in 2018, stated about pandemics:

> IMPROVE EMERGENCY RESPONSE: At home, we will strengthen our emergency response and unified coordination systems to rapidly characterize outbreaks, implement public health containment measures to limit the spread of disease, and provide surge medical care—including life-saving treatments.

At this writing, it was inexplicable that the United States, with about 4 percent of the global population, accounted for about one-quarter of confirmed cases and deaths, at one point placing it eighth from the bottom of 188 states that currently are inflicted with the disease. For the richest country in the world, these are staggering statistics and indicative of how poorly the US has fared in following its National Security Strategy and coping with this pandemic. Of course, India or Brazil may break this dreadful record.

President Biden made ending the pandemic his administration's top priority. The Trump administration argued it had a strategy: Keep the economy open in large part to reelect the president, put responsibility on the states, field a vaccine soonest, and downplay the danger in order to not panic the public and thus not necessitate lockdowns.

That was not a strategy, nor was it based on science. Even given that any administration would have been hard pressed to produce a perfect plan from the outset, Trump team failed. Trump's response was an excuse and a cynical aspiration in which the consequence was to infect more Americans with COVID and increase the number of lives lost. The lack of testing, contact tracing, and, most critically, plans for accelerating development of therapeutics and distributing vaccines remained glaring flaws.

Similarly, not having a national requirement for wearing masks just as seat belts are mandated was also inexplicable. Indeed, there was a time that to obtain a marriage license, both parties had to be tested for syphilis. And travel to some regions requires mandatory inoculations for entry. Why should the requirement to wear masks be any different?

To a large degree, the Biden administration was handicapped by what was and was not accomplished by its predecessor. The Biden administration produced a highly effective distribution plan that could have inoculated virtually all Americans by the end of 2021. However, too many Americans refused to take the vaccine. One reason was distrust of government that spilled over to vaccinations. Another was the absence of truth and fact, tarred by conspiracy theories and ignorance about COVID-19. Some even believed that being vaccinated was an infringement on the right to provide for their own health.

While it is too late for the administration to adopt this particular strategy for dealing with pandemics, it offers five guidelines for what a future contingency plan might include.

First, a national pandemic strategy must entail a universal testing program. Tests must be ubiquitous, cheap, self-administered, and quickly evaluated.

Second, a national coordination program best administered by the CDC needs to link all states in contact tracing.

Third, to prove effective, the universal wearing of masks in most public areas when people come in contact and social distancing must be mandated by law and tempered by common sense. A lone walk on a beach, for example, is far different from shopping in a supermarket or going to work in a crowded office, even with social distancing.

Fourth, guidelines for opening or restricting parts of the economy need to be sufficiently comprehensive and specific. While every region and state will differ in how each is affected by a pandemic, establishing infection rates as one criterion to determine opening and closing must be established.

Fifth, a strategy for creating, producing, distributing, and particularly administering vaccinations, as well as developing therapeutics at short notice, must be put in place before any future pandemic strikes. This includes maintaining a "hot" R&D base for vaccines and therapeutics.

The reality is that in a 51 percent nation, the pandemic was politicized. When a potentially fatal disease cannot rally near unanimity in response, the crisis facing the nation is serious and potentially fatal to millions of citizens. Politics, not science and medicine, dominated too many of the Trump pandemic responses. That was unconscionable.

The creation of a national investment fund, noted before and expanded in coming pages, would apply to the healthcare sector, creating new technologies and if done properly, contributing to explosive job growth. The goal would not only be a pandemic response. With aging populations and the possibility of further virus mutations, more healthcare professionals are needed. Healthcare can become one means for job creation. Of course, the Biden proposals address many of these needs. However, the approach will be based on increasing debt and not on public-private partnerships that, as with TARP, could be self-funding.

CLIMATE CHANGE

Fierce political debate has neutered comprehensive responses to climate change in the United States. Perhaps when coastal states and waterfront properties become permanently flooded and fires worsen, climate change will be taken more seriously. But can we wait?

The fundamental cause of climate change is man-made. As noted in Chapter 3, greenhouse gases and methane are raising global temperatures in many parts of the world. The only practical solutions must be through incentives—many monetary and others appealing to logic and the global good—and technology to move away from fossil fuels to cleaner energy. Transition from traditional energy employment in oil and natural gas to other sectors is imperative. And the geostrategic implications will be profound.

States dependent on oil and gas resources of the Persian Gulf region and Russia do not have obvious options. Within the United States, technology and money provide incentives and many options. The 1923 Fund would play a vital role for new initiatives not only in clean energy but healthcare and major revitalization of a failing twentieth-century network of highways, bridges, power transmission, and other infrastructure. Seeding technological incubators is a vital aspect of this.

Specifically regarding climate change, substantial investment of at least $2 trillion will be required both for developing cleaner and renewable power sources and for minimizing emissions from oil, coal, and gas through sequestration. Clearly, renewable energy will not power all aircraft, ships, and other forms of transportation. A substantial traditional fossil fuel energy sector will still be needed. And despite the drawbacks of spent fuel storage and memories of Chernobyl, nuclear power cannot be dismissed.

Using the Marshall Plan, the Manhattan Project, and the Vinson-Trammell Naval Construction Acts as models, the 1923 Fund can create highly innovative projects that will both hasten the transition to a twenty-first century economy and create millions of new jobs to replace others that will be lost. Money and investment cannot solve every problem. But properly focused, both can generate new revolutions. And appointment of the presidential envoy is an important first step.

For those who believe that governments can only print and not make money, the 2008–2009 Troubled Asset Relief Program (TARP) extended $800 billion in credit and convertible debt to the financial industry. Not only was that debt repaid quickly, the government made about $80 billion in interest and other returns. The same would happen with the 1923 Fund. Perhaps if the Biden proposals stall, then the 1923 Fund can be seen as an option.

CYBER AND SOCIAL MEDIA

The first requirement is to generate an overall national policy for cyber and social media. The US has not created an effective cyber strategy and has no substantive policy on social media beyond Congress debating how to regulate the four largest social platforms. Cyber policy must be directed firstly at cyber hygiene. As driving a car requires a test, a license and, for an automobile owner, insurance, anyone using or purchasing any device with Internet connectivity must pass a test or take a course on cyber hygiene.

Similarly, public companies must certify, as CEOs did vis-à-vis Sarbanes–Oxley affirming the accuracy of data, that all employees and associated IT systems are indeed meeting an acceptable standard of cyber hygiene. Ideally, that standard would be set by industry. Failing that, the government must act.

Second, all social media platforms must certify that any and all content carried meets certain levels of decency, truth, veracity, and common sense. Crying fire in a crowded theater is not free speech. But what happens if there is a fire? These platforms should issue standards as well and closely monitor content. Clearly, a fine line exists with freedom of expression. On the other hand, without any guidance, social media, like dynamite, has explosive potential and consequence.

Third, the US must embark on more offensive uses of cyber to take down dangerous websites. While the secret FISA (Foreign Intelligence Surveillance Act) Court monitors and approves surveillance warrants, a similar court should be convened for social media. A distinction between domestic and international cases exists. Domestic social media platforms can be warned or cautioned. If those warnings are disregarded, then, with court approval, some form of follow-on action can be taken.

Internationally, sites such as the Russian Internet Research Agency (IRA) in St. Petersburg, Building 3546 in Beijing, and similar locations in Pyongyang and Tehran can be targeted and shut down or disrupted. Again, this process must be closely monitored. But unless or until the United States adopts a comprehensive policy, cyber and social media will remain major disruptors that can do great damage to the US and its friends and allies. Potential disruption must be contained, mitigated, and where possible, legally and ethically prevented.

To prevent abuse, Congress should create an oversight committee, linked with FISA, to monitor these processes on a continuing basis to ensure that freedom of expression is balanced with the dangers that social media, wrongly or purposely used, produces. And internationally, perhaps the Five Eyes (US, UK, Australia, Canada, and New Zealand) plus NATO in some fashion can form the means to ensure that social media internationally is likewise kept from disrupting our joint interests.

DRONES

The Federal Aviation Administration estimates that approximately two million Americans own or operate drones. Chapter 6 explained how drones can be powerful engines of disruption for good or ill. In the summer of 2020, a drone flew close to Air Force One. Suppose that drone had carried an explosive charge or had been neutralized as a precaution? What and where are the rules of engagement?

Practically speaking, there are none. Further, drones are easily and cheaply manufactured by individuals in garages, basements, or backyards. Registration is not automatic nor practical other than on an honor system.

To take these gaps to a logical extreme, would drones armed to protect individuals be covered under the Second Amendment? Instead of hiring bodyguards, it would be less expensive to be accompanied by an armed drone, either in the form of a robot, land mobile system, or aerial vehicle. What case law applies here?

In the landmark *District of Columbia v. Heller* case (2008), the Supreme Court overturned Washington, DC's gun control laws, allowing individuals the right to carry. Is there a legal difference between carrying an assault rifle or Glock semiautomatic pistol by a person or by a drone? No one knows.

While massive drone attacks were postulated as one future contingency, this potential disruptor has not found its way onto the political agenda so far. It must. The next administration should direct the Justice Department to undertake a major review in conjunction with the Department of Homeland Security on the potential misuses and abuses posed by all forms of drones and propose actions and recommendations on sensible regulations to ensure authorized use.

TERRORISM

The good news is that since September 11, US intelligence and law enforcement agencies have been remarkably able to keep foreign terrorists offshore. The major dangers are domestic homegrown terrorists and virtual terrorism on the internet and through social media. The second category was addressed earlier.

While President Trump disagreed with his FBI and CIA director that right-wing, neo-fascist white supremacists constitute the most dangerous domestic terror threats, violence has been practiced by both extremes of left and right. Fortunately, the extent and danger posed by terrorism was worse a century ago. But the disruptive capability today far exceeds that of dynamite or gunshot. The extreme precautions taken with twenty-five thousand armed National Guard troops to ensure a "peaceful" transition of power during the inauguration underscore the domestic terror threat.

The physical use of violence always leaves evidence and some form of fingerprints that will ultimately bring perpetrators to justice. The internet and social media are less transparent and often invisible. Hence, one solution to containing, mitigating, and preventing terrorists from terrorizing rests in the proposed recommendations that follow regarding the internet and social media.

Internationally, causes of terrorism arise from many sources, desperation being one of the most powerful. Social, political, economic, and psychological injustices all lead to one form of desperation. The first identified female Palestinian suicide bomber was Wafa Idris. Driven by the desperate situation of Palestinians and, in her mind, no future options, she turned herself into a human bomb. While questions were raised about her authenticity, Israel declared it a suicide bombing in 2002. And the fact is that desperation has been a motivating factor for suicide bombers.

The only way terrorism can be countered and minimized, let alone defeated, is through international cooperation and exchange of intelligence and information. In prior administrations, this was usually well handled. Unfortunately, as the Trump administration pursued "America first" policies, according to interviews with many current and former senior officials in this area, cooperation was severely diminished.

While the US may be engaged in a great-power competition with China and Russia, it is in the national interest of all to counter terrorism. Yet when harsh rhetoric replaces engagement, arms races supplant arms control, and defiance trumps discourse, mutual interests suffer. Thus, as noted and reinforced below, fundamental change is needed in these relationships.

The crucial starting point in this effort must be knowledge driven. The advice to know one's adversaries—real and potential—is older than Sun Tzu. So how might this be achieved when the "enemy" range from thirteen-year-old female recruits to terrorists who may live in Birmingham or Boston or Berlin to the "faceless" members of al-Qaeda, Quorosan, and the Islamic State (a.k.a., Da'esh) or to understanding Russian and Chinese aims and intent, where national technical means have stumbled?

Many agencies and organizations are utilizing data mining to derive information and knowledge on potential enemies. But what is needed is a far larger and more focused effort. One model can be derived from World War II and the famous code breakers at Bletchley Park in England. It was Bletchley Park and its American counterparts that broke the Enigma and Purple code machines of Nazi Germany and Japan, greatly contributing to victory. What is less well known is that the Germans were at least as good in cracking the Allies' codes but of course ultimately were defeated by overwhelming force.

The equivalent of the Bletchley Park code breakers for the twenty-first century must be re-created to employ against our adversaries, new and old, to understand them better and use that knowledge to defeat them. This capability can be achieved by exploiting "big data," social media, and the universally available data from Google Earth and other public platforms. Examples of how this is being done at present are numerous.

The Atlantic Council, with which I am affiliated, presented a brilliant analysis and demonstration of these techniques. It provided incontrovertible proof of Russian forces in Ukraine, including tracing a young Russian paratrooper from his home in Siberia three thousand miles west to the battle zone inside eastern Ukraine through YouTube, "selfies," and other content posted on the internet. Similar reports from both government and nongovernmental agencies are common and provide proof of concept. The State Department, Pentagon, or intelligence community may be the appropriate place to create this new Bletchley Park.

Obviously, the amount of data is nearly infinite. Adversaries can take countermeasures to preclude texting or posting videos and to hide or dissemble. And unlike other wars, the Bletchley code breakers of today are vulnerable to being discovered in their electronic hunts for knowledge and at risk of being attacked on the internet or possibly even in person at home. Indeed, social media of four-star officers has already been targeted and hacked in retaliation or for disruptive purposes.

The British have already begun the first stages of such an effort. Two brigades—77 Brigade and 1 ISR (Intelligence, Surveillance, and Reconnaissance)—were formed. 77 Brigade is tasked with using non-kinetic forms of war to achieve purpose. The 1 ISR Brigade is tasked with using more open and civilian sources of information to gain knowledge. These could serve as models for the US to deal not only with terrorism but all forms of disruption.

DEBT

For all the tax cuts that have been approved for decades to stimulate economic growth, the national debt has never been higher or a larger proportion of GDP since the end of World War II. Excessive regulations can asphyxiate growth. But an absence of regulations and oversight can produce and even guarantee severe consequences for the environment and public health and for corruption in businesses and financial markets. Greenhouse gases and toxic waste pollute the atmosphere. Lead and other dangerous chemicals poison water supplies. And unchecked or unregulated, corporations often do not listen to their better angels.

Debt can kill. As of mid-2021, the federal debt was well over $30 trillion and climbing. Given the Biden administration's spending plans and proposed 2022 budget, the debt will only grow. As the population ages, Social Security receipts will not keep pace with expenses. While defense spending is unlikely to increase, it still will amount to the lion's share of the discretionary budget, crowding out other vital programs from healthcare to education to some entitlements.

The most recent Congressional Budget Office projections posit more red ink for the indefinite future. And while the Trump administration declared a tariff war with China to cut the trade deficit, America's trade imbalance with the rest of the world continues to rise. From a fiscal perspective, the country is growing insolvent. And from a monetary perspective, interest rates cannot remain close to zero forever, and the government can only print so much money before inflation returns.

Only two paths can defuse this ticking debt time bomb. Revenues must exceed expenditures. That means some combination of making massive spending cuts and imposing substantial tax hikes. If not done sensibly, both will seriously harm the economy until this tough medicine takes hold, and that could take years. This happened in the late 1970s.

The second is by stimulating the economy to produce at least 3 to 4 percent or greater annual real growth. Tax cuts alone offer temporary relief and are ideologically and not economically driven. History is unrelenting. Despite all the tax cuts and predictions of growth, since Bill Clinton balanced the federal budget for the first time in decades more than twenty years ago, annual national debt has continued to rise.

Nor does spending alone work. The onset of World War II and not FDR's New Deal ended the Great Depression and began the explosion of the US economy. It was an exception because the postwar period created huge consumer demand as in the early 1920s and the GI Bill educated and housed millions of veterans who became the backbone of the middle class.

Finally, the best and most intelligent plans will fail without the participation of very able and dedicated men and women. The simple answer that Einstein would have favored ("Solutions to the most difficult problems should be made as simple as possible but no simpler") is that government service must be remade into a noble calling and a privilege. Given how poisonous and partisan politics has spilled over and contaminated much of the key appointments and offices, Beethoven's lament that while deaf, he would hear in heaven may apply. However, many of the reforms and recommendations below are aimed at reversing the damage done by overly politicizing who can and cannot serve in government.

CORRALLING THE DISRUPTORS

What might be achievable is to combine many of these issues under the absolute need for a dramatic program to modernize America's infrastructure. The Vinson-Trammell Naval Construction Acts offer a far-reaching example of how forward thinking can become manifested by law. Following Japanese violation of naval limitation agreements, the two acts authorized the construction of a navy that would win World War II. Basically, construction of all the major ships had been started or authorized for construction before Pearl Harbor.

Where would a future Vinson-Trammell Act focus? The answer is evident: It is in infrastructure. Despite promises for some sort of infrastructure rejuvenation plan, the political divides between the two parties have so far prevented any action. In the broadest sense and in less polarized times, Democrats believed that a major infrastructure effort was best done under the federal government and cite FDR's New Deal and LBJ's Great Society as examples.

In earlier times, Republicans thought the private sector should take charge, arguing that government is too bureaucratic, slow, and overly regulated to provide management. Additionally, traditional Republicans rejected the huge debt that would accrue. But these are far from traditional times.

The Biden administration is using three bills as the most transformative social, political, cultural, and economic agenda since FDR. Republicans violently disagree. Senate Minority (then Majority) Leader Mitch McConnell declared in 2009 that his first priority was making Barack Obama a one-term president. A dozen years later, the leader declares that he is "100% opposed to the Biden plans." Readers can conclude where this is headed and where and how it is likely to end. Both answers are not reassuring.

The alternative to the Biden proposals for Jobs and Families is a public-private partnership National Investment Fund, named 1923 for the economic boom that followed the 1918–1920 Spanish flu pandemic.

The 1923 Fund would be monetized by bond issues underwritten and guaranteed by the government that would generate at least $2 trillion in investment. The fund would offer coupons at 200 or 300 basis points above prime interest rates, payable over thirty or forty years. The bonds would be repaid from user fees, tolls, and returns on investment in the technology areas based on taking equity positions in companies receiving federal funds as occurred with TARP. And the fund would be focused on several key sectors.

The fund was proposed as the engine for this growth. Technology grows asymptotically. Renewable energy, healthcare, information technologies, quantum physics, genetic research, and the exploitation of space, among others, offer potentially unlimited economic opportunities. This is what happened after the 1918–1920 Spanish flu.

After the Spanish flu, economic stimulus rested on electrification of the country and the massive production of automobiles and other technologies, to include radios, movies, and airplanes. Electrification meant greater industrialization as well as increases in standards of living as electricity brought lighting, refrigeration, and a range of products from radios and vacuum cleaners to freezers that changed life. Automobiles and the Highways Act accelerated demand for gasoline, steel, rubber, leather, and other materials for cars as well as gas stations, restaurants, and hospitality services as Americans took to the open road.

The parallel of electrification today is 5G technology and universal access to broadband. The demand for creating huge numbers of high-paying jobs equivalent to the old auto industry is in the climate change/environmental and healthcare sectors. This is harnessing the positive side of MAD.

Although a Green New Deal as envisaged by a number of progressives is unaffordable and unrealistic, climate change and the environment are rife with new opportunities. For those who believe coal is still vital, sequestration of CO_2 makes carbon usable once the technology is perfected. The creation of energy from renewable means should make "smart cities" and modern buildings energy self-sufficient.

Given the coronavirus and an aging population, healthcare is another industry that has potential for explosive growth. The same applies to virtually every sector affected by the information and technology revolutions. The 1923 Fund would seed technologies in these and other areas to modernize roads, the electrical grid, airports, water supplies, and other areas of critical infrastructure. A more detailed description of such a fund is given in my earlier book, *America's Promise Restored: Preventing Culture, Crusade, and Partisanship from Destroying America.*

The proposed recommendations apply to redressing the contradiction between advancements in society and the vulnerabilities and fragilities that are created. By acknowledging MAD, this contradiction becomes self-evident. The 1923 Fund must be directed in ensuring that vulnerabilities and fragilities are protected by technology. Climate change is a prime example. The fund will also provide for the means of making the economy competitive for the twenty-first century.

Fostering growth in technologies that pursue sustainability while strengthening the capacity of infrastructure to resist disruption is part of this. New materials and energy-producing products are part of this approach. Information technologies and AI provide enormous potential in sustainability and healthcare. The notion of smart cities is applicable.

Not only can structures become zero emission, they can produce electricity, too, whether from solar or friction generated merely by walking. IT/AI offers at-home virtual health treatment as well as remote education. Robots can obviously perform many tasks at some stage, even diagnostically, as well as conduct examinations and possibly surgery and other procedures.

Drones can also provide many services, from delivery of products and routine housework to construction. The 1923 Fund would underwrite a number of these uses. The FAA has a complete rulebook for manned aircraft. A similar rulebook is needed for drones along with a licensing program that would include background checks and some level of training.

To summarize: First an overarching strategy and concept is needed based on containing, mitigating, and preventing the dangerous aspects of the Fifth Horseman and MAD from disrupting society. The Marshall Plan, Manhattan Project, and Vinson-Trammell are guides for employing a Brains-Based Approach. Several sub-strategies were outlined for corralling the seven major disruptors.

The 1923 Fund was proposed to empower this restoration of the nation's vital infrastructure, advancing climate change mitigation and employment, and preparing for future pandemics. The next chapters focus on national security and defense, strategies for Russia and China, and regional challenges to deal with the Fifth Horseman and MAD. The main obstacle remains failed and failing government.

Roosevelt had the New Deal; Truman the Fair Deal. Kennedy challenged the nation to put a man on the moon. Johnson had visions of the Great Society. Since then, despite much rhetoric, words and deeds have not been synonymous. Assuming that the Biden bills for Jobs and Families are not fully approved, the nation must have an alternative. The 1923 Fund is precisely that. As the Fund will be revenue neutral or even positive for the federal government, that is another inducement for its adoption.

MAD threatens the soul and body of this nation, unlike any other time since the Civil War. The Fifth Horseman and the seven disruptors can be corralled. However, it will take powerful leadership.

Chapter Nine

RESTORING AMERICA II: NEW NATIONAL SECURITY AND DEFENSE STRATEGIES IN A MAD-DRIVEN WORLD

The United States needs smart and clever National Security and Defense Strategies that cite specific ends, outcomes, and means rather than aspirations in an era of MAD. Realism must trump idealism and unobtainable expectations. But will the nation understand and act accordingly? That is the challenge. We cannot allow failure.

Because each of the MAD-driven disruptors—failed and failing government, climate change, cyber, social media, terrorism, debt, and drones—has a direct impact on national security as national security has on each of them, developing a relevant national security architecture, strategy, and plan is of prime importance. Unfortunately, a coherent national security construct, as well as the elusive and badly named whole of government approach, is still missing in action. A Brains-Based Approach to Strategic Thinking, along with important organizational changes to government, should rectify these deficiencies.

As Sun Tzu argued, defeating an enemy's strategy short of war is by far the best outcome. In constructing a strategy, the major flaws of the current US national security concepts must be avoided, namely largely aspirational, descriptive, and often ill-defined strategic aims. Specifically, both the US National Security Strategy (NSS) and National Defense Strategy (NDS), issued by the Trump administration and continued under Biden, called for a great-power competition with peer or near peer competitors in which the US military must compete, deter China and Russia (and North Korea and Iran), and if war comes, defeat that adversary.

One lesson from the Cold War should not be dismissed as the US strategy focuses again on two peer or near pear threats. During the Cold War, the US argued for a "2 1/2 war strategy" to defeat the Soviet Union and China simultaneously while having the capacity to win a "half war" elsewhere. The elsewhere turned out to be Vietnam. That should give Americans pause in accepting the NDS.

However, both the NSS and NDS were fatally flawed for three reasons. First, in 1914, great-power rivalry was a large factor in causing World War I. No off-ramp has been envisaged in today's great-power competition. The Chairman of the Joint Chiefs of Staff, Army General Mark Milley, told the US Air Force Academy graduating class of 2021 in late May that one of their principal objectives was to prevent the global competition with China from escalating into conflict. That is not a good sign if the nation's most senior military officer is depending on second lieutenants for help.

Second, the terms "compete, deter, and defeat" are aspirational and have not been defined to determine which, if any, are achievable, affordable, or appropriate, and which are not. Indeed, the strategic objectives that are to be achieved to compete, deter, and defeat like-wise are missing so far.

Third, while lip service has been given to the importance of allies and partners, both were largely ignored or diminished by the former president. The jury is still out on the Biden policies, although the president has been an internationalist for his entire career. Neither strategy has dealt with these contradictions:

- As societies became more advanced, they became more vulnerable and susceptible to disruption and especially to MAD.
- Bounding MAD will require more and not less international cooperation at a time when powerful centrifugal political forces were headed in the opposite direction under America's last president.
- And last is the conundrum of whether and how to allocate substantial resources to anticipate disruptions and crises that may never occur while assuring traditional challenges are met.

To underscore why these flaws are fatal to the strategies, from what are China and Russia to be deterred? Is it war; Belt and Road Initiative; militarizing islets in the China Seas; active measures; incursions into neighbors such as Taiwan, Georgia, and Ukraine; or more indirectly into Moldova, Serbia, and possibly Bulgaria? How to defeat both in a war that could be nuclear is likewise undefined, as are the explicit roles of NATO and other allies in this great-power competition.

The failure to incorporate allies and partners, as well as international and nongovernmental organizations, more fully into this competition, at face value, would seem sufficient to invalidate the strategies. So far, concepts of operations to deter and defeat are works in progress. The Chinese critique of American strategy hits squarely on exploiting these flaws.

The Chinese observe that American strategy has been technologically driven and not the reverse. Exploiting technology did not work in Vietnam or against the Taliban. While precision and deep strike were successful applications of technology, the strategy was clear and a driving factor: defeat the Soviet military at great range and not on the front lines. Today, new types of weapons systems such as unmanned vehicles and hypersonics are defining the strategy rather than strategy directing what is or should be in the military kit from a technological perspective. That stands Sun Tzu (or George Marshall) on his head.

The Congressional Research Service (CRS) provided a further critique in its September 30, 2020 paper, *Renewed Great Power Competition: Implications for Defense—Issues for Congress*. In its questioning, the CRS challenged the Department of Defense's strategy by asking how "preventing emergence of regional hegemons [*sic*]" was to be achieved. This question encapsulates the main criticisms of the NSS and NDS, namely in failing to define success in a great-power competition without provoking conflict or war.

Effective analysis demands a crisp and clear definition of what national security means; establishes which components are vital, necessary; or discretionary; decides how each is to be integrated and aligned; and carries out a cost-benefit analysis to ensure sufficient resources will be available to sustain the strategy. The starting point for a Brains-Based Approach to Strategic Thinking is to set the outcomes that are to be achieved and determine the most effective and affordable means to obtain them.

From this foundation, specific capabilities and well-defined objectives for each of the agencies of government with national security responsibilities can be set that apply to a MAD-driven world. Then a disciplined cross-governmental approach must be put in place with the necessary resources used effectively and efficiently along with means of ensuring compliance and oversight. Two options for ensuring this compliance and oversight were offered earlier.

Assumptions that underpin any national security strategy must be ruthlessly challenged and tested. No strategy or policy can overcome mistaken or erroneous assumptions just as no structure can long survive atop a flawed or faulty foundation in an earthquake, tornado, flood, or other environmental catastrophe. Last, this alternative strategy must be compared against the NSS and the ability, or lack, of the various government agencies to coordinate and to assure that security. In summary, the NSS and NDS have failed in acknowledging, incorporating and then containing, mitigating, and preventing the challenges of MAD and the Fifth Horseman.

The National Security and Defense Strategies for a MAD-driven world are derived from the overarching policy previously defined:

> The purposes of the new National Security Strategy must be based on achieving peace and prosperity through partnerships that will contain, mitigate, and prevent Massive Acts of Disruption, whether of man or nature, from threatening and destroying the safety, security, prosperity, and health of the United States and its friends and allies.

> This strategy requires an integrated, cross-governmental approach that must intimately engage both legislative and executive branches and friends and allies, and, in parallel, the National Defense Strategy must be able to contain, defend, and engage potential adversaries and other threats.

From this overarching statement, supporting sub-strategies and plans of action will and do follow below. The NSS and NDS list five actual and potential adversaries. China is the primary or pacing threat, followed by Russia and then North Korea, Iran, and violent extremism. Unlike the last two and the current administrations, this author regards Russia as the more imminent challenge given its actions, intent, and ability to penetrate, destabilize, and divide the United States, NATO, and EU to erode or weaken coherence and unity both domestically and internationally.

Indeed, the author fears the "threats" posed by China are still ambiguous and, in many ways, the military components have been exaggerated. As will be shown, China lacks the military capability for an armed assault and invasion to occupy Taiwan. It has, as Clausewitz described, "other means." These should be understood and the focus of strategy.

The March 2021 testimony of America's two most senior admirals in Asia, Philip Davidson, Commander Indo-Pacific Command and John Aquilino, Commander Pacific Fleet, before Congress, was chilling. Both cited the growing threat of China to the region and especially to Taiwan. Admiral Aquilino contended that a Chinese "military takeover" of Taiwan sometime in the future was one of, if not, his greatest concern.

These warnings not only must be taken very seriously given China's crackdown in Hong Kong. More importantly, these warnings and the assumptions or assertions underlying them must be rigorously scrutinized and challenged. No matter the credibility, too often the US has greatly exaggerated the nature of threats and at least twice gone to war over reasons that proved wrong.

In August 1964, after North Vietnamese PT boats allegedly staged a second attack against two US Navy destroyers (USS Maddox and Turner Joy) in the Tonkin Gulf, President Lyndon Johnson got from Congress the resolution to use force opposed by only two votes. The Tonkin Gulf Resolution trapped the United States in the Vietnam quagmire as it finally lost at the cost of 58,000 American and countless Vietnamese lives on both sides. But the second attack never occurred, and the first was the result of a local North Vietnamese commander acting without authority.

Thirty-eight years later, by a large majority, Congress passed the Authorization to Use Military Force to deprive Iraq and Saddam Hussein of weapons of mass destruction it did not possess. The region was thrown into geostrategic turmoil that has yet to be settled.

Both political parties and House of Congress are in agreement about the Chinese threat. However, consensus on the nature of the threat and its political, economic, ideological, and military dimensions is lacking. Thus, a thorough assessment of Chinese policies and options toward Taiwan is essential.

To that end, a number of questions must be addressed. First, what is meant by a "military takeover?" Is it a direct military amphibious assault and a twenty-first century version of the Normandy landing but on cyber and modern electronic steroids? Does China possess or will it possess the actual capability needed for a full scale opposed invasion of Taiwan that could require hundreds of thousands of troops, given that during World War II, US plans for retaking the island demanded 4,000 ships and 400,000 soldiers and marines?

Of course, China could threaten massive physical, cyber, or financial destruction as leverage or other pressure that will not require a massive opposed assault. Will China subvert the government from within for a regime change in Taiwan? Will China use economic and other forms of pressure? Or will China threaten a blockade or quarantine or measure well short of war to force re-unification?

Finally, what are the range of options to ensure Taiwan's independence not just for Taiwan but the US and other possible allies? Would the US Congress vote to go to war over Taiwan and would the public support the use of force to respond to Chinese aggression? What options short of war are available?

Would any allies join the US in protecting Taiwan and if so, under what circumstances and with what capabilities? Can any of this be agreed to in advance and is that wise?

Should the Taiwan Relations Act and other agreements be modified or remain based on strategic ambiguity? Would a presidential declaration that the US would come to Taiwan's assistance if attacked enrage, engage, or deter China's intent to "re-unify" the island? Should Taiwan be allowed to buy more advanced military systems to prevent any Chinese attack? Would Taiwan consider a nuclear option to avoid the fate of Hong Kong?

Finally, how and where can the Pacific Deterrence Initiative (PDI) be applied specifically to a Taiwan scenario? Or is PDI self-defeating by reinforcing the likelihood of an outcome we do not want, namely provoking China to assimilate the island with or without the use of force?

These and other questions should be the subject of broader public examination to avoid falling into the trap of either exaggerating or underestimating China's actual capability and intentions and options vis-à-vis Taiwan instead of what we would do if we were China.

Regarding Russia, it has no intention of occupying the Baltics or any NATO member. Today, NATO is seen by many once again at death's door, made moribund by the withdrawal of American forces and commitments during the Trump administration and by the failure or indifference of many of its European members to mount a credible defense against an increasingly aggressive Russia. One benchmark of this decline is the reluctance of a majority of NATO members to allocate at least 2 percent of GDP to defense spending, a commitment made seven years ago at the Heads of State and Government summit held in Wales.

Critics also note the deplorable status of many of Europe's military forces in readiness, training, and numbers. The entire UK military, for example, is smaller than the US Marine Corps (175,000 versus 160,000). Many German tanks are unserviceable and pilot training does not provide ample flying hours. Similar observations apply elsewhere.

On the other hand, Russia is seen as modernizing its conventional military of about 900,000 active-duty troops for twenty-first century war as fought in Syria and Ukraine and its strategic nuclear forces. Its aggressive use of exercises such as the one underway in the Black Sea aimed at Ukraine and overflights of NATO ships at sea or in the air is taken as a further side of hostile Russian intent. The fixation of the US on China as the "pacing threat" and the "tilt" of the UK to the Pacific reaffirm these concerns about NATO's ability to deter and defend against Russian encroachment.

But is Russia really ten feet tall? Or is NATO underplaying its strengths? From the Kremlin's perspective, Russia is surrounded by the powerful, thirty-member NATO alliance. Russia knows its economy is too energy dependent and that its population is in numerical decline and ill health. And geography is no friend.

East of the Urals, Russia is largely unpopulated. China may be a tactical ally. It has never been a long-term partner. Despite Moscow's fear of being surrounded by NATO, of the thirty members, only four directly border Russia: Norway in the north; Estonia and Latvia in the Baltics; and fourth is the United States in the Barents Sea. America's Little Diomede is only a mortar round distance from a nearby Russian island. Poland and Lithuania cut Kaliningrad, a Russian enclave, off from Russia.

Russia is confined to the Black Sea by restricted passage through the Bosporus Straits guarded on both sides by NATO member Turkey and in the Baltic by seven NATO members. It is also severely outgunned by NATO.

Using open sources, in virtually every category, the numerical military balance is vastly in NATO's favor. According to the International Institute for Strategic Studies, NATO spent over $1 trillion on defense last year with the US accounting for about three-fourths. Russia, whose defense spending is declining, declared it spent about $65 billion. But if Russia spent twice that, NATO still has an 8 to 1 advantage. NATO has about 3.3 million active-duty troops and another 2.1 million in reserve; Russia has about 900,000 and 2 million reserves.

NATO possesses about five times as many tanks; four times as many combat aircraft; three times as many attack helicopters; and 300 large surface combatants and 140 submarines to Russia's 35 warships and 50 submarines. Concerning the strategic nuclear balance, New Start limits the US and Russia to a total of 1,550 warheads (each with 700 deployed and 800 deployed or non-deployed launchers), and does not include the British and French nuclear deterrent of about 400 warheads total.

Quantitative military inferiority and Russian paranoia about encirclement has led Moscow to rely on nuclear weapons to overcome conventional force imbalances and "active measures," those short of the direct use of military force to divide and disrupt using cyber, social media, intimidation, and leveraging its supply of natural gas to Europe as an economic weapon.

Several conclusions are clear. First, NATO spends more than enough on defense, provided that spending is done wisely to develop alliance as opposed to individual member states' capabilities. Second, NATO discounts Russia's weaknesses. Third, NATO is failing in not countering Russian "active measures."

With that understanding, NATO can readily enhance its posture vis-à-vis Russia. But it needs a strategy and plan for the twenty-first century information age of warfare and not one rooted in the twentieth century industrial age. Furthermore, it needs forward thinking leadership to make that happen.

Strategy must also be targeted and focused on specific individuals in leadership positions of authority, elites, domestic publics, media, and of course allies, friends, partners, as well as potential adversaries and competitors and others who may be uncommitted. For Russia, the primary target is Putin and those around him, the Russian national security apparatus, to some degree the Russian people, and of course allies and partners. A similar grouping applies to China and the three other potential adversaries. The intellectual challenge is understanding and utilizing the most effective means for affecting, influencing, and where possible, controlling will and perception to protect our interests.

The strategy to counter Russia must be accomplished with the assistance of allies and friends, focusing on the requirements to "contain, defend, and engage" so that Moscow will be cajoled, convinced, or coerced to act in our interests or to cease actions that are damaging to those interests. To some degree, this recalls the Nixon Doctrine of fifty years ago when the United States was to provide the responsibility for strategic reassurance and leadership and regional states were to assume greater responsibilities for local security with full support of America to complement and add missing capabilities.

Contain means to prevent expansion, whether territorial such as Russian incursion into Ukraine or directed against NATO, or soft-power, ideological, or influence operations encompassed by active measures. *Defend* means having sufficient military power to deter, respond to, and disrupt any uses of force against the United States and its allies. And *engage* means to find areas of mutual agreement such as in terms of arms control, climate change, countering terrorism and proliferation, confidence-building measures, deconfliction to prevent unintended escalation, and other areas to reduce tensions and even improve relations.

Putin must be convinced that any military aggression will be too costly, that active measures and intimidation will be blunted and answered at least in kind, and that cooperation noted above are in his interest. As was shown in Chapters 4 and 5, straightforward communication of intentions is vital. Putin and Xi were transparent in delivering those messages. American and allied leadership must be as clear and direct in this matter, as Russian and Chinese leadership actively read and analyze the statements and actions of Western leadership for content and intent.

Indeed, President Biden must hold summits with Presidents Xi and Putin lasting more than a day to ensure a full dialogue. At these summits, the president must meet privately with each and state candidly and directly areas of competition and cooperation and be forthright about where "red lines" are set and will not tolerate interference. The aim is to achieve a modus operandi to avoid conflict and controversy where possible, to cooperate where suitable, and to agree to certain rules of engagement for future engagement and interaction.

The Porcupine Defense explained below is based on the "contain, defend, and engage" foundation, with emphasis on neutralizing active measures through affecting will and perception. Similarly, China must be engaged with allies and friends diplomatically, economically, and ideologically, downplaying the military competition that inevitably will produce an arms race that is not in anyone's interest. The Mobile Maritime Defense likewise incorporates these components.

THE NATIONAL SECURITY CRISES

Upon taking office, President Joe Biden and his administration faced a daunting array of formidable and seemingly insurmountable challenges, many the legacies of his predecessor, unlike any other president. An assessment of the state of his principal national security departments likewise was discouraging.

The State Department was dramatically understaffed, underused, and overly politicized. Rebuilding a diplomatic corps takes time. The Office of the Director of National Intelligence was compromised by two directors whose loyalty, again according to actions and to former officials, was to the forty-fifth president and not the Constitution. The CIA and FBI were demeaned and discredited by the last president.

While the US military seemed relatively unscathed by these crises, make no mistake: providing for the common defense is in trouble. Defense budgets, strategies, and organization comprise the major reasons for concern. This means that the Biden administration must pay serious attention to these issues if a highly capable and ready military is to be maintained.

One of the top priorities will be to restore appropriate civil military relations badly damaged by how the last president tried to manipulate and use the armed forces and personnel to his own political advantage. The disgraceful "photo op" in Lafayette Square with the short walk to St. John's Church after the outbreak of protests over the murder of George Floyd joined by the Secretary of Defense and Chairman of the Joint Chiefs was among the more grievous examples, as was the pardoning of convicted war criminals, of the impact of failed civilian leadership on the US military.

First the budget: sustaining $715 billion a year for defense spending will be impossible for the long term because of growing deficits, a national debt that now exceeds the annual GDP, and most importantly, lack of a compelling rationale. Barring a crisis or war, defense spending will shrink, possibly more dramatically than most expect.

The nasty not-so secret is that to maintain the current force at equivalent levels of readiness and modernization, at least 5 to 7 percent annual real growth in spending is needed. At 7 percent, principal doubles every ten years, showing the insidious nature of uncontrolled cost growth and compound interest. Indeed, that cost growth figure may be underestimated as funding for space, hypersonics, AI, and myriad other known technologies will be expensive. Modernizing the entire strategic nuclear triad (land-, sea-, and air-based nuclear weapons), with fixed or declining budgets, will come at the expense of the conventional forces. And the costs of nuclear modernization have almost doubled from the past 4 percent to as much as 7 or 8 percent of the budget.

The Marine Corps is undergoing a major transformation. The Army is refocusing on Asia. But those needs will require more, not less, funding. The decision to buy two more *Ford*-class nuclear aircraft carriers and air wings, along with supporting escort and logistics forces, will require in excess of $60 billion over time. Without profound reform not seen in the Navy for fifty years to overhaul and revamp a force structure oriented toward big decks and nuclear submarines or Congress approving hundreds of billions of additional dollars, the proposed 500-plus-ship navy called for in Battle Force 2045 will never be achieved.

The second factor is strategy. The Trump administration's National Defense Strategy expanded the Obama 4+1 scenario from the requirement "to deter and if war comes defeat" China, Russia, North Korea, or Iran to making great-power competition its central theme. The Biden administration, so far, has continued this strategy.

Unlike the Cold War and after Nixon went to China in 1972, the competition with Moscow was geostrategic and ideological because the Soviet Union was not an economic power. China is. That extends the global competition well beyond the Pentagon.

For the Pentagon, does competition mean engaging in an arms race (and recall the pre–World War I naval arms race) and continuing freedom of navigation operations (FON) in the South China and Black Seas? Or is competition more than that? And if it is more, where does that lead and are future conflicts and collisions inevitable or avoidable?

If war comes, what constitutes success or victory especially if thermonuclear weapons are used? Neither has been defined. How are China or Russia to be defeated in a conflict that could escalate to the use of nuclear weapons? Few answers are there either.

The third issue is the DoD's organization. As described, the basic organization of the legislature and the presidency is neither suitable nor structured for a MAD-driven (or any other) world; the same failing applies to the US military. The National Security Act, the Unified Command Plan, and Goldwater-Nichols Act are the basic organizational foundations. In the intervening seventy-four years since the National Security Act was first passed in 1947, much has changed, including the growth of bloat, unresponsiveness, and too much redundancy.

The Department of Homeland Security and a Director of National Intelligence were created after September 11. The Chairman of the Joint Chiefs was made the principal military advisor to the president. A vice chairman and other members were added to the Joint Chiefs. The influence and power of the Joint Staff likewise grew. In 2020, a separate Space Force was approved, the first new service since the US Air Force was created in 1947.

Goldwater-Nichols mandated more "jointness." Jointness means more than interservice cooperation. It means integrating war-fighting capabilities in what was called the "joint force" and not the naval, land, or air force. Joint assignments on combatant command and joint staffs were required for promotion to senior ranks. However, jointness for the sake of jointness makes little sense. And rather than forcing more competition among the services, Goldwater-Nichols had the unintended consequence of fostering collusion.

In this case, collusion means that as long as each service has the autonomy to decide what weapons and supporting systems it needs without competing for those capabilities, it will support the requirements set by the other services for their forces. For example, if the Navy is allowed to procure nuclear aircraft carriers, it will not oppose the Air Force or the Army in obtaining weapons systems each deems important—and vice versa. Each service will conveniently support the others, virtually eliminating competition.

Under the Unified Command Plan, the former "CinCs," now combatant commanders, were expanded to seven geographic and four functional commands. Each command has staff numbering in the hundreds or thousands. The Offices of the Secretary of Defense and the Joint Staff swelled to about five thousand personnel each, including contractors. And the Army has more four-star generals than it did in World War II. As the other branches of government became bloated, the same effect infected the Pentagon.

One wonders how the United States won that war with such a streamlined chain of command. Admiral Ernest King, Chief of Naval Operations and Commander-in-Chief, had Admiral Chester Nimitz, Commander-in-Chief Pacific Fleet, and Admiral Harold R. ("Betty") Stark, Commander-in-Chief Naval Forces Europe, reporting to him. General of the Army George Marshall likewise had two principal subordinates: General Douglas MacArthur in the Pacific and General Dwight Eisenhower in Europe.

For reform to work, any national security overhaul must include Congress. To ensure all the members have worthy assignments and responsibilities, the number of committees and subcommittees has soared, leading to an excess of overlapping national security jurisdictions. Worse, the legislative process is broken. The current triple-spaced House Defense Authorization Bill is 3,468 pages long. Clearly, no member of Congress has read or fully understands what is in that bill despite having voted on it.

What is to be done? First, the NDS and a global competition must go. Instead, the foundations for the strategy should be to contain, defend, and engage potential adversaries without specifically naming any. Then, a Porcupine Defense for Europe and a Mobile Maritime Defense in Asia should be implemented.

A Porcupine Defense is based on the requirements to contain, defend, and engage by affecting, influencing, and controlling an enemy's will and perception to believe that the costs imposed through "disruptive" tactics and weapons systems to confuse, deceive, and derail any potential military attack are simply unacceptable. Targeting command and control and vital choke points with massive numbers of missiles, drones, and other unmanned, highly distributed systems and electronic and information warfare capabilities, supported by conventional forces, would overwhelm and thus deter an adversary from contemplating a first strike or attack.

A Mobile Maritime Defense in the Pacific would likewise focus on will and perception to convince China's military that in a war, its forces would be confined to within the boundaries set by the first island chain. This chain runs from the southern tip of Japan, through the Ryukyu Islands to Taiwan, the northern tip of the Philippines to Vietnam.

Using Porcupine Defense tactics and systems emphasizing undersea warfare (and sea mines) and a World War II island-hopping campaign to dismantle China's Belt and Road Initiative well beyond its borders would deny access to overseas resources and markets, making a war too costly for China even to contemplate. The 2017–2018 Breaking the Mold conferences held at the Naval War College described both defenses in detail. They could be affordable at about $600–$650 billion a year. More on both strategies follow.

Second, the National Security Act must be revised and the UCP streamlined. Regarding the first, as recommended earlier, a small number of senior members of Congress must be given de facto membership in the NSC so that Congress is aboard for the takeoff as well as the landing for national security policies. And Combatant Commands should be broadened to have foreign officer/civilian deputies or even commanders.

Northern and Southern Commands would be amalgamated into an Americas Command and European and Africa Commands into a Western Command. Indo-Pacific would be renamed Eastern Command, while Central Command would remain unchanged. The two new commands should have a four-star deputy or the equivalent civilian rank.

Strategic and Space Commands should merge given the amount of overlap. Similarly, in age of "hyper" or speed of light war, Cyber Command, NSA, and DIA would form a new Information and Intelligence Command with a four-star commander. As Special Operations have an assistant secretary of defense, the need for a separate combatant command is superfluous.

The Joint Chiefs should serve in that capacity on a full-time basis to focus specifically on strategic thinking and planning. A separate set of service chiefs would be appointed to manage each service. Many of the functions of the Joint and OSD staffs can be merged. Finally, professional military education must be integrated, aligned, and more closely coordinated. The Navy's Education for Seapower study, rejected by a former Chief of Naval Operations, is the model for necessary reform. The study called for greater coordination and integration of the naval educational assets into a Naval University headed by a three-star vice admiral and more focus on improving critical strategic thinking and analysis across all domains.

Will this happen? Absent a crisis, the answer is no. But if another and perhaps more destructive Pearl Harbor or September 11 strikes, it will be too late. The reality is that the nation has a twentieth-century defense organization that will not work in nor is suitable for the twenty-first century.

The conclusion: The US has a superb military. To maintain that military advantage, profound change is necessary to provide for the common defense in the coming decades of the twenty-first century. These changes will also strengthen the nation's ability to deal with the disruptions caused by cyber, social media, and terrorism as the military will be in a better position to contain, mitigate, and prevent them.

PORCUPINE AND MOBILE MARITIME DEFENSE

Analysis begins with using the Brains-Based Approach to Strategic Thinking and the first requirement of obtaining far greater knowledge and understanding of Russia and China and their respective strategies and policies. Russian policy under Putin is clear. It is highly exploitive in increasing Russian security and influence given severe societal and economic constraints.

While Russia is a resource-rich country with a declining population of about 140 million, it has never been able to make full use of those assets nor of its technically educated population. Centuries of autocratic rule have contained the "animal spirits" of free enterprise. Corruption has empowered a small number of Russians at the expense of the majority. And dependence on oil and gas has made Russia vulnerable to markets and in early 2020 a price war with Saudi Arabia that drove prices to unprecedented low levels.

Simply put, Russia is a smaller version of the old Soviet Union without the constraining communist ideology that made the political system ultimately unworkable. While Putin is not out to re-create the old Soviet empire, he intends to increase its influence, standing, prestige, and respect. To do so, he is relying on old Russian and Soviet tactics built on active measures and military power and prowess.

Putin's Russia has relied on its military to expand its access and influence and use weapons sales to accumulate foreign currency, offsetting economic and financial sanctions and relatively low oil prices. Putin has brilliantly and sometimes heavy-handedly employed active measures that date back to the early days of the Soviet Union. Regarding Russia's military, Putin has certainly created a formidable force fully knowledgeable of American and NATO strategy and exploiting both its strengths and weaknesses. It is no accident that Chief of Defense General Valery Gerasimov has observed that in the twenty-first century, "information warfare" is three to kinetic warfare's one.

From these conclusions, the United States requires, first of all, far greater knowledge and understanding of the international environment to include rivals, allies, and friends. US leadership and its public must recognize that American strategic thinking is not universal, and not everyone outside our borders thinks or wishes to think as we do. In this pursuit of greater knowledge must come recognition of Russian insecurity that yearns for respect. Indeed, one secret weapon, if we are clever enough to use it, is to play on the Russian psyche and the need for respect.

Second, Russia has many vulnerabilities that we ignore. During the Cold War, the USSR was not seven feet tall. Perhaps it stood five feet eight. And not all its vital organs were properly developed. Today, Russia does not want a war with the West, believing that with clever diplomacy, active measures, and a lack of coherence on the part of the West, all are sufficient to keep Russia safe, secure, and with growing power, influence, and respect.

Third, Russia is better at relating strategy with forces, objectives, and affordable levels of defense spending than the West and NATO are. Putin has been tactically brilliant at exploiting Western weaknesses and openings.

Fourth, the aim of the West and the US is to focus on affecting, influencing, and controlling Russia's will and perception with an objective, culturally relevant, geostrategic analysis of Russian military strengths and weaknesses. That includes developing an effective cost-exchange ratio in which it costs Russia far more to respond to us than it does for us to cause that response. That is an effective way of dealing with will and perception. From that departure point, creating a strategy may not be as easy as George Marshall once observed that if you set the aims, a lieutenant can do the job. Without that basis, however, no strategy can work.

Finally, and this applies to China, the most difficult task is changing the trajectory of US-Russian-Chinese relations to a more positive and less combative direction. The goal should be a respectful rivalry. Russia and China crave respect. That may be the most important leverage point the West and the US have.

China has many problems, including a shadow banking system, excessive real estate, an underclass of almost half a billion, and a history of peasant revolts and revolutions. China's Belt and Road Initiative and Russia's active measures present far greater challenges than a possible military confrontation in the various Chinese coastal seas or over Taiwan or the Baltics. Both China and Russia face enormous social and demographic issues, with both an increasing elderly cohort and a decline in total populations that will take hold over the coming decades.

China is betting its future economic growth on Belt and Road to provide access to resources and, most importantly, to larger markets for Chinese goods and services. But spending potentially trillions of renminbi on Belt and Road means less money for domestic consumption, particularly for raising standards of living for hundreds of millions of Chinese and modernizing infrastructure, already grounds for discontent and criticism at home.

Russian active measures are aimed to disrupt and extend beyond propaganda, cyber, mis- and disinformation, and interference in domestic affairs of other states. Putin has made Russia more influential abroad. The interventions in Syria and Libya, improved relations with Israel and Saudi Arabia, sales of S-400 missiles to Turkey, Nord Stream 2 to make Europe more dependent on Russian energy, and efforts to break NATO's cohesion present more immediate challenges and tests than does its military, a military that is far smaller than that possessed by the entirety of NATO.

History offers a lesson in thinking about Westphalia II. In Vietnam, Afghanistan, and the second Iraq War, the United States had total air, sea, and land dominance. Initially in Vietnam and in Afghanistan and

Iraq after 2003, the enemy had no army, navy, or air force. Yet the US and its allies could not "win."

What is needed is an "unconventional" approach using will and perception to countering Russia (and China) to reverse the cost-exchange ratio in our favor strategically and militarily and to protect and defend against disruptive events.

Both Porcupine and Maritime Defenses are predicated on finishing the transformation of a largely twentieth-century industrial-based military to a twenty-first century information-based structure. The intention is to outflank Russian and Chinese conventional and industrial-based capabilities with unmanned systems, long-range strike, electronic and information warfare, standoff weapons, deception, decoys, diesel submarines, and other pain-imposing capabilities to blunt any potential attack, reversing the cost-exchange ratio to our favor and thus altering will and perception to our advantage.

Finally, engagement is vital. NATO and the EU are strategic tools for engaging Russia on confidence-building measures, arms control, and means to reduce unwanted or accidental interactions between militaries. Officer exchanges should not be discounted but probably at war colleges or staffs that deconflict zones where both sides are operating military forces. For the United States, engaging China more succinctly and effectively runs first through Europe to bring NATO and the EU into closer cooperation along with other Asian states noted below.

The geostrategic and political purposes of the Porcupine and Mobile Maritime Defenses are to demonstrate to Russia and China that any form of interference not only will be countered, the cost will be so great as to discourage and therefore deter hostile acts by Moscow and Beijing. Since the current NDS is designed to prevent faits accomplis—against the Baltics and Black Sea in Europe and Taiwan in Asia—both defenses must deal with these contingencies.

Additionally, nonmilitary and soft-power tools are important. Regarding the Black Sea, access by non-riparian states is controlled by the 1936 Montreux Convention. That convention is long out of date since one of the signatories, the USSR, is no longer in existence and Ukraine and Georgia were not independent then. Realizing the friction with Turkey, merely mentioning the prospect of revising the convention to allow freer access for external states, for example, can be a very powerful negotiating point with Russia, which clearly will steadfastly oppose any change as will Turkey. But that opposition could be a negotiating advantage as a tradeoff and incentive for other concessions.

The military purpose is to disrupt any initial military attack by targeting command and control, logistics lines, and other weaknesses with kinetic and non-kinetic systems; threatening bases with long-range missiles; neutralizing enemy fleets; and supporting rapidly deployable forces to both regions. Because the Black Sea is Russia's strategic center of gravity, it will be used as the case study for examining Porcupine and Mobile Maritime Defenses, as similar analysis applies to Europe and the Baltics and to Asia and Taiwan.

To deal with the Black Sea first, Constanta, the largest seaport on Romania's southern coast, should become a version of the highly defended Russian Kaliningrad enclave on the Baltic Sea with the capacity for an active coastal defense. With Aegis Ashore and the M-K (Mihail Kogalniceanu) air base as well as NATO's multinational headquarters nearby, Constanta would be the strategic focal point for stationing cruise missiles as well as an array of electronic warfare systems to disrupt, confuse, and deceive any attacker. Naval capability would be expanded with the stationing of stealth missile boats and at least two Romanian submarines to be built by Romania to conform with the present Montreux Convention along with developing the equivalent of Captor sea mines and other anti-ship weapons.

The ground forces would be equipped with systems to disrupt, delay, and achieve mission kills rather than wholesale destruction of the Russian ground and air forces. Despite the addition of Patriot missiles (and Aegis Ashore), Russia would dominate the air. Hence dispersion is vital. In dispersing forces, however, each unit from the battalion down should have combat systems that form the quills of the porcupine and are highly sharpened.

For example, consider a company- or battalion-size force equipped with thousands of inexpensive drones; long range missiles; upgraded Stinger and Javelin missiles; new electronic and information warfare systems for deception, mis-, and disinformation; lighter than air and aerostats as well as low Earth orbiters for reconnaissance and C3I; and IEDs with twenty thousand pounds of explosive to block potential points of advance on the ground.

In this case, drones would form the main battery designed to attack command and control and logistical choke points. Inexpensive and autonomous "swarm" attacks would confound and confuse any attacker. For those who doubt this capacity, the 2018 Seoul Winter Olympics featured several thousand drones intricately maneuvering in mass formations to produce an extraordinary sound and light show. China now argues that it has broken this record using some three thousand plus drones in a coordinated exercise.

Deception is crucial. During World War II, General George Patton commanded the fictitious First US Army Group (FUSAG) armed with rubber and papier-mâché aircraft, tanks, and field artillery, all designed to convince Hitler that the invasion would come at the Pas-de-Calais and not Normandy. Deception in all domains is vital, especially cyber and electronic. In that regard, new vulnerabilities exist, as many soldiers will carry cell phones despite orders to the contrary.

As the Russians showed in Donbass, cell phones can kill. Recall the senior Ukrainian Army officer who posed a serious threat to Russian forces. Russian intelligence sent a doctored text to the officer's mother asking her to call him immediately. She did. The Russians pinpointed his location and with an artillery strike killed the officer. The information age is now central to warfare.

Deployed in large unmarked trailers or vans, five or ten tons of high explosives as super-destructive IEDs to destroy logistics routes is an effective and inexpensive technology. The aim is to disrupt and thereby delay or confound an attack. Soldiers are dependent on resupply not only of ammunition and reinforcements; in terms of weight requirements, water and batteries to power all the electronics equipment are considerable. This is not World War II.

Upgraded anti-air Stinger and anti-vehicle Javelin missiles likewise would be formidable defenses. While the Russians are dependent on heavy artillery and fire support, dispersion and the use of drones and deception would harass and complicate the targeting problems as they can operate well behind the forward edge of the battlefield (FEBA), leaving the leading elements vulnerable to man-portable missiles. And as the US learned in Vietnam (and Somalia) and the Soviets in Afghanistan, helicopters are not bulletproof.

AI would be vital in providing unit commanders near-instantaneous operational options. Obviously, command, control, and communications would be attacked. Local jam-proof internet would be part of the kit. And as satellite communications too are vulnerable, procurement of low-cost low Earth orbiter (LEO) satellites that could be launched in crisis would be needed. That said, Romania also must maintain a capability for intervention for up to three battalions to include not only its coasts and borders but the Danube.

NATO needs the capability to threaten Crimea and contain the Black Sea Fleet. Cruise missiles with a range of four hundred miles that can be fired from air, surface, or submerged platforms need not be expensive. As "low fliers" operating tens of feet above the surface even at subsonic speeds, detection is difficult, especially if jamming and "window"—that is, radar-blocking metal strips dropped or fired into the air—are used.

In that regard, NATO needs to encourage the Romanian Navy to build and deploy diesel-electric propulsion submarines along the lines of the German 209 class. Four would suffice, meaning at least one and possibly two can be kept at sea, armed with cruise missiles. Acquiring modernized stealth missile boats such as China's Type-22 and Sweden's Visby class and sea mines such as the Captor Mk-46 torpedo likewise will present a major threat to the Russia fleet. Fixed and towed sonar arrays can threaten Russian submarines with the risk of detection and are not expensive.

To complement surveillance and command and control, three systems are applicable. The first is the aerostat or "blimp" that is a lighter-than-air system. Second, long-range radars can be mounted on these aerostats that can look deeply into the Black Sea for example. And third, ground-based over-the-horizon (OTH) radars likewise complement surveillance even though fixed land-based sites are readily targetable.

As the ground forces would be reconfigured for the Porcupine Defense, a vital complement is using the Reserves as the base for an insurgency force and home guard. This force would be prepared to wage guerrilla warfare against an advancing force to harass, disrupt, and confuse. During World War II, in some cases resistance forces were effective. In Vietnam, the insurgents were very effective in imposing casualties and forcing the US to spend an inordinate amount of time and resources in largely wasteful and counterproductive "search and destroy" missions.

Surely this force would be a powerful reminder of the Soviet experience with the mujahideen in Afghanistan. Along with the Reserves, it could be oriented toward Moldova and, in the west, Serbia, in the event either or both were used for active measures and hybrid warfare, including the presence of mercenaries in Moscow's equivalent of Academi (originally Blackwater)—the Wagner Group.

This force along with Reserves would have a secondary task of dealing with disruptive crises from environmental catastrophes of weather or floods, pandemics, and other dangers.

TWO SCENARIOS

NATO/EUROPE

It is 202X. A new, more virulent form of the coronavirus had dramatically crippled global economic growth and led to more states turning inward. NATO support for the wars in Afghanistan and Iraq had ended with the exception of a few train-and-assist teams still deployed. NATO cohesion had weakened. "America first" had taken its toll despite the attempts of the Biden administration to reassert American leadership. America continued to place its geographic priorities on Asia, shifting away from its traditional alliance with Europe. China intensified its belligerent attitude towards Taiwan. Japan and South Korea relations worsened as South Korea continued reconciliation with the North. The China Seas became largely Chinese-dominated lakes.

The calamitous hard Brexit finally separating the UK from the EU also reduced Britain's influence in NATO. After butting heads with France and Greece, President Erdogan withdrew Turkey from NATO's military structure as Charles de Gaulle had done sixty years before with France. Russia continued to put greater pressure on Ukraine to move back into Moscow's orbit.

NATO had abandoned any idea of granting Ukraine or Georgia membership as it struggled to maintain its own coherence. NATO was impotent to prevent the near war between the Gulf States and Israel against Iran and its allies. War was averted only after Iran lifted its blockade of the Strait of Hormuz that had sent oil prices to new heights and suspended attacks against Saudi oil facilities after an Israeli-UAE joint F-35 air raid destroyed much of the Natanz nuclear facility.

Believing that the Black Sea could be made a Russian lake, Kremlin leaders embarked on a plan to accomplish that aim, creating the crisis that forms the scenario for testing the Porcupine Defense.

In June, Moscow imposed an ultimatum on Ukraine: join the CSTO and sign an act of friendship with Russia or risk the annexation of Donbass into Russia. Moscow sailed the Black Sea Fleet, declared a blockade of Ukrainian seaports, and sent a small detachment to occupy Serpent Island, a scarce twenty miles off the mouth of the Danube River and Romania.

The Black Sea Fleet had sortied to enforce the blockade and a no-fly, no-sail zone around Serpent Island extending fifteen miles in all directions. Moscow implied that Constanta, Romania's major seaport and the second largest in Europe, could be affected if it allowed entry of Ukrainian-flagged ships. That zone was a direct infringement on Romanian territorial claims as well as its sovereignty.

Russia activated its internet warriors with a propaganda campaign alleging Ukrainian attacks against Russian-speaking citizens and posted videos of a Ukrainian frigate attacking a Russian merchantman and then being quickly sunk by Kalibr missiles fired from one Russia's smaller, stealthy surface combatants.

NATO immediately convened an Article 4 meeting to consult on this growing crisis. After tumultuous debate, the alliance decided that Russia's actions fell short of the Article 5 criterion of an attack against one and that Romania had the option of using international law and the International Court of Justice for resolution of the threatened blockade. However, the alliance did not prevent individual NATO members from coming to Romania's aid. Turkey objected from its now more remote status, threatening to close the Bosporus and not permit transit of warships of states that were non-signatories of the

Montreux Convention. Despite strenuous objections, Turkey was adamant in preventing passage. That left only the land and air routes.

In this crisis, Serbia initially declared neutrality; it backed Russia and closed off land and ground passage east to Romania, asserting that was the best way to contain the conflict. Its media was filled with anti-NATO and anti-Romanian propaganda.

A divided NATO could not force the issue. Hungary, with its authoritarian rule, abstained from the Article 4 meeting and was ambiguous about permitting transit to the conflict region. Practically, the Black Sea was isolated with Bulgaria as the only access point. Bulgaria chose to be silent on the issue of access.

Despite its weakened position, the US responded to force NATO action. The president announced on national television that the US was acting on the basis that Article 5 was in force even though not all NATO members had agreed. In conjunction, Romania's president also declared on national television that any state violating Romanian territory and territorial waters of twelve miles would be met by deadly force. Bluntly, that translated to mean that "Little Green Men" would be shot on sight and warships in violation would be sunk.

Instead of acting as an alliance, a coalition of twenty-two NATO states led by the US formed to support Romania. This coalition understood that the strategy had to be to induce, coerce, compel, or cajole Russia to evacuate Serpent Island, although Ukrainian, as it was a clear and present danger to Romanian sovereignty and, ultimately, to NATO cohesion. This was a very high-risk strategy.

But the option of giving Moscow a free hand smacked of capitulation and appeasement. The NATO coalition began a preplanned exercise with Romania to reinforce its borders with Moldova and Serbia, deploying the Porcupine Defense as well as moving large unmarked trailers to critical logistical choke points. These vans reportedly were loaded with twenty thousand pounds of high explosives. The Reserve/guerrilla force was part of this exercise.

Two Romanian submarines were deployed to trail the Black Sea Fleet in proximity to Serpent Island along with stealth patrol boats to shadow that fleet as well. Romania also flew numerous drones over the Black Sea to show that capability along with activating its Aerostat fleet. It also published a notice to mariners that it was preparing to test-fly a long-range cruise missile over the Black Sea.

NATO's Chairman of the Military Committee and coalition chiefs of defense met with Ukrainian counterparts to begin planning for a joint Ukrainian-NATO amphibious assault to recover Serpent Island. Ukrainian amphibious ships would carry both Romanian and Ukrainian troops for the mission. The military kit for a Porcupine Defense that was light and lethal was perfect for retaking the island. A-10s also were on station to provide fire support for any assault on Serpent Island as well as supporting the border exercises.

Brilliantly, the NATO coalition practiced creative information warfare. The local NATO commander in Romania told the press that while he did not believe reports of "Little Green Men" being shot by Romanian troops upon crossing the border, they were being investigated. Although the story was invented, Moscow was listening.

A deep-fake video of the Russian president being medevaced from the Kremlin to a Moscow hospital materialized and went viral in minutes, registering over half a billion hits. Concurrently, a cyberattack with IPs originating in Serbia and Moldova was launched against the Black Sea Fleet Headquarters, interrupting communications with the deployed units. Stories circulated that Moldova and Serbia wanted no part of a wider conflict. This dis- and misinformation so confused the Kremlin that it would take several days for it to recover.

When the Russian president went on television to refute the rumors, the link was interrupted by another cyber hack, and manufactured stories that seemed to originate from China reported that the broadcast was another deep fake. Electrons and not bullets were turning the tide against Russia.

To circumvent Turkey's refusal to allow passage through the Dardanelles, the example of the so-called Tanker War of the 1980s in the Gulf would be repeated in an equally innovative manner. Then, the United States had reflagged foreign-owned oil tankers, with the clear meaning that any attack by Iran risked a wider war with America.

In this crisis, a US nuclear submarine was reflagged to Romania. While the submarine was still manned by a US crew, legally she was Romanian and hence had standing to transit from the Mediterranean to the Black Sea. That she was nuclear was not mentioned, only that a submarine had been purchased.

To ensure Turkey would not block the transit, the submarine sailed at night at modified periscope depth, avoiding detection. Now Russia had to contend with Romania possibly having nuclear weapons at its disposal when the submarine surfaced and was identified in the Black Sea.

In this scenario, Russia retracted from Serpent Island as Khrushchev had from Cuba seventy years before, claiming a diplomatic victory. Some will assert NATO or even a coalition of the willing would never resort to such a bold and risky strategy. On the other hand, given the geostrategic scenario, NATO leadership would likely conclude that this was an existential danger to the alliance. It would have been unacceptable if Russia had been able to control access to the Black Sea and threaten blockade of Romanian seaports.

The history that comes to mind is the Cuban Missile Crisis of 1962. To circumvent American superiority in nuclear weapons and intercontinental ballistic missiles, Soviet leader Nikita Khrushchev ordered shorter-range Soviet nuclear missiles to be stationed in Cuba. He reasoned that no president would object, as America had Jupiter missiles in Turkey aimed at Russia and once the weapons were in situ, using force to remove them would be rejected as too dangerous. Khrushchev could not have been less correct.

President John F. Kennedy responded with a quarantine to isolate Cuba with a de facto blockade. Khrushchev blinked. Russian missiles and military forces would be withdrawn. The parallel with this scenario is clear.

TAIWAN

The NDS has used the concept of a preventing a fait accompli as its basis. That is a huge flaw and probably a surrogate for the argument to increase numbers of US forces. The fact is that for the foreseeable future, China lacks the military capacity and capability to invade and occupy Taiwan. The strait is about one hundred miles wide. That Hitler was incapable of crossing the twenty-five-mile English Channel is suggestive. But history has a better example: Operation Causeway and the US plan to invade Taiwan in 1944.

The force required by the plan entailed four thousand ships and about four hundred thousand soldiers and marines landing at four sites on the southwest tip of Taiwan. The landing force faced about thirty thousand Japanese soldiers on the island. Instead, the decision was made to retake the Philippines. Today, Taiwan's military, active and reserve, is many times larger than the occupying Japanese force of World War II.

Of course, China could obliterate Taiwan with missiles and bombs. It could intimidate Taiwan using diplomatic and financial leverage. And it could work politically from within to orchestrate empowering a regime amenable to annexation.

Given the makeup of the Biden team, it is likely its view would be as follows. Given China's neuralgic regard for Taiwan, attempting some form of annexation will be one Indo-Pacific scenario. China, for geopolitical, domestic, or opportunistic reasons, concludes that it will abrogate the "one China, two systems" agreement and annex Taiwan by intimidation or force short of a military invasion or strike.

The preferred means to achieve that aim and prevent direct conflict would be an air, sea, and financial blockade of Taiwan to disrupt commerce and transport, ultimately forcing Taiwan to submit to Beijing's sovereignty. China's maritime militia of fishing and commercial boats would form the physical blockade, supported by its coast guard.

The PLA Navy would be kept in reserve so as not to overly militarize the scenario. China would extend its Air Defense Identification Zone (ADIZ) to include Taiwanese airspace and declare it off-limits. Concurrently, China could mobilize the PLA, threatening an invasion of the island. However, at present, China is not fully capable of conducting a successful amphibious assault on Taiwan.

How would the United States respond? Assuming the US were to transform its military for such contingencies, that will take time. The foundations for its naval power are its carrier strike groups, nuclear submarines, and long-range missiles. But no matter how capable or invisible these forces may be, the range at which strike aircraft could operate even with refueling is less than the range of Chinese hypersonic, cruise, and ballistic missiles. One tactical option could be for US surface warships to intermingle with maritime militias to complicate counter-targeting. But that would raise the stakes, and resupply would be difficult.

The critical question is what would induce the United States to use military force to deter or repel an assault on Taiwan. The Taiwan Relations Act is not a mutual defense treaty that extends a NATO Article 5–like guarantee. Answering that question is impossible unless the US pledged to come to Taiwan's defense. However, the Chinese reaction is certain—conflict.

If a conflict started, the Mobile Maritime Defense would contain the Chinese military to the first island chain off its coasts, providing defensive measures such as sea mines and standoff weapons to target a Taiwan-bound invasion fleet. Even though the US military focused its strategy on the Indo-Pacific region, it is still based on the ability to attack the Chinese homeland directly. In the Mobile Maritime Defense, the aim is to contain PLA forces, and not just the navy, to the first island chain. With vast numbers of unmanned vehicles and anti-ship missiles in defense, an amphibious assault by China could be prohibitive. Ideally, Taiwan would be provided these systems.

Because China lacks the capacity to invade Taiwan, a fact not likely to change in the short term, it would rely on its nonmilitary coercive instruments. Thus, the Chinese blockade could be challenged at sea and the ADIZ in the air by providing fighter escorts for commercial airliners—a reverse Cuban Missile Crisis of sorts. In the event that actual hostilities broke out, the Mobile Maritime Defense would conduct an island-hopping campaign similar to World War II to isolate China and remove or occupy its Belt and Road outposts. But to be effective, allies and partners would have to be engaged. The worst of all scenarios would be a US-China conflict. Given geography and lack of US bases or allies, it is clear who has the advantage.

IS NATO CRITICAL TO THE INDO-PACIFIC?

Both the Trump and Biden administrations have urged NATO to play a larger role in the Pacific. In the summer of 2021, a combined task force centered around the new British aircraft carrier *HMS Queen Elizabeth II* deployed to Asia. But the larger issue of an expanded NATO role raises important issues. For one, trade and investment with China can conflict with greater military engagement in the region. For another, Europe still shares the same continent with Russia. A shift to Asia as the UK's Integrated Report announces can dilute focus on the more proximate adversary. Final, what would greater interest in the Pacific yield as benefits and costs?

The US argues that to prevent conflict and engage the PRC meaningfully, the road to China must move east across the Atlantic to incorporate Europe, the EU, and NATO. For seventy-one years, NATO, the most successful military alliance in history, has been at one crossroads or another, often wrestling with the question of how to remain relevant or risk becoming a relic. Meant to deter the Soviet Union from attacking Europe, the centerpiece of the Washington Treaty is Article 5, namely that "an attack against one is an attack against all."

While NATO members Turkey and Greece clashed over Cyprus and Britain's Falkland Islands were seized by Argentina in 1982, the first and only time Article 5 was invoked was on September 12, 2001, after the terrorist attacks in New York and Washington by what turned out to be al-Qaeda. The fathers of NATO would have been aghast to learn that the alliance went to war not in the Fulda Gap in Germany against a Soviet onslaught but in distant Afghanistan.

For decades, NATO had adjusted its strategy to deal with a changing security environment. By 1967, the strategy of "massive retaliation" underwritten by superior nuclear forces was being eroded by advancing Russian military capabilities. The result was a strategy of flexible response designed to deter conventional and nuclear war.

In 1991, when the Soviet Union finally imploded, the alliance determined that it needed to expand beyond the European and Atlantic boundaries. The phrase was "out of area or out of business" and the strategy was to use the alliance to promote regional stability. The alliance also embarked on expansion to allow former members of the Warsaw Pact, once fully democratized, to join. Russia ultimately found this expansion to be unacceptable.

After Moscow's interventions first into Georgia in 2008 and then Ukraine six years later, NATO reacted to this violation of long-recognized national borders by rebuilding its defenses against what was viewed as an increasingly aggressive Russia. A European Defense Initiative was created. Three "battle groups" were deployed to the Baltics and the US stationed additional forces in Poland, all as deterrents to Russian encroachment.

Beyond a resurgent Russia, China too has become a major international player. It is building a formidable military. By virtue of its huge economy, China is investing in the West, purchasing ports and rail lines. Through Huawei, it is trying to monopolize 5G technology. It is also pressuring its neighbors to move closer to China and away from the West.

As a result, NATO has recognized that China must be incorporated into its strategic thinking and planning. NATO's secretary general, Norway's former prime minister Jens Stoltenberg, has convened an outside group to propose strategic options for the alliance to consider. China will be part of that review, to be finished in late 2021.

The question for NATO is how to approach China given the constraints of Article 5. It is problematic that any NATO member, if war with China for whatever reasons arose against the US, would allow Article 5 to be invoked.

To prevent Russia from being isolated as NATO expanded, the NATO-Russia Council was created to include Moscow as a direct alliance participant. While a NATO-China Council sounds promising, would China be interested and why would China see this as beneficial? After all, the NATO-Russian Council is now moribund.

The key to engaging China is through increasing partnerships such as the Trans-Pacific Partnership that Trump left. NATO already has eight global partners in Asia: Afghanistan, Australia, Iraq, Japan, Mongolia, New Zealand, Pakistan, and South Korea. Of those, Australia and New Zealand are the most relevant.

NATO should consider an Asian equivalent of expanding the alliance but with non-Article 5 status. In this case, Australia and New Zealand would enjoy full access to the alliance, including the North

Atlantic Council (NAC), the Military Committee, and Article 4 protection, namely the right to consult in crisis. Using Australia and New Zealand as a base, the next steps would be to expand both military partnerships and diplomatic activity to engage China in areas of mutual benefit. An incident-at-sea agreement with the alliance similar to the 1972 US-Soviet pact is one possibility. Climate change also must be a high priority to engage China, along with confidence-building measures to prevent conflict and miscalculation.

Embracing Australia and New Zealand in this manner would be an unmistakable signal to Beijing. Growing partnerships in Asia are the most effective way of engaging China. The US would be foolish to persist in going it alone. And NATO would miss this opportunity. That the RCEP is in force is another reason for more US engagement. China has since signed a trade agreement with the European Union, further freezing the US out.

This decade of the twenty-first century will be the most demanding for NATO since the end of the Cold War. Disruption and the new MAD form the new strategic paradigm. Other disruptors beyond COVID-19, to include climate change, cyber, social media, debt, terrorism, drones, and failed and failing government, will likely consume nations. NATO must accommodate and respond to this new MAD-induced environment.

To do so, the most important weapon is using collective intellect, innovation, and imagination in safeguarding national security. To repeat Winston Churchill's famous advice, "Now that we have run out of money, we must think our way out of danger." No better advice could apply today. Brains, not brawn nor bullets, are the not-so-secret secret weapon—but only if we use them. So here are two out of the box suggestions Churchill might appreciate.

First a revolution in education is vital across government. Except for the Defense Department, education in the other agencies and departments is sporadic and usually underutilized. One immediate solution is to open the service and JCS war colleges more broadly to permit greater attendance by government workers. In fact, promotion to Senior Executive Service (SES) ranks could mandate such attendance. And the war colleges offer enough elective courses beyond the defense that this education along with exposure to some of the best and brightest of civil servants—uniform and civilian—would surely expand intellectual horizons.

Second, genuine breaking the mold thinking is essential regarding both strategy and the means to implement that strategy. Beyond the Porcupine and Mobile Maritime Defenses, suppose examination of alternative uses of resources attempted to stretch innovative and imaginative options. For example, the services have historically been platform orientated; the Army relied on tanks, armored personnel carriers, helicopters, mobile artillery and air defense and indeed trucks for logistics.

The Air Force likewise bought many types of aircraft from stealthy fighters and bombers to cargo, transport, and reconnaissance planes to long-range ballistic missiles and fleets of helicopters. The Navy has procured aircraft carriers, surface combatants, submarines, and supporting air wings and logistics platforms, and the Marines a combination of the above in its pursuit of forcible entry amphibious operations and now its shift to the Indo-Pacific region.

Suppose, instead of spending $1 billion for ten F-35s at $100 million each (or the current cost), 10,000 $100,000 advanced drones with an operating range of up to 200 miles were procured. Similarly, in lieu of the nearly $30 billion cost of a Ford Class nuclear aircraft carrier and its air wing, 30,000 long-range cruise missiles at $1 million each could be purchased. Of course, basing and operating these drones and missiles must be considered.

But if a potential adversary faced 10,000 drones and 30,000 long-range cruise missiles, that is daunting in the extreme. Other such tradeoffs can be made. That does not mean this is an acceptable alternative. However, the purpose of this exercise is to demonstrate how far these what if's can be taken. And we need more what if's in dealing with a MAD-driven world.

Chapter Ten

RESTORING AMERICA III: SMART FOREIGN POLICIES IN THE AGE OF MAD

There is a lot of ruin in a nation.
—Professor Adam Smith
Edinburgh, Scotland,
after the disastrous Battle at Saratoga and
Gentleman Johnny Burgoyne's defeat in 1777

Great-power rivalries were one of the major causes of World War I. And while America won a two-front war a quarter of a century later in a second global conflict in the Atlantic and Pacific, does it make strategic sense in the twenty-first century to have two concurrent potential enemies again?

The Biden administration's first foreign policy priorities were undoing the damage done over the past four years by his predecessor, reassuring friends and allies of American commitment and engagement, and working out a modus operandi with China and Russia. Ruthlessly critiquing the aims and assumptions underlying any policy choices as a first step is essential. While necessary, that will not be sufficient in assuring and implementing a successful policy or strategy. Recognizing and incorporating the impact of the Fifth Horseman and the new MAD on domestic and international politics on foreign policy is also vital. But that may not happen.

THE TRUMP LEGACY: UNDOING THE DAMAGE

Is America safer and more secure today than it was four years ago?

The answer is a resounding *no*! NATO is weaker. China and Russia are more influential. Allies and partners no longer trust America to honor its commitments in the wake of the Trump administration's disengagement and rejection of multilateralism. And America's reputation abroad is stained.

Iraq and Afghanistan remain in political chaos, still wracked by violence. Arms control seems to be becoming uncontrollable. Iran is not constrained in its regional ambitions and, if it so chooses, its pursuit of nuclear weapons. North Korea has refused to denuclearize. And the coronavirus/COVID-19 continues to take its toll.

Many of these problems were the direct result of former President Donald Trump. It may be ironic or coincidental, that in the age of a new MAD, Americans elected the most disruptive chief executive in history. Trump was never silent and indeed was super willing to make his ideas and policies very public through his countless tweets and pronouncements that were as plentiful as snowflakes in a blizzard and could appear at virtually any time day or night.

In shaping foreign policy, listening to what Presidents Putin and Xi both said and wrote publicly is important in revealing future actions.

The same predictability applied to former President Trump underscoring the many errors and flaws in his foreign policy that must be rectified. He delivered, for good or ill, on what he said he would. In his inaugural address, the former president was forthright and candid.

According to Trump, America needed to put itself first. Allies in NATO were "free riders" not paying their fair share for defense. Why should America shoulder these security burdens, he asked, including "endless wars" in Iraq and Afghanistan?

"America first" meant striving to achieve better relations with Russia and China. It meant pursuing unilateral and transactional rather than multilateral-based actions in putting America first and making it great again. The result was a rejection of seven decades of bipartisan American foreign policy.

Not only did a profound lack of knowledge and understanding pervade the president's handling of foreign policy. His hubris was impossible to underestimate. Trump boasted, "I am smarter than my generals."

His key initial foreign and defense appointees resigned or were fired: Rex Tillerson from the State Department, James Mattis from Defense, and National Security Advisors H. R. McMaster and John Bolton. Trump depended on his instincts, Fox News, and a few sycophants, including family members with zero government experience, in making decisions. With the exception of the Israel-UAE-Bahrain agreement, despite the administration's self-adulation, any other foreign policy success is difficult to identify. Indeed, Trump called himself the greatest president, even asserting he has done more for African Americans than even Lincoln.

His first overseas visit in early 2017 was to Riyadh, Saudi Arabia, to gain support from and cement financial deals with Mohammed bin Salman (MBS) for American weapons systems and aircraft. With the macabre murder and dismemberment of Saudi American journalist

Adnan Khashoggi, despite the intelligence communities' assessment that MBS was involved, Trump said nothing.

During his administration, Trump refused to address Saudi Arabia's human rights record. Because he seemed more comfortable with authoritarians, to include Putin, Xi, and Kim, a similar courtesy was extended to MBS. And the US continued to sell weapons to the Saudis that have been used extensively in the Yemen civil war, often against civilians.

Among Trump's most disruptive decisions was to withdraw from the Joint Comprehensive Plan of Action (JCPOA) with Iran to which the permanent five members of the UN Security Council (Britain, China, France, the US, and Russia), the EU, and Germany were also signatories. If Iran complied with the agreement—it was not a treaty, as the Senate could not muster sufficient votes to provide advise and consent—then it would *never* develop nuclear weapons.

Iran could cheat. However, the intrusive inspection regimen would have detected noncompliance. Since then, Iran has increased uranium enrichment and upgraded some of its nuclear facilities. However, so far, Iran has not moved to produce nuclear weapons.

Trump mistakenly asserted it was the worst treaty ever, that America gave Iran billions of dollars in return, and that by using a campaign of maximum pressure, Iran would be forced to renegotiate and, possibly, the regime might be replaced. Trump was wrong on all counts. The money Iran received was from payments made in advance by the shah in 1979 for weapons purchases and impounded after the Iranian Revolution, where the funds accrued substantial interest payments the US would have to make.

The maximum pressure campaign has been a maximum failure. Iran became more hostile and aggressive, expanding its influence in Iraq, Yemen, Syria, and Lebanon, all with tragic consequences for those countries. If the JCPOA were followed, as noted, Iran could not build nuclear weapons.

The Trump administration claimed it had reacted more vigorously to Moscow's interventions than past presidents by imposing sanctions and withdrawing from various treaties to "punish" Russia for repeated violations. But Trump refused to confront Putin on a number of issues, from hacking into US elections and databases to allegations of paying bounties to Taliban in Afghanistan to hunt and kill American service personnel. All this has raised concerns that Putin may have had damning information on President Trump, a charge that Trump has vigorously denied. In any event, that is no longer relevant with a new occupant in the White House.

Trump withdrew from the Intermediate-Range Nuclear Forces Treaty (INF) with Russia that banned land-based missiles with ranges between 500 and 5,500 kilometers. One cause célèbre was Russia's 9M929/SSC-8 missile allegedly accused of violating the treaty. Russia denied that allegation, having previously countered by arguing that the US Aegis Ashore missile defense system in Europe violated the treaty because, with a software update, it was capable of firing a Tomahawk cruise missile with a range of 1,000 miles and that the US had tested a two-stage missile that likewise was a range violation. Those two issues were minor and could have been resolved.

The Trump administration also wanted to extend nuclear arms control discussions to include China, even though China was adamantly opposed to negotiations. Without Chinese participation, the administration argued this was a further reason to leave the INF regime. Abrogating the treaty meant that Russia no longer had any restrictions for its land-based missile systems.

The New START Treaty that ultimately was extended before the February 2021 deadline was also questioned. As the Defense Department began developing land-based missiles that could operate in the 500–5,500 km range, the specter of a new arms race loomed. That concern was intensified by the need to modernize and replace simultaneously all three legs of the US nuclear triad at huge expense that could break the defense budget. Meanwhile, Russia had already modernized its strategic systems, another advantage for Moscow.

As a result, the abrogation of the INF treaty favored Russia because range constraints on land-based missiles were lifted. To counter the latest Russian threat, the US began developing relatively smaller nuclear warheads, arguing that these weapons reinforced deterrence against Russia. That concept was flawed in that even with a smaller warhead, a nuclear weapon is a nuclear weapon. There is no reason to believe that if used, Russian escalation would not follow, a conclusion wiser heads reached during the Cold War when the notion of tactical nuclear war was raised and rejected.

The net result was disruption of the arms control process that had greatly contributed to easing the tensions of the Cold War and indeed probably assisting in the final implosion of the Soviet Union. Perhaps needed more in a MAD-driven world, the future of arms control is bleak as China is unwilling and the triangular politics of the Cold War, along with a Nixon who could go to China politically, are no longer in play. This is not a good sign as the great power competition seems to offer no off-ramp.

But of all the blunders and disruptions the Trump administration made, the most grievous was the unnecessary confrontation provoked with China. The administration withdrew from the Trans-Pacific Partnership, preferring bilateralism to multilateralism. (In fairness, Hillary Clinton had also promised to do so if elected.) The more effective way to deal with China is multilaterally with allies and friends to pressure and negotiate with Beijing. But Beijing preempted American attempts at restarting multilateralism by entering into the fifteen-nation RCEP in late 2020.

Trade became Trump's cause célèbre. He was somehow convinced that the $400 billion trade deficit with China had to be corrected. Had he or his key trade advisors studied accounting, they would have learned that a balance sheet consists of current and capital accounts.

The current account covers all goods and services involved in trade; the capital account registers investments and money flows.

The $400 billion trade imbalance was matched by a $2 trillion to $3 trillion surplus in the capital account with Chinese ownership of US Treasuries and stocks and bonds. Instead of bleeding off jobs, China was underwriting America's deficit spending, very much in America's favor. By imposing tariffs that raised prices, it was the American consumer who picked up the tab, not the government. The tariff war damaged US-China relations and generated greater anti-China attitudes even by Democrats who opposed Trump's trade levies. Disruption trumped again.

The arrival of what Trump called the China virus or Wuhan flu made the relationship even more bitter. The closing of consulates and imposing sanctions on politicians in both countries was childish even though China was rightly accused of massive intellectual property theft. The crackdown on Hong Kong, noted before, was further evidence of malign Chinese intentions. The consequence was that both Republicans and Democrats were largely united on one and only issue: China, and how to constrain its ambitions and actions.

Having disrupted Europe over NATO, Trump raised grave concerns in America and elsewhere with his friendly attitude toward Putin. He sent Asia into turmoil not only over a tariff war with China but his erratic stances on North Korea. From first threatening "fire and fury," Trump then claimed he "fell in love" with North Korea's Kim Jung-un.

The Middle East, Southwest Asia, and the Persian Gulf were the next targets. Trump's mandate for a withdrawal from Afghanistan by year's end, opposed by the Pentagon, was nonetheless ordered. Negotiations with the Taliban in Afghanistan stalled and the government in Kabul remained dangerously divided, with Ashraf Ghani as president and his main rival Abdullah Abdullah as chief executive.

In the summer of 2020, intelligence reported that Russia's military intelligence arm (GRU) was paying bounties to kill American and British troops in Afghanistan. The report was never confirmed or denied, and Trump never took the intelligence seriously. But no commander-in-chief could be seen as not defending the men and women in uniform. However, two other events occurred, one more positive than the other.

The head of ISIS, Abu Bakr al-Baghdadi, was killed by a US raid in Syria in October 2019, a major event. In January 2020, Trump approved a drone strike to kill Iranian major general Qasem Soleimani, head of the Quds Force, shortly after he landed at Baghdad Airport. Whether that assassination was legal, as it took place on the soil of an ally, Trump again claimed great credit. Soleimani was immediately replaced by his deputy, Esmail Qaani.

The major accomplishment of the Trump administration was the recognition of Israel by the United Arab Emirates and Bahrain in August 2020 with the Abraham Accords, joining Egypt and Jordan as the other Arab states to recognize Israel followed by Morocco and Sudan, for a price. While the UAE and Israel have had close unofficial ties and this agreement was not necessarily a surprise, it could have very positive results if properly handled. In essence, Israel traded off nothing in that it would not annex the West Bank and in return will have access to the UAE treasury, no doubt using UAE money to finance leading-edge Israeli technology.

The agreement also extended a lifeline to Israeli prime minister Benjamin Netanyahu, who is under indictment possibly facing conviction and jail time and was finally replaced as prime minister by a new government in mid-2021. Moving the embassy from Tel Aviv to Jerusalem also was a boon to Netanyahu while pointlessly provoking Arabs and Palestinians and seen as rejection of a two-state solution.

At the end of November 2020, Netanyahu met secretly with the Saudi crown prince, MBS. This meeting was unprecedented. Whether it presaged a breakthrough now that Netanyahu is gone is unclear. Clearly, Iran could be the target of a new Saudi-Israeli relationship. The Biden administration no doubt is exploring this possibility.

The vagaries and idiosyncrasies of Trump's other foreign policies, such as threatening to cut US forces in Germany by a third over pique with Chancellor Merkel over the Nord Stream 2 pipeline and criticizing allied leaders and other friends, were not conducive to enhancing American prestige and influence. The net result of these disruptions was at least partial dismantlement and erosion of American foreign policy in place since World War II. The status and standing of America in virtually all polls are at the lowest points since the Vietnam War. Most concerning is that many Europeans placed greater trust in Putin and Xi than in Trump.

In this MAD-driven world, perhaps it was predictable that the forty-fifth president of the United States would become the principal and often reckless disruptor in abandoning multilateralism and ending decades of traditional and successful American foreign policies concerning allies, partners, commitments, treaties, and agreements. Ending "endless wars" was a fine slogan provided vacuums were not created that made bad situations worse. In one sentence, the most disruptive president in American history has been the most destructive of its foreign policies since the end of World War I.

All presidents make mistakes. George W. Bush's decision to invade Iraq was the most disastrous since the Vietnam War. But Bush's errors were in misjudgment. Trump's errors were malfeasance. That was inexcusable.

NEEDED: A SMART FOREIGN POLICY

The purposes of the new National Security Strategy must be based on achieving peace and prosperity through partnerships that will contain, mitigate, and prevent Massive Acts of Disruption, whether of man or nature, from threatening and destroying the safety, security, prosperity, and health of the United States and its friends and allies.

This strategy requires an integrated, cross-governmental approach that must intimately engage both legislative and executive branches and friends and allies, and, in parallel, the National Defense Strategy must be able to contain, defend, and engage potential adversaries and other threats.

Make no mistake: unless the Biden administration acts quickly and decisively to make fundamental changes in foreign policy, it will be impossible to repair all the damage done during the Trump years. Since control of the Senate was not determined until the January 2021 Georgia runoffs, that was a further complication. One additional concern was how much the Biden administration was an extension of Obama's, as many appointments went to Obama alumni.

As cited earlier, when Joe Biden became president on January 20, 2021, he faced an even worse hand at home and abroad than Obama or FDR. The national security structure was in disarray. The State Department and Foreign Service had been emasculated. The Pentagon had been without consistent or firm civilian leadership since Jim Mattis's resignation. And the intelligence agencies were battered by Trump's successful attempts at politicizing the leadership.

Biden's first tasks were to respond immediately to rectify these deficiencies. He appointed his cabinet and key staff. But his team was four years out of office and not current on the latest intelligence. A Republican Senate complicated a long confirmation process that normally takes well in excess of six months before a full administration is in place. That transition was done "virtually" with social distancing in light of COVID.

The new administration, under the national security advisor, began a formal interagency foreign policy review. In normal times, this process takes about a year. But today is far from normal, and a profound reexamination of America's global role is long overdue. Recommending change on the margin—often the outcome—will not work.

President Biden would have been well advised to follow President Dwight Eisenhower's example in creating a modern version of Ike's Project Solarium: a no-holds-barred examination of foreign and national security policy. Solarium was also the name used by the cyberspace commission that issued a hard-hitting and sadly underread report earlier this year. But there is no reason a Solarium-like effort could not still be re-initiated.

After taking office in January 1953, Ike's priority was to end the Korean War. But Stalin's death in March, with a cabinet already divided over the Soviet Union, demanded a thorough reexamination of Kremlin policy. Eisenhower also harbored grave concerns that by overly militarizing the Cold War, the economy would suffer. Solarium was Ike's answer.

Named for the top floor of the White House, Solarium was conducted under the cover of a policy review at the National War College at Fort Lesley J. McNair in Washington. Three teams were convened. The conclusions led to the policy of containment and directive NSC 162/2 that set direction for much of the Cold War and reinforced what would become Ike's "strategic new look" emphasizing nuclear deterrence and "massive retaliation." And the option of more aggressive actions such as "roll back" of Soviet control of satellite states was rejected.

Solarium took six weeks, completed in July 1953. Members were largely serving military officers who fought in World War II and Korea and some in the First World War. All were male, white, and did not reflect what would be later called the interagency process.

In a 2021 Solarium, four teams should be convened with members drawn from the private sector. The objectives would be to challenge conventional wisdom by reevaluating the relevance of great-power competition as the foundation for current strategy; to identify and prioritize possibly existential and other major security challenges and threats, including failed government, climate change, and future pandemics; and to propose policy responses. A deadline of two months should be set.

Team A would be chartered to analyze and critique great-power competition with emphasis on China and Russia; Team B to focus on the government's organization and ability to provide for national security; Team C to identify possible existential and major threats to include climate change, pandemics, debt, and other disruptors; and Team D to identify the roles of alliances, partnerships, and international and nongovernmental organizations.

The results of such a Solarium exercise could be used for immediate decisions and as the basis for challenging the longer-term interagency process to overcome the bureaucratic tendency for producing compromised and watered-down strategies. The Foreign Affairs, Foreign Relations, and Armed Services Committees of both chambers of Congress should be invited to provide inputs as well.

The reasons for urgency are evident. The nation is in crisis at home and abroad. Many current policies and strategies are not working. And the government is gridlocked.

Under these circumstances, the new administration must apply creative, innovative, and bold strategic thinking if the nation is to be made safer, more secure, and prosperous. Using the model of Eisenhower's Project Solarium is an ideal place to start.

A BIDEN FOREIGN POLICY

Successful foreign policy matches national interests with achievable goals and resources using diplomacy to negotiate favorable terms with friends, allies, and rivals. That means understanding what motivates the other sides and what incentives and disincentives could be applied to ensure successful outcomes for foreign policy. Foreign policies that worked followed this model, combining both pragmatism and sensible idealism. Those that failed did not.

Under the Brains-Based Approach, instead of defining aims, a more useful exercise is to specify the outcomes that policy and strategy are to obtain. The general outcomes must be to enhance peace and prosperity through partnerships and renewed American leadership. The first step must be to reject great-power competition as the foundation for strategy and policy. The flaws and negative consequences of that policy were fully described in earlier chapters.

Here, history is useful. Failing to recall or worse, ignoring past successes in shaping future foreign policies, is inexcusable. Despite his fall from grace, Richard Nixon had major foreign policy triumphs. The first was the Nixon Doctrine. In this doctrine, the United States assumed responsibility for maintaining the strategic balance with the USSR. That led to successful arms control agreements. Regional states and allies were asked to assume more responsibility for local security supported by American assistance. This policy had great application in the Persian Gulf.

Called the two-pillar policy, Nixon was able to mobilize Shia Iran under the shah and Sunni Saudi Arabia under the royals to ally against the Soviet Union. Clearly, the perceived threat posed by the USSR overcame the religious animosity in Islam. That alliance persisted until the 1979 Iranian Revolution.

Second was triangular diplomacy and outreach to China to counterbalance the Soviet Union. Of course, on the other side of the ledger was the facetious claim of a "secret plan" to end the Vietnam War. However, the two-pillar and triangular diplomacy policies are very relevant today if the current administration is able to seize on those constructs. Because Russia and China have few real allies, both of these past initiatives assume greater relevance.

Are there equivalents today of Nixon's triangular and two-pillar policies as applied to Russia and other states? China no longer can balance Russia, and Saudi Arabia and Iran are hardened enemies. NATO could be the cornerstone for a new version of triangular diplomacy. Here, the United States must reassume aggressive leadership. While domestic politics require demanding NATO allies spend more on defense, that will not happen until long after the pandemic ends. As previously argued, it is not the most relevant geo-strategic issue.

The intellectual challenge is finding new leverage in foreign policy in which two and not one major adversary confronts the United States. Although some argue that the rivalry with China is over both power and ideology, that is a false dichotomy. While the Communist Party of China is seen as the "enemy," that too is an oversimplification.

The other challenge is to balance the need to respond to the Fifth Horseman and MAD with these traditional threats and issues. In this case, Russia and China are critical. However, Russia and China cannot ignore MAD, as it has similarly sinister prospects for them that are not restricted by borders. Mobilizing the need to address MAD can and must engage China and Russia.

The tools that Biden can muster are powerful. These could constitute a twelve-point foreign policy agenda. The first is the energy and dynamism of America and its entrepreneurial-driven economy. Of course, COVID-19 must be overcome. Once that occurs, America can almost certainly repeat the economic success after the Spanish flu receded a century ago if the 1923 Fund, or one like it, can be put in place.

Second, America has far more allies, partners, and states disposed to it than China and Russia—once the damage done by Trump is repaired. NATO, the EU, treaty parties and friends in Asia, Israel and the Arab states recognizing Israel, and African and Western Hemisphere states must be utilized and be made part of the actions that follow.

India plays a special role because of its size and geography. But India is not Nixon's China. It is, however, very important because many of the contentious issues with China such as climate change and free and fair trade are germane to India.

Third, because government is subject to gridlock and inertia, the private sector can and must be mobilized to complement, reinforce, and fill gaps in policy. As Putin has militarized private companies such as the Wagner Group (and the US had with Blackwater) and China weaponized Belt and Road, the Biden team must "civilianize" the private sector and private foundations as key tools. If billions can be raised for campaigns and for presidential inaugurations, surely the private sector can be mobilized for this effort.

For example, the Gates Foundation has been exemplary in fighting disease and pandemics. The list of other philanthropic organizations can fill libraries. These must be mobilized with civilian forms of "soft power."

Coordination of policy can be done in the White House and execution in the State Department. The three most pressing areas are healthcare, climate change, and information, including education. By having private sector resources applied in a focused and coordinated fashion, the US will have powerful tools to complement its resources and policies. New MAD mandates such an approach because without it, the government is unlikely to succeed, especially if politicization continues and Republicans and Democrats remain intractably divided.

Fourth, neither China nor Russia must be regarded as enemies or even competitors. As noted, respectful rivals should be the endpoint even given the hostility in Congress toward both. Each is a sovereign state with whom some form of relations must be established. The Cold War term of "peaceful coexistence" might apply. Not every action either state takes is disruptive or dangerous. That leads to the next requirement.

Fifth, focus must be on specific issues that are contentious, conflictual, and concerning. That will not be difficult to compile. Regarding China, among these issues are intellectual property theft, unfair trade and investment practices as seen from the US and the West, Belt and Road projects that could be debt traps, climate change, military escalation, and technologies such as 5G, AI, and quantum computing that could be used as Trojan horses to provide China intrusive means of information gathering.

No doubt some would like to make human rights, Hong Kong, treatment of Uighurs, and the dictatorship of the CCP central to American foreign policy. The flaw here is that until other issues can be resolved, no chance exists of China accepting this agenda. And frankly, the other issues will not be easily resolved.

Regarding Russia, the issues that require resolution include active measures, occupation of the Donbass in Ukraine and Crimea, an arms race, military miscalculation, intrusion into domestic politics, cyber espionage and theft, and disinformation.

But there is a certain sense of inferiority in Washington over fears that China or Russia will dominate new technologies of 5G, AI, quantum computing, genomes, and others. The reality is that technology is fungible. A temporary lead does not guarantee permanency.

No state can maintain technological superiority in perpetuity. But the US does not seem to recognize that. Perhaps America is more paranoid than Russia after all.

Sixth, using allies, partners, and others noted above, a series of conferences must be created to develop approaches to resolving each of the main issues. Theoretically, this should be part of the UN's mandate. Certainly, the UN must be integrated into any approach. However, with nearly two hundred members, the UN may be too large and too politically divided to be fully effective.

NATO indeed has greater strategic relevance to both Russia and China. For the US, the road to the Pacific first runs east through Europe. As noted earlier, bringing Australia and New Zealand into closer cooperation with NATO, as well as Japan and South Korea, will have an impact in counterbalancing China's influence. Likewise, India and Vietnam have value in balancing China.

To enable this strategy, NATO must return to having greater global reach and influence while not compromising Article 5. Instead of making the 2 percent of GDP spending goal, updating the old phrase of "out of area or out of business" to one of "the cornerstone for global stability" captures this intent. And even small amounts of NATO presence in the Pacific through staff meetings, conferences, and assist visits are significant. That Britain and France have deployed warships to Asia is important, and perhaps an annual visit to the region by a reconstituted NATO naval squadron is possible.

Seventh, incentives as well as disincentives are needed. Relief of sanctions, for example, is a possible quid pro quo for Russian movement on Ukraine. Here, Russian withdrawal from eastern Ukraine could be balanced by a free and fair referendum on Crimea to allow residents the chance to decide, realizing that the majority would vote to remain with Russia. But the largest potential breakthrough is in arms control beyond New START.

Arms control could be one means of improving relations by limiting an arms race and preventing future unintended escalation. The withdrawal from the Open Skies Treaty by the Biden administration was a setback. And this is not the 1970s, for arms control is greatly complicated by cyber, "gray zone" operations, hypersonics, non-nuclear standoff weapons with the capacity to destroy hardened targets, drones, and nuclear powered and armed torpedoes with intercontinental range, intermixed with defenses.

Similarly, the incentives for China must be economic and environmental that de-emphasize military rivalry and competition. Could China not invest in the 1923 Fund, particularly in the international sectors of environment and healthcare? Can some form of a free and fair trade agreement be negotiated once tariffs are lifted?

Eighth, other policies should incorporate these ideas. The US and NATO should be making maximum effort on a range of arms control and confidence-building measures (CBM) with Russia. The more Russia may attempt to backtrack, the more aggressive NATO should become to return to the Treaty on Conventional Armed Forces in Europe and even new agreements on exchanges of observers and staffs as part of CBM. Counterterrorism should be part of this new intensified engagement along with counter-proliferation.

At the same time, social media and twenty-first century equivalents of Radio Free Europe and other communications should be countering Russian propaganda and targeting the Russian public with factual reporting of news. Putin and the leadership are very sensitive to domestic intrusion, particularly on their personal lives and personal wealth. This can provide leverage if cleverly done in other areas where, if progress is made, then perhaps these counter-influence operations can be reduced depending on future Russian behavior.

Strategy also requires brilliance in identifying issues about which Russian leaders are hypersensitive to create incentives and disincentives. For example, merely raising the need to update or abolish the obsolete Montreux Convention of 1936 that regulates access of non-riparian warships to the Black Sea will certainly get Moscow's attention, especially since Russia views that region as its strategic center of gravity.

While some will argue that extending and even suggesting to extend NATO membership to Georgia and Ukraine is essential to containing Russia, given the sensitivity of the region to Moscow, a quid pro quo for deferring that conversation might encourage discussion of how Georgia and Ukraine can be kept secure and thus may be more effective negotiating options.

Exposing the extent of wealth that has accrued to Russian leaders, while understood by most Russians, still will erode the legitimacy of the regime and Putin. For example, Russia continues waging propaganda and other forms of information warfare against the West. This is an area that must be turned against Moscow. Challenging directly and where necessary with subtlety Putin's legitimacy can be both an incentive and disincentive for Russian behavior.

Ninth, in that regard, if adopted and if not, the more the US can show how the 1923 Fund, or other initiatives, is developing renewable and clean energy, the more Russia is put at economic risk for the long term given its dependence on fossil fuels. While the so-called Reagan strategy of using defense spending to bankrupt the Soviet Union failed, a policy that aims at undercutting Russian dependence on fossil fuels certainly should be effective in affecting Russian reactions.

During the Cold War, the West was prepared for a lengthy struggle. Similarly, by exposing potential future weaknesses when less global demand will exist for oil and gas, Russian prosperity is being put at risk. Part of this strategy must include deriving analysis of what happens in this future when oil and gas are less economically viable and the aspiration for aiding Russia in this transition so as not to repeat the mistakes of the collapse of the USSR and to give Russia incentives for its behavior.

Since President Putin believes that the greatest geopolitical disaster of the twentieth century was the implosion of the Soviet Union, what happens when Russia no longer can depend on oil and gas revenues and the nation faces great economic disruption? Merely raising this question clearly will get Putin's attention.

Tenth, regarding China, the argument has been for a more confrontational approach. That should be discouraged based on an understanding of China's culture, history, society, and needs. That does not mean toughness and firmness do not apply. Both do.

Toughness and firmness, however, need not be entirely adversarial, as both countries have many common interests over climate change, economic growth, and preventing conflict. The late and great thinker Zbigniew Brzezinski understood this. He foresaw that China would be the economic colossus of Asia and the United States of the Western Hemisphere.

The choice was to cooperate with or confront the other. The latter made no sense. To achieve the former required a modus operandi. Earlier reference was made to Nixon's policies. The executive agent of the China policy was America's other great foreign policy force, Henry Kissinger. Kissinger spent many days in Beijing working out a modus operandi.

President Biden does not have a Kissinger or a Brzezinski. That doesn't mean he cannot work out a modus operandi with China and Russia. When he does, in addition to defeating COVID, that accomplishment will make him one of the greatest presidents in history. If he can mitigate the fierce politicization, Pope Francis should consider him for sainthood.

One opportunity is to use the Pacific Deterrence Initiative directed by Congress to counter China and expanded to focus more on partnerships than confrontation. Partnerships, whether economic, political, or military, are the most appropriate means to deal with China. Militarization of foreign policy will only provoke a response in kind by China. An arms race is in no one's interest. To make the point again, the great-power rivalry and naval arms race were major causes of the First World War.

The intent must be to move to a respectful rivalry.

Eleventh, all states need to respond to the Fifth Horseman and MAD. Russia and China are not immune. Making the case that a global response to MAD is a societal good can be used to engage China and Russia. China and Russia cannot be isolated from MAD. Each of these disruptors impact universally. No amount of population control can completely avoid them.

Twelfth and last, optimism is essential. That the end of the Spanish flu led to the greatest economic boom in American history is not confined to the new world. This, too, can be a powerful argument.

A FINAL WARNING AND WISH

Many will not immediately absorb the consequences of the arrival of the Fifth Horseman and MAD. A military aphorism warns that the only task more difficult than introducing a new idea is shedding an old one. The Westphalian tradition of a state-centric system of international politics and interstate conflict remains powerfully embedded. Of course, great and small power rivalries will persist. The critical difference is that these conflicts and rivalries have been replaced and overshadowed by this Fifth Horseman and MAD. The coronavirus was the first messenger. It will not be the last.

Lurking are two more potential massive disruptors: arms control or its failure and demographics. The failure of arms control will provoke an arms race that is unnecessary, and for the United States, will require a transfer of resources from the conventional land, sea, air, and space forces to replace the strategic nuclear deterrent triad. Space, cyber, and hypersonics, among other technologies, will likewise complicate arms control and means to reduce conflict. Here, the nation is not fully prepared for this form of MAD.

As populations age and/or are forced to migrate, social pressures will be exacerbated. People and populations have always been sources of massive disruption. China, Japan, and the United States face an older society. The ratio of workers to retirees will approach low single digits, raising profound questions about allocation of resources with an increasingly older population. The exodus of millions from North Africa and the Middle East/Southwest Asia has already overstressed receiving states, rekindled populism and anti-immigration attitudes, and magnified the size of these humanitarian disasters. If shortages in food, water, and energy resources continue over access, these pressures will turn demographics into another MAD. Are states prepared for this?

For the United States to corral the Fifth Horseman and MAD, the most important weapon is our collective intellect striving to be innovative and imaginative in fielding solutions for safeguarding the safety, security, prosperity, well-being, and health of our nation and our friends and allies. To repeat Winston Churchill's famous advice, "Now that we have run out of money, we must think our way out of danger."

But will we have the fortitude, common sense, and brains to do that? On this the fate of the nation rests.

Endnote

2021 AND 2037

Will we understand, respond, and lead in a MAD-driven world? Too often America's actions have been reactive, too late, or, worse, non-existent. As COVID-19 tragically revealed, failure to react in a timely fashion led to tens of thousands of unnecessary deaths. What happens if or when an even greater disruption erupts, incited by one of the seven disruptors, and the nation is overwhelmed by catastrophic events whether due to man or to nature? Is the Constitution still viable, adaptable, and fit for the twenty-first century and MAD?

Most critically, can failed and failing government be reversed? If it cannot, then it is not overstatement to conclude that the nation is at perhaps one of the gravest periods of risk in its history. On the answer to this question of governance, America's future rests.

What happens in 2037 after President Bennett finishes her second term will be largely determined by actions taken or deferred in 2021 and 2022. In terms of an action plan, the nation needs first an overarching construct for governing that will preserve and defend the Constitution against all enemies—foreign and increasingly domestic. And make no mistake: America is at grave risk at home.

The basic reason is that the conflict between MAD and the vulnerabilities and fragilities of modern society created by the combined forces of the diffusion of power and globalization is potentially existential, unlike any time in the nation's history, certainly since 1861. And the Constitution, along with checks and balances, is surely at grave risk as is the future viability of that great document.

That twenty-five thousand armed National Guardsman and fifteen thousand law enforcement officers were required to ensure the safety and security of the inauguration of Joe Biden as forty-sixth president on January 20, 2021, meant something was indeed very rotten not in Denmark but in America. The cause was a pandemic more infectious and life-threatening to the political health of the nation than the coronavirus/COVID-19 pandemic has been to its physical health even after having claimed six hundred thousand American lives so far.

This pandemic is political, ideological, cultural, and spiritual. Both Republicans and Democrats bear equal responsibility and accountability for its virulence. Yet, without demanding and assigning accountability, will this occur? And if both do not take place, will this pandemic mutate to an even more deadly strain that further infects and threatens the Constitution, government, and the American way of life?

It is easy to blame Donald Trump and "Trumpism." Democrats certainly do. The former president certainly has contributed to the degradation of truth, fact, and credibility of government. Trump also widened the already huge political divides.

Trump's embrace of dog whistle–like slogans such as "fake news" and "alternative facts" was exacerbated by an irrational willingness to ignore truth and spread lies, falsehoods, and misstatements—according to the *Washington Post* by the many tens of thousands—to advance his interests and suit his ego. Trump supporters that gathered in Washington on January 6, 2021 and those that stormed the Capitol were largely incited by Trump's repeated lies that the presidential election was stolen by Democrats. Trump claimed a massive landslide victory, asserting that Joe Biden was an illegitimate president. He demanded wrongly that Vice President Mike Pence could reverse the election results as Electoral College ballots were counted.

These, as Voltaire would have defined them, were all "damn lies." Yet, according to polls, a majority of Republicans believed Trump's rants and a greater majority were more supportive of him than of the party. How can a nation function when truth and fact are missing in action and the most outrageous of lies, distortions, and untruths are accepted without question?

But while Democrats do not have a leader with the personality and control of the party that Trump still has, their party has been driven to the far left and its ultra-progressive agenda. The Green New Deal is unworkable. Embracing Black Lives Matter and taking so-called "woke" politics to extremes, likewise provokes a strong backlash. The Biden spending proposals indeed would impose a radical transformation of American society that is not universally acceptable.

In a 51 percent nation, when the majority of Americans are broadly center left and center right and without real representation and both political parties are united only on destroying the other, without an overriding force, it is difficult to see how government can indeed be more productive. Indeed, and impossible to know, had Hillary Clinton been elected president in 2016, would that have led to a better outcome?

The answer is probably no because Mrs. Clinton was as politically polarizing as Donald Trump. Her White House could not have been more chaotic than Trump's. But, if her campaign promises were followed, her policies toward China and Russia would have not substantially differed from Trump's except for his extraordinary treatment of and seeming regard for Putin. She may not have called for tax cuts and indeed would have tried to raise rates on the wealthier Americans.

How the Clinton administration would have dealt with COVID, likewise, is unknowable. It would have been hard-pressed to improve on the creation of vaccines. It would not have been hard-pressed to improve on Trump's distribution and inoculation plans.

Proof of how politics have become even more pernicious and bitter is Joe Biden. Biden is the most experienced politician to assume the presidency since George H.W. Bush and possibly ever. While Biden is a man of great decency who respects the traditions of the Senate and the presidency, nonetheless, partisan politics in the first months of his presidency worsened. To some degree, Trump's long shadow is still present. Even if he were to disappear or become less relevant, the government would still be failing.

The reality is that MAD, like COVID, has deeply infected the nation and its government. Recognizing and responding to MAD will not be the magic vaccine that provides the cure to our political ills. It is a necessary start.

A happier answer may rest in history. After the 1918–1920 Spanish flu pandemic ended, it was erased from the public's memory as if a bad dream. By 1923, the nation was embarked on the greatest economic boom in its history. A year or so from now, once vaccines are broadly administered and work against COVID mutations, a similar memory loss could follow as and if the economy takes off. Or, if mutations prove resistant to vaccines and COVID-19 continues, this crisis could be far from over.

A more sinister outcome, however, may be more likely. Suppose divisions over politics and disparities of race, gender, and income widen rather than contract? Suppose that increases in crime, gun violence, and other societal disruptions continue? That alone will create huge political pressures on the White House for responses, exacerbated by the onset of the 2022 Congressional elections and Republican efforts to win both Houses back.

Making Washington an armed fortress to ensure the "peaceful" transition of power following a duly administered election, an extraordinary oxymoron, seemed unthinkable a year ago, as did a pandemic infecting the globe. But the unthinkable may become too thinkable.

The United States, we are constantly told, is a 250-year-old experiment, meaning that at some point the experiment could fail. As long as truth and fact are dismissed by fake news and alternative facts, America and Americans are at grave risk. Will that make a difference? And will a cure be found in time?

Domestically, recommendations for reform and modernization of the branches of government were made to that end. Hopefully, if implemented—and that is a big if given past failures to accept necessary changes in governing—basic ambiguities in the statutes about presidential succession will be reconciled. A degree of greater relevance as well as efficiency and effectiveness will follow in how America governs and how Americans are governed. A crucial measure of civility and compromise will be restored. And the Constitution will endure for another quarter of a millennium at the least.

The 1923 Fund would have spurred economic growth by creating new jobs as part of containing climate change and rebuilding infrastructure. Modernizing healthcare likewise will be an engine of economic growth and the means not only to contain, mitigate, and prevent the further spread of coronavirus but to prepare for future pandemics. Expansion of access to the internet and 5G systems can be the equivalent of the automobile and associated infrastructure that created the greatest economic growth in the nation's history in the wake of the 1918–1920 Spanish flu pandemic. As the economy expands, debt shrinks.

But the 1923 Fund can only be an alternative to be considered if or when the Biden Jobs and Families proposals are defeated or cut.

In terms of the proposals for national security, defense, and foreign policy strategies, the aims must be to deal not only with peer and near peers but also to contain, mitigate, and prevent Massive Acts of Disruption, whether of man or nature. Both MAD and state and non-state actors threaten the safety, security, prosperity, and health of the United States and its friends and allies. Solutions require an integrated, cross-governmental approach that must intimately engage legislative and executive branches and friends and allies and, in parallel, support the National Defense Strategy to contain, defend, and engage potential adversaries and other threats.

The Porcupine and Mobile Maritime Defense strategies give body to this framework. Cyber, social media, terrorism, and drones will be harnessed so that the beneficial sides of MAD are additive to society while not unduly restricting access to these technologies. And the most likely new disruptor—arms control—can be used to prevent the dangerous excesses of arms races in space, cyber, technology, and other sectors that not only threaten stability but raise the prospect of conflict.

On the other hand, the nation can allow great-power competition to spawn even harsher rivalries that, unchecked, put the United States on what could be an inevitable path to conflict or worse, and not only with China and Russia. The US could see allies turning away, seeking better relations with Beijing and Moscow for economic and political reasons.

Those are the stark choices. The year 2021 could prove to be the most important inflection point in the nation's history since 1861, 1914, 1939, or 2001 if we take the wrong path. Fast-forward to 2037.

Prior to the June 6, 1944, Normandy landings, the Supreme Commander, Allied Forces Europe, General Dwight D. Eisenhower drafted two communiques. One reported the success of the landings. The second did not. Fortunately, Ike did not have to send the handwritten message that stated:

Our landings in the Cherbourg-Havre area have failed to gain a satisfactory foothold and I have withdrawn the troops. My decision to attack at this time and place was based on the best information available. The troops, the air, and the navy did all that bravery and devotion to duty could do. If any blame or fault attaches to the attempt it is mine alone.

In her Farewell Address to the nation in January 2037, depending upon how events evolved, President Anne Jackson Bennett could face the same Hobson's choice as Ike did nearly a century earlier. Unlike her initial address eight years before, if prior presidents had indeed accepted the reality and challenge of the Fifth Horseman and MAD and put in place strategies and programs to corral both, it would be self-evident what she would say. But who knows what will happen over the next fifteen years? And at this stage, optimism may not prevail.

After General "Johnny" Burgoyne was defeated at the Battle of Saratoga in 1777, a student approached the venerable Professor Adam Smith at the University of Edinburgh with the admonition, "Burgoyne defeated. We are ruined." Smith responded with what could be America's saving grace. "My boy," he said, "there is a lot of ruin in a nation."

Let us hope that is not the best answer to our ills.

Appendix

A BRAINS-BASED APPROACH TO STRATEGIC THINKING

A Brains-Based Approach to Strategic Thinking consists of three parts: complete knowledge and full understanding of all aspects of the problem set and solutions; a twenty-first century mindset that facilitates innovation, imagination, and rigor; and the means for affecting, influencing, and controlling the will and perception of real and potential enemies.

In waging war and defending the nation's interests and security, since the earliest days of the republic, presidents and administrations have been accused of having no strategy, the wrong strategy, or a strategy unconnected to resources. Underscoring this criticism, over the past sixty years, every war the US started, it lost. And today, the greatest threat to the US is not the Islamic State, a recrudescent Russia, or an expanding China.

The major threat is a badly broken government torn apart by the fiercest partisan differences since the end of the Cold War, with little expectation of this condition repairing itself in the short-term or absent an existential crisis. Translated to the US military, the greatest danger is not from abroad; it is at home. The issue is uncontrollable internal-cost growth that if not contained will do more damage to the US military than the wars in Iraq and Afghanistan.

On the current trajectory, uncontrollable internal-cost growth for personnel, healthcare, retirees, overhead and administration, operations, and weapons systems will produce a "hollow force" unready and underequipped to carry out its duties even at current levels of defense spending—which, in constant dollars, exceeds the largest defense budgets of the Reagan buildup and an active force nearly a million stronger.

Regarding the wars of the past sixty-five years, the Korean War, which the West did not start, was at best a draw. Vietnam was a complete defeat and humiliation. The 1990–1991 Iraq War was a tactical victory that would postpone a second confrontation. Critics (wrongly) blamed the first Bush administration for not marching to Baghdad and toppling Saddam Hussein. When his son did that in 2003 and succeeded, the second Iraq War arguably became the worst geostrategic catastrophe in America's history, accelerating the unraveling of the greater Middle East and precipitating many of the crises unfolding today. Sadly, Afghanistan is in greater turmoil and disarray as the Taliban appear to be increasingly contesting Kabul's control of that war-torn country.

A Brains-Based Approach to Strategic Thinking can be defined in three parts.

First, this approach must be knowledge-based to allow and facilitate as complete an understanding of all aspects of strategy as possible, from basic aims to intimate analysis of the adversary, various courses of actions and assumptions underlying each, and the consequences, including the resource implications, costs, and the objective calculation of affordability in blood and treasure.

Second, this approach must have a twenty-first century mindset based on understanding of the end of the Westphalian system of state-centric politics, the arrival of the Fifth Horseman and MAD and its fundamental importance and relevance to protecting the nation and its prosperity and democracy.

Third, the aim of strategy and policy must be to affect, influence, and control the will and perception of the other side by greater power of intellect employing innovation, ingenuity, and inventiveness, often called "out of the box" thinking.

The basis for a Brains-Based Strategic Approach must rest in understanding the forces that are at play have changed and are changing international politics. Driving these changes is the assault on the Westphalian system found in three largely invisible and accompanying overarching realities that have been ignored or dismissed.

First, the most powerful armies, navies, and air forces in the world are hard-pressed to and usually will not defeat a determined adversary who lacks those capabilities and chooses to wage war with what Carl von Clausewitz called "other means" and with great resolve and tenacity. The Islamic State, a.k.a., Da'esh, is the most relevant example.

Second, while we use the term "asymmetrical" as promiscuously as hybrid warfare, the reality is that these adversaries are beating us badly in cost-exchange ratios and particularly in winning the political and propaganda narratives as well. Da'esh was ahead in both areas, and Russia's Putin is sweeping the PR battlefield.

Third and most importantly, the strategic linkages between and among many disparate conflicts must form the foundations for responses in this post-Westphalian world along with understanding the effects of Mutual Assured Disruption.

Regarding the first two issues, the US spent around $70 billion to counter IEDs that cost the other side relative pennies. Ironically, having abandoned multimillions of dollars on weapons systems and other equipment that were captured by the enemy in Afghanistan and

Iraq that cost them nothing, America is spending another fortune in destroying them. And, being brutally frank, suicide bombers likewise are cheap.

Compounding these advantages that favor the enemy, our strategies are too often reactive, overly sensitive to "political" pressures rather than the Clausewitzian view that war is a conflict of wills with an admixture of policy, and address symptoms rather than causes of violence. And, of course, having a single overarching or existential state-based threat common to 350 years of the Westphalian world such as Nazi Germany or the Soviet Union made strategizing easier.

In World War II, the strategy became clear: win first in Europe and then in the Pacific through mobilizing America's arsenal of democracy and Russian manpower to force the Axis enemies to surrender unconditionally. The strategy of containment and deterrence produced the bloodless Cold War victory with the collapse of the Soviet Union in 1989. Unfortunately, the twenty-first century has not offered a single or principal adversary around which one strategy could be crafted.

Yet unifying linkages among today's many disparate threats, dangers, and challenges exist. Globalization and the diffusion of power have made the world far more interdependent and interconnected. It is this interconnectivity and interdependence that form these linkages and hence the need for a mindset for the twenty-first century.

The consequence is that events in Russia, Ukraine, and Europe are directly related to events in Iraq, Syria, and the Gulf (of which Iran is a vital part) either through common interests in defeating terrorism or in preventing destabilization from one region contaminating the other. Because of the flaws in fashioning our policies, we have failed to grasp this vital truth of a post-Westphalian world, too often substituting twentieth-century thinking.

What else constitutes a Brains-Based Approach and how might it be implemented? Twenty-five years ago, "shock and awe" was developed by a group of former senior persons that included Donald

Rumsfeld for a time. The group argued that the aim of policy was to affect, influence, and control the will and perception of the adversary. In simple terms, get the other person to do what we wanted and stop doing what we found objectionable. Force was but one and not necessarily the sufficient or only tool. Unfortunately, shock and awe was turned into a sound bite and not a strategy in the second Gulf War and thus had been discredited by this misuse.

This short statement of the intent of shock and awe, however, should be the centerpiece for a Brains-Based Approach: the overriding requirement to affect, influence, and control the will and perception of an adversary. In other words, use our brains to defeat theirs!

Shock and awe also set four criteria: obtaining great knowledge and understanding of the enemy at all levels, brilliance in execution, rapidity, and gaining sufficient control of the environment in all dimensions to impose our will. These criteria can form the basis for any Brains-Based Approach, particularly the knowledge requirement.

Whether we like it or not, absent a debacle, miscalculation, or crisis à la September 11, defense budgets at best will not grow and more likely will contract. This is surely the case. Because of the increasing costs for people—from pay and incentives to retirement and healthcare—and for even more capable weapons (e.g., aircraft carriers, Trident replacement, and F-35s) and the cost asymmetries that favor adversaries who do not have the same need for expensive conventional forces, the consequences are self-evident. The West is facing the return of the dreaded "hollow force" that plagued America after the Vietnam War.

The only questions are how much will our forces contract and when, and if that contraction will yield a "hollow force" that inevitably results from lack of resources and the failure or refusal to take these consequences seriously.

To mitigate these effects, we need to think our way out of this conundrum and not rely on the tactic of substituting pounds or dollars for brains or rely on obsolete worldviews. October marks the anniversary of the Battle of Agincourt in 1415. As we know, Henry V's relatively small army of about five to ten thousand defeated a force many times larger thanks to the longbow and a battlefield turned into an impassable quagmire, halting French cavalry literally in its tracks. With a Brains-Based Approach to Strategic Thinking, drawing on that battle, we would ask what are the new longbows of the future and how do we make future geostrategic battlefields such that the enemy (rather than us) is trapped in them? The same logic applies to containing, mitigating, and preventing the negative aspects of MAD from harming society.

In summary, a Brains-Based Approach to Strategic Thinking consists of three parts: complete knowledge and full understanding of all aspects of the problem set and solutions; a twenty-first century mindset that facilitates innovation, imagination, and rigor; and the means for affecting, influencing, and controlling the will and perception of real and potential enemies.

A Brains-Based Approach will not guarantee favorable outcomes. But absence of one along with the failure to embrace a twenty-first century mindset and lack of recognition of the descending fiscal Damoclean sword will guarantee for the United States that future battles and conflicts could too easily be lost and a hollow and impotent military made inevitable. That would mean more potential Vietnams, Afghanistans, and Iraqs and failing wars on terror. But who will listen? And who will lead?

Acknowledgments

I want to acknowledge and thank my agent Ian Kleinert for his sage advice and skillful navigation of the industry; Anthony Scaramucci for his example of grace under fire; and to the team at Post Hill especially my editor Maddie Sturgeon and the extraordinarily creative group who designed the cover.